Cannibals

The New Historicism: Studies in Cultural Poetics, edited by Stephen Greenblatt, volume 37.

CANNIBALS

The Discovery and Representation of the Cannibal from Columbus to Jules Verne

FRANK LESTRINGANT

*Translated by
Rosemary Morris*

University of California Press
Berkeley   Los Angeles

University of California Press
Berkeley and Los Angeles, California

Published by arrangement with Polity Press

This translation © 1997 by Polity Press
This translation first published by the University of California Press 1997
First published in France as *Le Cannibale: Grandeur et Décadence* © 1994 by Librairie
Académique Perrin

Library of Congress Cataloging-in-Publication Data

Lestringant, Frank.
    [Cannibale. English]
    Cannibals: the discovery and representation of the cannibal from Columbus to Jules
Verne/Frank Lestringant; translated by Rosemary Morris.
        p.   cm. – (The new historicism; 37)
    Includes bibliographical references and index.
    ISBN 0-520-20240-6
    1. French literature—History and criticism. 2. Cannibalism in literature. I. Morris,
Rosemary. II. Title. III. Series.
    PQ145.1.C35L4713 1997
    840.9'355—dc21   96-39830
                                                                                    CIP

Printed in Great Britain

9   8   7   6   5   4   3   2   1

Contents

vi

List of Illustrations

‿∴‿

In memory of Auguste Lestringant, bookseller at Rouen
To my parents

Introduction
To Meet a Cannibal

ᨑ᠄ᨕ

And so the cannibal shows through the working man's overall, like the skull of the Carib under the bourgeoise's black silk bonnet.

Gustave Flaubert, letter to Louise Colet, 2 January 1854

What do the essayist Montaigne, the painter Géricault and the novelist Flaubert have in common?

There are two possible answers: one a place, the other an object. The place is the town of Rouen, open to the Atlantic, ocean of the Great Discoveries, gateway to the Lesser Antilles and to tropical Brazil (later, much later, it was to turn inwards, snug in the embracing arms of the Seine, in its bourgeois security and its narrow outlook); the object is the Cannibal, whose representatives disembarked there as ambassadors for a world that, amidst the piles of undressed timber, the bales of cotton and sacks of feathers, was truly new. This book can be seen as a search for that place of common origin, that almost undetectable threshold, in the heart of deeply inland Normandy, of a distantly ramifying, powerfully breathing, wholly distressed and alien ocean.

The first encounter took place in November 1562. Rouen had just been reconquered from the Protestants by the armies of the King. The royal troops, commanded by the duke François de Guise and the High Constable Anne de Montmorency, had entered through a breach in the ramparts near the Saint-Hilaire Gate, and had pillaged the town for twenty-four hours. In the days and weeks that followed, the punishment of the heretical party, which had governed the city unchallenged for six months, allowed the settling of many an account. When order was finally restored, King Charles IX, then aged twelve, and his mother, Catherine de' Medici, made their solemn entry into the town.[1] It was at this point that Montaigne made his appearance.

Here, then, is Montaigne, against the background of a city that has been taken by storm and laid half in ruin, talking to us about a subject which seems quite irrelevant: the Cannibals, who had just disembarked from Brazil and were, to say the least, taken aback by the disorder which they found in this highly civilized Europe, whose merits the missionaries had so insistently described to them during their voyage. They were treated with the utmost consideration. The King received them personally and talked to them for some time. The magnificence of the royal entourage was paraded before them, the pomp of the itinerant Court, 'the form of a fine city' – or what was left of it after a month of siege and tribulation. Far from voicing the expected admiration, they expressed only doubt and astonishment (though the word 'admiration' could have that meaning in the sixteenth century, when prodigies and 'monsters' of every kind were a frequent occurrence). Certainly, their proud replies were such as to perplex their royal interlocutor. They were astonished by this child king, still more taken aback by the juxtaposition of rich and poor, and wondered how the latter 'could endure such injustice without taking the others by the throat and setting fire to their houses'.[2]

Montaigne ventured to ask them some questions of his own. His questions, unlike the King's, were entirely political, as if he had consented to enter the Cannibals' own chosen territory and so become their spokesman. His curiosity focused on the function of monarchy among the savages. What were the privileges of the King of Brazil? To 'go foremost into battle', he was told. How many men does he have in his army? Four or five thousand, as many as would fit into the 'extent of space' indicated to him with a sweep of the arm by the captain who was answering Montaigne's questions, and whom the sailors called 'the King'. What authority remains to him when there is no war? When he visits the villages under his jurisdiction, they make for him 'paths through the hedges of their woods along which he can pass very easily'.

In that autumn of 1562, 'new horizons' were assuming a distinctly critical function, and it took a savage to denounce the glaring injustices of a ravaged town swarming with beggars. This was very different from the entry of Henri II in 1550, when two worlds, one on each side of the Seine, had exchanged competing and complementary images of a golden age. On that occasion, for the pleasure of the Court on its progress, 'three hundred naked men, tanned and bristling like hedgehogs, with no attempt to cover the parts that Nature commands' had mimed the alternation of peace and war among a savage people.[3] The Indians were still there, but there was no longer anything picturesque about their presence. Now, it pointed up a contrast, between the egalitarian community of the free Brazilians and the flagrant disparities within a civilized society based on unequal wealth and arbitrary laws.

Rouen 1853, 26 December: a busy day for Gustave Flaubert. He visited his barber and his doctor, called on the mistress of his friend

Louis Bouilhet and, most important, went to see the 'savages'. These were no longer the 'Topinambu' of three centuries earlier, who had long since been exterminated, but Kaffirs from South Africa (known for their particularly uncouth customs), who were 'on show at 11, Grande-Rue' for the sum of five *sous*.[4] Colonialism has evidently been at work. Instead of the free and proud speakers whom the King of France had considered fit to be received and heard at some length, we now have a kind of hairy animal 'uttering inarticulate cries', 'crouching like monkeys round a cookpot', in the depths of a smoke-filled room, and considered unworthy of a visit by decent Rouennais society. Such spectacles were considered more suitable for the working classes – 'seven or eight working men' were there – and for a novelist with a taste for the exotic. Montaigne had delighted to see the Brazilians as nudists, naked knights 'without fear and without reproach'. Flaubert saw only a 'horde of primitives', whose appearance inspired him almost with awe: 'I thought I beheld the first men on earth. They were newborn, still crawling amongst the toads and crocodiles.' There could be no very sustained dialogue with such pitiful creatures.

As Flaubert's Kaffirs did not seem to have reached even the rudiments of political organization, the interchange was confined to a flashing of eyes and some body contact. In a word, the dialogue, which with Montaigne had been political, had now descended into badinage. Moreover, it was in dumb show. The miserable driver of this train of savages could say what he liked, but 'Although he claims that they know a little English, they do not understand a word of it.' Happily, there remained the language of the senses: 'Among them there is an old woman of fifty who made *lubricious* advances to me and tried to kiss me. Everyone's hair stood on end.'[5] The whole of Flaubert's interview was reduced to this lengthy animal flirtation, which lasted a good quarter of an hour. Afterwards, the novelist was quite tempted to prolong the experiment and transport her to the solitude of Croisset, *pour épater le bourgeois*. But some strange misgiving held him back. The fear of 'being seen trying to pose', the fear of a sort of inverted conformism, deterred him from inviting the savages to dinner. So the Kaffir woman never went to Croisset.

Montaigne and Flaubert had the same initial difficulty in communicating. Montaigne said he was hampered by the 'stupidity' of his interpreter, who proved unable to follow his flights of fancy and spoiled the pleasure of the conversation. However, this obstacle did not prevent him from conveying the lofty political concepts of his Cannibals. Flaubert remembered Montaigne's difficulties 'when he also saw Brazilians at Rouen, for the coronation of Charles IX'.[6] The difference was simply that there was no longer any message to convey.

The (very relative) failure of Montaigne's dialogue with the Brazilians was due to a superabundance of meaning: the loss of a question and of the yet more valuable reply; breakdowns in simultaneous interpretation; the imbecility of the interpreter.[7] Flaubert, on the other hand, does not tell us of any questions that he wanted to ask, and he probably had no more to say than what he actually does convey: an unexpressed desire, sexual rather than linguistic; a dimly felt urge to unite with living matter in its simplest and most bestial form. Here, the meaning errs by default.

This gives us the measure of the erosion suffered by the savage body in the period between the two meetings. Already disturbed at the outset by the incompetence of the interpreter, the notion of relating to the Other has become impossible, even scandalous. Flaubert never did admit the Kaffirs into his personal life, however much he was tempted to do so. Montaigne was not so particular: not only did he hold long conversations with the Cannibals at Rouen, he later took into his household at Saint-Michel du Périgord a 'man who had dwelt ten or twelve years in that other world'[8] – in other words, since he could not get a household savage, he settled for a genuine man of the woods, who had become suitably 'savage-like' and had turned late in life to the more peaceable role of domestic servant.

During the three centuries which separated the two meetings in Rouen, a series of events progressively downgraded the relationship between the West and those Others. Towards the end of this period the Great Revolution and its sporadic aftershocks had muddied the waters of a political discourse which had passed untroubled from La Boétie (Montaigne's friend and fellow philosopher) to Marat, but had then been travestied in Marat's 'The Chains of Slavery', and re-used shortly afterwards in the service of the Terror.[9] Plagiarizing La Boétie's *Discours de la Servitude Volontaire* ('Discourse on Voluntary Servitude'), the author and future member of the Convention dragged the eloquence of the Cannibals in the direction of mere banality: 'The love of domination is natural to the human heart.' This was enough to constitute an advance justification of revolutionary dictatorship, spurning the free and proud speech attributed by Montaigne to the Brazilians in sympathy with the thinking of his dead friend. At about the same time, the works of Sade, for whom Flaubert professed a particular interest and veneration – that 'extract from the abyss' flung into the midst of the Enlightenment[10] – shook the moral certainties which underlay the assumed superiority of civilized peoples and exterminated the alleged 'savages', or reduced them to subservience. Finally, an ever-widening material and technical gap opened up between Europe and the other worlds, which thus became its prey, or its immediate vassals.

In the process, the figure of the savage was blackened, in every sense of the word. No longer were they free and fair-skinned Brazilians, partners in an economy based on barter: they became Negroes, potential slaves and probable commodities, or, at best, fairground attractions.

Nonetheless, we must counterbalance this figure of the Kaffir by that of the Negro in Géricault's *The Raft of the Medusa*. Géricault, like Flaubert, was born in Rouen, but their visions of the Other had nothing in common. At the top of the desperate human pyramid on the raft, the Negro, waving the red rag, channels all the energy of this mass of flesh straining toward heaven. His muscular back, unwithered by starvation, stands firm against the threat of a stormy sky, the clinging heaviness of torrid air. Unlike the waxen-faced, cadaverous whites, the four Negroes in the composition seem to be holding out against the corruption of matter which is turning the raft into a sort of floating morgue. Up to the time of his death, Géricault was planning a vast painting which would deal a great blow to the Negro slave-trade.[11] *The Raft of the Medusa* is an advanced contribution to this abolitionist programme, but it was doomed to remain unnoticed or misunderstood. When Alexandre Corréard, the most voluble survivor of the actual shipwreck, ventured to describe the painting, putting himself in the starring role of the man who is pointing towards the horizon, he ignored the flag-bearing Negro, perilously balanced on his barrel, and remembered only one of his fellow blacks, whose attitude was more conventional: 'An African fails to understand anything that is happening around him; he is in a state of gloom, and his motionless figure reveals the state of his soul.'[12] In a word, if we are to believe Corréard, who is quite indifferent to the dramatic backlighting and powerful plasticity of that pensive figure, that mulatto Michelangelo seated at the centre of the painting, all we have is a living image of dumb resignation.

From the caravel to the raft

The degrading of the image of the Other, from the heroic idealization of the Renaissance to the stormy twilight of Romanticism, is paralleled over the same stretch of time by an increasing inability to make sense of anthropophagy. The explanatory model based on the

notion of cannibalism as a rite, which came first, was soon superseded
– at the dictates of philosophy and science – by a determinism which
reduced habit to the merely material, and custom to natural constraint. Cannibals, subject to a hostile environment and bereft of all
liberty, became no more than eaters, predators without conscience or
ideal, who, in times of severe famine, turned their hunger against their
own race.

For this reason, readers may feel increasingly uneasy as they peruse
the following series of documents on the cannibal theme. The voyage
of exploration, which began enthusiastically with the long navigation
towards the discovery of a new world and a new humanity, ended in
pangs of hunger. As a token of this progressive degeneration, we may
take the change from Columbus's caravels to the raft of the *Medusa*:
not the raft as painted by Géricault, on which the downrush of bodies
is inverted into an ascent, but the real and rudimentary 'machine', so
overloaded that it sank almost three feet into the water when the last
survivors of the shipwreck climbed on to it on the evening of 5 July
1816. Anticipating certain death, fifteen of them owed their salvation
to the methodical removal of their companions.[13]

Rouen, 1992. Four centuries after the death of Montaigne and over a
hundred years after that of Flaubert, the wharves today are deserted,
the entire port has moved downriver with its ships laden with fibres
and timber: the hum of commerce has shifted westwards en bloc,
towards the river mouth which once gaped emptily and is now tacked
shut by two bridges. The flood of questions which used to flow out
towards the visitors from another world, along with their firm and
laconic replies, have given place to silence. Nothing remains even of
the dumb and bewitching enigma which brought Flaubert and his
Kaffirs together in the fifteen-minute promiscuity of a smoky furnished room: 'We are not going.'[14]

What has the Cannibal to say to us now? Did such a person ever
really exist? In point of fact, the easiest and most radical solution is
simply to deny cultural anthropophagy. This is the kind of crazed
revisionism which has been indulged in recently – with considerable
popular success – by the essayist William Arens.[15] He alleges that the
Cannibal of the Antilles or Brazil sprang, naked and bloody, from the
heads of hurrying travellers, Europeans greedy for living space and
conquest and quick to project their own devouring fantasies on the
Other, whom they hated and despised. Arens – who is more of a sen-
sation-hungry journalist than an exact historian – has received all too
much attention. Others have followed in his footsteps, spreading the
denial of the Cannibal through five continents.[16] Sufficient answer is

the argument advanced two centuries ago by Cornélius de Pauw against Atkins:

> How [he asks] can it be possible that animals formed in the image of the Divinity should have been capable of thus degrading the dignity of their nature? Let us in turn ask the plausible Atkins how these animals have been capable of descending to such vileness as calumny, avarice, envy, barbarity, superstition, treachery, murder, parricide, despotism and slavery . . .[17]

These moral objections can easily be supplemented by converging ethnological evidence,[18] thus demolishing a position which, under cover of idealism and intellectual high-mindedness, actually leads back to the misrepresentation of the Other. And archaeologists have discovered, in the broken, burned and gnawed human bones in tombs in Provence and the American South-West, probable evidence of anthropophagous or necrophagous practices at various periods of prehistory.[19]

For the Cannibals did really exist, and have never ceased to speak to us.[20] Their loquacity – or rather their proud and cruel eloquence – have probably never been equalled since that historical period between Columbus's discoveries and the death of Montaigne a century later, the period with which my investigation begins. Today, their voices have sunk, sometimes to the point of inaudibility. Their retrieval from beneath the stratagems, excuses and prim attenuations of the learned on the one hand, and, on the other, the sensational exaggerations beloved of the public at large (witnessed by the success of Delorge's *Contes du Grand-Guignol* in the last century, and of horror films in this), is the aim of the present book.

For a long time the oratorical facility of the Cannibals was considered directly proportional to the fear aroused by their monstrous appetites. Their alleged eloquence, which in turn borrows Ciceronian cadences and a clipped Senecan style, was designed to transcend the horror of an act which was inherently incomprehensible. The most notable of such attempts remains the story of the cannibalistic act of noble revenge, made familiar by a long tradition in medieval courtly literature of hearts eternally being eaten by deceived maidens and vindictive lovers. This revenge cannibalism, linked with the aristocratic values whose embers were still glowing at the dawn of the modern age, was the explanation adopted by the first missionaries to the New World and, after many others, by Montaigne. Such a token of magnanimity and chivalry had the advantage of transforming famine into abundance, and the devouring of another into a generous act of self-giving. It restored the Cannibal to a precarious liberty, which was soon to be challenged by the greed of the conquistadors and the excessive zeal of missionaries.

This explanatory schema was progressively accepted to describe the ritual practices of certain American peoples, chiefly the Tupinambas of Brazil, and was later attached to the Caribbean islanders – initially reviled, deported and exterminated, later to be tardily rehabilitated for strategic reasons during French colonization. At the same time, the contrary hypothesis, which also proceeded through allegorization, turned cannibalism into the emblem of an unendurable constraint. All tyrannical regimes could be seen as anthropophagous. The Ancient Greeks themselves called tyrants *demoroboi* – demovores, eaters of the people – and this was the title later bestowed by Philo of Alexandria upon the bloodthirsty Emperor Caligula. With Montaigne, the question of the American Cannibal came to be connected with politics. The author of the *Essays* transports to the New World the paradox of voluntary servitude, which so fascinated his friend La Boétie. The scandal of eating the dead gives way to the even more intolerable scandal of devouring the living. The slave-trade, usury, feudal services, judicial torture, were all ways of eating one's fellow creatures – not to mention the wars of conquest and the mass round-ups of slaves which were common currency in the first decades of European overseas expansion.

Before Montaigne, the Cannibal, pitching in the wake of Columbus and Vespucci, was seeking an identity, from the Windward Isles to the coasts of Brazil. After Montaigne, that identity disintegrated into universality. Everything became cannibalistic: politics, society, interest on loans, matrimonial law, the relationships between fathers and children, masters and pupils. To generalize the allegorization of anthropophagy in this way runs the risk of losing sight of the reality, underestimating it, or, worse still, denying it. It might imply that cannibalism exists only as a figure of speech.

Recently, René Girard has seen Tupinamba ritual as an example of the universal notion of the scapegoat; his reading has been challenged by Isabelle Combès, who thinks that ritual cannibalism may *not* be 'a sacrificial rite similar to any other'.[21] Here again, the attempt to discover a universal – in this case 'the unity of all rites'[22] – threatens to lose sight of what is specific about the eating of human flesh.

Another difficulty is that in the case of Montaigne the allegorical reading is twofold. The body of the Cannibal represents the body of 'Dame Policy' (in the words of Christine de Pisan),[23] but also, and principally, the mystical body of the Church. This goes to show that one should always look for multiple levels of meaning in allegory. The second figure, in which the eaten body is central – indeed, the epicentre – is, of course, the Eucharist. Catholics, Anglicans and

Lutherans see this as an indestructible body which can be eaten indefinitely, and by which, week by week, year by year and century by century, the community of the faithful is sustained and fed. That body, which Calvinists relegate to heaven, infinitely removed from an earth sticky with scattered flesh and shed blood, is endlessly offered by Catholics as a propitiatory sacrifice. This is indisputably the core of the cannibal question, which it would take many more books to explain. In our own culture, at the very least, theophagy is the religious substratum of anthropophagy, its half-buried plinth and ultimate justification. It is this that makes the cannibalism of the Cannibal at once unacceptable and comprehensible. Unacceptable, because there is no further need for sacrificial anthropophagy once Christ's death on the Cross has redeemed all mankind and delivered it from the constraints of murder; and at the same time comprehensible, because of the striking similarity between the Eucharistic symbol and the actual anthropological rituals observable in some variety in the New World. The communal aspect of the rite, its relation to the worship of the dead – through the renewal of the sepulchre – and the hope of a substantial benefit to an entire group are all common points of belief between the New World and the Old. An inferior and distorting mirror of the chief sacrament of the Christian religion: this is what the first western voyagers saw in the cannibalism of the Cannibals, which could be interpreted, according to taste, either as the repulsive remains of an archaic stage of development, or as a caricature of obviously diabolical inspiration – Satan (known to be a born plagiarist) aping his betters.

It will be seen that Montaigne, who invites us to admire the fraternal conviviality of the Brazilians and the happy harmony which prevails in their society, is trying to surmount the insurmountable. By proposing a secular version of the communion of saints, he is obliged to take a route unknown to the thinkers of Greek and Latin antiquity. The dispute over the Mass, which was at its height when he was writing, during the cruel wars of religion, was to him both a starting-point and an obstacle. He uses it to leap from sign to meaning, and, scorning the more garish aspects of his subject, to concentrate his attention on the symbolism. Hence the importance which he gives, at every stage in the ritual, to what the Cannibal says, turning the very real and anthropophagous repast into a pure cannibalism of words. The primitiveness of the culinary preparations is accordingly sublimated; the eater of human flesh is compared with the Christian, whom the Cannibal surpasses in virtue, courage and generosity. The real physical presence of the plumed and tattooed Indian, with his necklace of teeth and his bone flute, is forgotten in favour of an evanescent and idealized double, a modern avatar of the naked philosopher beloved of Plato and Sextus Empiricus.

The move from the literal to the figurative, and from theology to grammar in the *Essays* was in the same direction: away from realism, towards nominalism. In his 'Apology for Raymond Sebon' Montaigne says, with reference to the wars then rending France asunder, that 'for the most part the occasions of the troubles of the world are Grammarian'.[24] And, he continues, alluding to Christ's words at the Last Supper: 'How many quarrels, and how serious, have been produced in the world by the doubt over the meaning of this syllable, HOC!' It is indeed true that that hiccup in the Latin text of the Vulgate, the beginning of the sacramental formula *Hoc est corpus meum* ('This is my body'), was the principal bone of contention between Roman Catholics and Calvinists in Geneva and elsewhere.

However, Montaigne, as a practising Catholic, had no intention of renouncing the dogma of transubstantiation, and this is without doubt what remains unsaid in the chapter 'Of Cannibals'. Bolder when discussing a distant anthropophagy with a spicy breath of exoticism rather than the familiar theophagy, Montaigne, like most of his readers and plagiarists over the next two or three centuries, nevertheless (and with good reason) says nothing of a parallelism which had seemed obvious to the pastor Jean de Léry who was his direct inspiration. It will be seen that the drawbacks are equal to the advantages.

Montaigne thus abstains from giving a decisive answer to the crucial question of sacred anthropophagy. Having ventured onto dangerous ground, he stops halfway, leaving obscure an essential point of doctrine, which the title – 'Of Cannibals' – and still more the context – the Wars of Religion – necessarily seemed to be evoking. The censorship here is patent. However, Montaigne stops short of the irreparable – that is, of outright condemnation of an anthropophagy based on bestial appetite, signifying nothing.

In the history of the Cannibal's reception in Europe one can, up to a point, observe a kind of solidarity between the Christian affirmation of the mystical body and the tendency to adopt the hypothesis most favourable to the savage: that this was a rite of vengeance, in which appetite, hunger and the need for food played only a negligible part. This was the strategy adopted, in particular, by the missionaries in Brazil and Canada, who would use any means to refute the hypothesis of cannibalism for nutritional ends in their determination to save the soul of the Indian, however deeply it might be enmeshed in the dark snares of Satan. But when the world was returned to the dominion of secular custom, with the advance of conquering reason and a new technological assurance, the vision of the Cannibal was to be downgraded. This movement of rejection arose first of all in the domain of Protestantism (in the broadest sense), whether in the form of Abbé Prévost – that errant mind inclining to Anglicanism – or of Daniel Defoe, whose Robinson Crusoe turns from peaceable householder into exterminating angel when his island home is threatened by Caribs from the mainland.

The 'end of an illusion', to borrow a phrase from Freud, cost the Cannibal dear. The liquidation of religion (which Freud describes as an 'infantile neurosis'[25]), and especially of the Christian religion, was shortly to bring about the liquidation of the Cannibal, a victim of the triumph of reason and the progress of the Enlightenment. Anthropophagy, bereft of its religious overdetermination, had no further excuses. It had to be swept from the face of the earth, and the sooner the better; at the very least, it had to be eliminated from all parts of the world whose fruits were to be enjoyed by civilized men. That was more or less the attitude of two men writing a century apart and from opposing viewpoints: the anti-colonialist Cornelius de Pauw and Jules Verne, who sang the praises of the new empires which Europe was establishing overseas.

The age of the caravel gave way to the age of the steamer and the raft. The Cannibals, relegated to the narrow confines of lost Pacific islets or the remaining inaccessible regions of Africa, were presumed to have forgotten not only their language and their eloquence, but also their rituals and fears, even their birthplace and baptism, and would no longer subsist except as remnants. It would take all the imagination of a Sade or a Flaubert to re-embody them and restore to them, if not their voices, at least their fearful appetites.

Today, as the second millennium draws to a close, the outcome of the centuries-long battle between the advocates of the haughty Cannibals and the horrified observers of their primitive bestiality is still in doubt. The magnanimity of Nurture is no more likely now than it was then to triumph over a distinctly ill-intentioned Nature. The negative hypothesis, reinforced by the current upsurge of interest in environmental questions, has returned in force. The stress is once more upon the dependence of human beings on their natural environment: 'ecologism' is at grips with 'culturalism'. The old pessimism about the origins of man is abroad once more, albeit wearing new clothes.

There is one difference from the last century, when the triumph of colonialism was supported by an unshakeable faith in progress: the worse option is no longer necessarily associated with contempt for the Other. The theory of cannibalism by constraint has become, at most, a comfortable and selfish solution. It is an easy way of relegating an unacceptable sort of savagery to pre-history, or to some untamed region on the fringes of the known world. It is also a way of removing this burden from the back of a dominant, civilized society, which is now more incapable than ever of thinking out its relationship with the world and with nature. The culturalist hypothesis tended to idealize the violent act of eating, to shift the noise of teeth and lips towards the domain of language. Similarly, but by a less carefully considered and obscurer route, the determinist hypothesis, or its ecological variant, achieves at little cost a continuous exorcism.[26] The body of the savage (who has now declined into a primitive) pays the price. Thrust back into the ancestral forest, penned into a distant island, the Cannibal nonetheless continues to people our imagination and haunt our present day.

At the end of my own voyage in contrary winds over high seas, let me take this opportunity of expressing my gratitude to all those who assisted it, beginning with Pierre Chaunu, to whom this book owes its form and title. Over the long winter of 1993 my friend Claude Rawson and my colleagues at Yale helped, by their friendly and familiar conversation, to shape several chapters. I am grateful to Michel Delon for his information about everything outside the century of Montaigne.

PART I
From Cynocephali to Cannibals

1
Birth of the Cannibal
౼‧ᔍ

Columbus discovers the Cannibal

The noun 'cannibal' derives from the Arawak *caniba*, apparently a corruption of *cariba*, the name (meaning 'bold', it is said) which the Caribbean Indians of the Lesser Antilles gave to themselves.[1] To their enemies, however, the peace-loving Arawaks of Cuba, the name had a distinctly pejorative connotation of extreme ferocity and barbarity. It was from the latter that Christopher Columbus first heard the word during his epoch-making voyage of 1492.

For Columbus can be credited with the discovery not only of America, but also of the Cannibal. In his journal of the voyage, preserved by Bartolomé de Las Casas, the Admiral noted on Sunday, 4 November 1492, a few days after reaching the northern coast of Cuba, what his interpreters had told him: that 'further on [eastwards] there were men with only one eye and others with dogs' snouts who ate men' (*'hombres de un ojo e otros con hoçicos de perro que comian los hombres'*).[2]

The word 'cannibal' does not yet appear. It seems that the two strange peoples mentioned here derive from the geographical lore of antiquity: *monoculi* and Cynocephali are included in the list of monstrous races which passed almost without alteration from Pliny and Solinus to St Augustine and thence into Isidore of Seville's *Etymologiae*. In the latter work, the one-eyed Cyclops come directly after the Cynocephali. Isidore's list of monstrous races continues with the Blemmyes, the Panoti ('all-ears'), the Artabites, the Satyres and cloven-footed Faunes, the Sciopodes, the Antipodes, the light-footed Hippopodes, the legendarily long-lived Macrobes and the Pygmies, who, mounted on goats, wage perpetual warfare against the cranes. It was in that form that the fabulous list was included in Pierre d'Ailly's *Imago Mundi* at the very beginning of the fifteenth century.[3] This work, which was printed dozens of times in the late fifteenth and early sixteenth centuries, became the discoverers' *vademecum*.

The dog-headed man and the one-eyed Cyclops begin the sequence of twenty-one woodcuts of monstrous races which opens Hartmann

Schedel's World Chronicle, published at Nuremberg in 1493. The authorities cited in the accompanying commentary are the inevitable trio, *'Plinius, Augustinus und Ysidorus'* – Pliny, St Augustine and Isidore of Seville.[4]

It is clear that Columbus translated the insulting names which the Arawaks had bestowed on their cannibalistic neighbours in terms of an existing 'scientific' world view. No lesser an authority than Pliny – *Plinius dixit* – is invoked to equip these ferocious eaters of human flesh and drinkers of human blood with the heads of dogs.

It is symptomatic that in Columbus's Journal the Cynocephalus should precede the Cannibal. The latter does not appear under that precise designation until a few pages further on, in an entry dated 23 November 1492. The similarity between this context and the verbal exchange of 4 November reveals that the word 'cannibal' is used as an exact equivalent for the earlier dog-headed people. Associated, once again, with the *monoculi*, these redoubtable individuals strike terror into the local inhabitants by their savage greed for human flesh (by now Columbus is nearing Moa Grande, following the coast in the direction of Haiti).[5] On Monday, 26 November 1492, a curious metamorphosis takes place: the *caniba* or *canima*, still wearing canine headgear, are suddenly telescoped into identity with the one-eyed Cyclops.[6] The two monster races, which appear one after the other in Isidore and in Schedel's 'Chronicle',[7] are now fused to produce a twofold monster, the dog-headed Cyclops.

By a concomitant effect, which, following Lewis Carroll, we might call a 'portmanteau word', the roots of the two words become confused, as the two images merge. Columbus vaguely perceives in the word 'cannibal' – or, more accurately, 'canibal' – the root of the Latin *canis*: hence the assimilation to the Cynocephalus. But on this same Monday, 26 November, the confusion is worse confounded: 'canibal', already caninized by the Latin root, is endowed by apocope with the majesty of the Great Khan of Tartary. A nominal 'allusion' of that kind was, from Columbus's point of view, entirely logical, since he believed he was approaching the western coasts of Asia. Indeed, not long afterwards, on 24 December, he confused the native name 'Civao' (Haiti) with the contemporary name for Japan, Cipango, which he hoped shortly to reach.[8] Hence, the Admiral, who in his heart of hearts had always doubted the existence of the dog-headed Cyclops, resolutely plumped for the much more gratifying second etymology: the Cannibals really belonged to 'the lordship of the Great Khan'.[9]

This was also a convenient way of eliminating the growing menace of the dog-headed Cannibal. As late as 11 December, however,

Columbus, continuing his eastward voyage along the north coast of Hispaniola, came back to that besetting question and offered what seemed to him to be the most rational solution: 'I therefore repeat what I have said several times already: that the Caniba are none other than the people of the Great Khan, who must be neighbours to these. They have ships, they come and capture these people, and as those who are taken never return, the others believe that they have been eaten.'[10]

Shortly after this, the Admiral was shown some unhappy Indians who had lost 'pieces of their flesh'.[11] He refused to see this as the terrible stigmata of a monstrous appetite. In the teeth of growing evidence in favour of cannibalism, he clung desperately to the word which seemed to open to him the road to all the marvels of Asia. He followed the coasts of Hispaniola another month before abandoning them, on 16 January 1493, and turning back towards Spain. Thus, the Great Khan hypothesis remained unproved, and the dog-head hypothesis, though becoming ever more improbable, remained a faint possibility. However that might be, Columbus did not, on his first voyage, encounter any of the real Caribs who made meals of the Arawaks.

This he was not to do until two years later, on his second great journey. Reaching the Antilles via the Dominica passage, he came upon a newly abandoned Carib village on Guadeloupe, where he discovered intact evidence of an anthropophagous feast. The scene is described, with a wealth of culinary detail (albeit tempered by a fitting sense of pathos) in the first of the eight 'Decades' of Peter Martyr of Anghiera, an Italian humanist resident at the Court of Spain, who, as a member of the Council of the Indies, was ideally placed to obtain first-hand information for his chronicle of the Great Discoveries.[12] The cannibalistic tableau is described as an imaginary stage-set, empty of living actors and strewn with dismembered bodies: legs and arms spiked on spits; human flesh cooking in cauldrons along with parrot meat; a freshly severed head, still dripping blood, hanging from a beam. This nightmarish vision was well calculated to afford the Cannibals some durable publicity. The images were to proliferate throughout Europe: though the Cannibals were soon to lose their legendary canine head-pieces, their monstrous table manners were to provide ample compensation for such a limited degree of humanization.

The Cannibal, son of a dog

Thus the word 'cannibal' is occidental in origin and rooted in America; but from the very first it was at the heart of a complex semantic nexus. By means of verbal allusions – the lateral etymologies which enjoyed such an immense vogue throughout the Renaissance – the Arawak word came up against the improbable Cynocephalus, bequeathed by Pliny and Isidore, and the historical Great Khan, Kublai, the contemporary of Marco Polo. The Mongol allusion died with Columbus: it was too closely bound up with his personal mythology to outlive him. In any case, it had not been proof against the trials and disappointments of his last three voyages. The memory of the Asiatic emperor soon faded from the shores of the New World, falling before the successive forays among the islands and on to the mainland which were conducted both by the great Genoese and by his 'follower', the Florentine Vespucci.[13] Nonetheless, the canine etymology survived for an unexpectedly long time. For generations of sailors and navigators – as well as humanists and the merely curious – the Cannibal undoubtedly remained the son of a dog.

The most striking illustration of this stubborn legend is probably a woodcut published in Strasbourg in 1525, in a work by the learned Lorenz Fries entitled *Uslegung der Mercarthen oder Cartha Marina*.[14] In this small-scale cosmography, intended as an accompaniment to Waldseemüller's nautical chart, America has difficulty in emerging above the sea of marvels bequeathed by the medieval imagination.

Figure 1 Dog-headed cannibals butchering human flesh. Lorenz Fries, Strasbourg, 1525 and 1527. Woodcut.

Thus, in a woodcut purporting to illustrate the inhabitants of Brazil, a naked couple, wearing only necklaces of teeth, poses with bows and bucklers in hand, while two unicorns with lowered heads, appearing on the left, seem about to charge them. But the most extraordinary image relates to the 'Canibali' of the Lesser Antilles. The commentary, which owes something to the exaggerations of Vespucci (as we shall see in the next chapter), but elaborates even on him, not only asserts that these cruel people prefer human flesh to any other food, and that to satisfy this preference they fatten up young boys and breed from female prisoners of child-bearing age, helping themselves to the issue: it also declares that in this island, discovered by 'Christofel Dauber von Janua' (Christopher Columbus of Genoa), the men have dogs' heads. And, accordingly, the woodcut shows dog-headed Cannibals chopping up human meat and devouring it with relish. The strange beast of burden, carrying a victim tied hand and foot by a single cord, is probably meant to be a South American llama, as described a few years earlier by Antonio Pigafetta, companion of Magellan and chronicler of the first circumnavigation of the world.[15] He, too, following Vespucci, had encountered Cannibals in the latitudes of Brazil.

In the Strasbourg woodcut (see Figure 1), note the details such as the wattle-and-daub hut which shelters the gruesome feast, and the row of human limbs hanging like hams or sides of bacon – to borrow a comparison attributed to Vespucci.[16] These diverse elements, together with the archaic nature of the image, indicate that it belongs among the very earliest representations of the American savage. As Hugh Honour suggests, it can usefully be compared with a very rare woodcut from Augsburg or Nuremberg, dated 1505, which shows plumed barbarians indulging in the delights of free love, while others, infringing an even weightier taboo, munch human limbs which have been smoked over a wood fire.[17]

This intrusion of dog-headed extras onto the stage of the New World shows the remarkable suggestiveness of the myths of antiquity. It also brings about a sort of phantasmagorical conflation. The dog-headed butchers of the Strasbourg illustration, a sample of imagined America at its most primitive stage, associate the genuine cannibalism of the peoples of the Far West with the reputedly dog-like appearance of peoples in the Far East. The link is made through a play on words, *canis-caniba*. Thus, from Arawak into Latin, a Freudian *Witz* creates the necessary dream structure.

A century later the polygraph Loys Guyon de La Nauche, contemplating the disorder which imaginative reports of the Great

Discoveries offered to a scholarly eye, and attempting to introduce some kind of rationality, strove to reconcile academic tradition with the new anthropological data. But it was no easy task to 'pick up the pieces' when the entire conglomeration flew in the face of common sense.

In his *Diverses Leçons* ('Diverse Readings'), a curious miscellany continuing those compiled by the Spaniard Pero Mexia (Pierre Messie in French) and his friend, the councillor Antoine du Verdier de Vauprivas, Louis Guyon, gentleman of La Nauche, initially affirms his belief in the existence of the Cynocephali. The chapter in which he discusses this delicate question is assertively entitled '*Que les peuples Cinocephales, c'est-à-dire ayans testes de chiens, ont esté descouvers, et qu'on habite journellement avec eux*' ('that the Cynocaphalous, that is dog-headed, peoples have been discovered, and that men are dwelling day by day with them').[18] By adhering to this paradox he accepts the evidence of both the ancients and the moderns. Pliny and Aulus Gellius are not 'liars', though they have often been accused of it. But the long-distance voyagers, who, following in the wake of Columbus and Vespucci, have confirmed that there are no monster races are not wrong either.

Louis Guyon, whose compilation was first published at Lyon in 1604, had read Jean de Léry's *Histoire d'un voyage faict en la terre du Brésil* ('History of a Voyage to the Land of Brazil'), the French and European best seller among Protestant works on America at the turn of the seventeenth century;[19] and he was thoroughly familiar with the *Essays* of the 'sieur des Montagnes de Bourdeaux', as he calls him.[20] From the former writer he learned that the Tupinikin Indians of Rio de Janeiro 'considered their children beautiful only if they had squat noses'. Therefore, as soon as they issue from their mother's womb 'they have their noses crushed and flattened with a thumb'. And Léry adds a comparison which is taken up by Guyon: 'just as you can see we do in France to spaniels and lapdogs'.[21] Thus, 'these peoples who were discovered sixty years ago' have the same pug faces as the lapdogs which 'ladies and unmarried girls keep in their rooms as pets'.[22] And, in fact, the literature of the discoveries – and until recently the racist laws of South Africa – saw a squat nose as characteristic of lower races destined for subjugation: primitive, indeed, but quite tameable.[23]

In reality there was nothing final about such a malediction as regards the savages of Brazil. Their squashed noses were not congenital, but the result of a perverse custom. The Cynocephali were not dog-headed 'naturally, but artificially'. Or, as we would say today, they belonged not to nature, but to culture. Deeply immersed as he was in the overblown pages of the 'ethnologist's *vade-mecum*' (as Léry's masterpiece has been dubbed),[24] Louis Guyon used them as a basis for correcting the negative, and indeed thoroughly repulsive, image that classical writers had given of the people whose only speech consisted of howls and barks. In spite of their flattened noses, they could in fact 'speak a tolerably learned, concise and properly accented language which might be Greek'. This impeccable diction, bringing a gleam of renaissance Hellenism to the wildernesses of Brazil, was coupled with the moral virtues of prudence, magnanimity and liberality. Perhaps they did happen to eat human flesh occasionally, but nobody is perfect – and they did at least eat it cooked, and confined themselves to the flesh of their enemies.

To complete his rehabilitation of the legendary Cynocephali, Guyon, who has read Montaigne, shamelessly plagiarizes the latter's 'Of Cannibals', giving the reader to understand that he, too, was present at Rouen to see and question the famous man-eaters straight from Brazil.[25] Guyon, more fortunate than Montaigne (who was able to speak with only three cannibals), saw a 'dozen of these men at Rouen, whom certain Normans had brought'. Without mentioning the need for an interpreter, he declares that he 'conferred and spoke with them, as with the lords of Villegagnon and Léry'.[26] Villegagnon, who died in 1572, had been the leader of the short-lived 'France Antarctique' venture to Brazil, and Jean de Léry, though he had judged the enterprise harshly, was considered to be the most reliable historian of the expedition. Thus it is easy to see why Guyon, anxious to endow his narrative with the greatest possible veracity, took out all necessary safeguards, even if it meant inventing the little conversation with those affable Cannibals.

To Columbus and his contemporaries, the Cynocephalus seemed like the legendary ancestor of the newly discovered Cannibal, the modern myth answering to that of antiquity. This recognition mingled with an understandable feeling of alarm, as if the tendrils of a long-suppressed nightmare were stretching out into waking life. Hence, Guyon saw the passage from Cynocephalus to Cannibal as a moral and social promotion. It was not accomplished without repeated sleight of hand: in the first place, the Asiatic (or more accurately Scythian) origins of the dog-headed people had to be forgotten so that they could be transported to the western fringes of the known world; then their flat noses had to be replaced by childlike features, and their canine appetite by an appetite for vengeance that seemed considerably more human and certainly less repellent; finally, they had to be seen as paragons of the loftiest virtues, instead of expressing needs so primitive that they verged on the bestial.

So the Cynocephalus was promoted to Cannibal – a revolution of thought resulting from a long century of discoveries and reinterpretations, and from the living presence of Montaigne. At the dawn of their history, Cannibals were incontestably worse than the ancient Cynocephali who, according to some sources, were neither so cruel nor so barbarous as their modern rivals. The Cannibal, as seen by Columbus and Vespucci, was far removed from the inoffensive stupidity of the dog-headed races whom Aelian locates in the Indies, in the country of the purple beetles – where, though they spoke in grunts and led a most frugal existence among their flocks and herds, they showed themselves to be fair-minded and very hospitable. Only their lack of an articulate language barred them from classification amongst rational beings.[27] Cannibals, on the other hand, had a sinister colouring from birth: not content with barking and going about naked, they also ate their fellow creatures. Their literary prestige was the token of the horror which they commonly provoked. If it had not been for their ever-increasing familiarity to discoverers, and especially for the change of mental outlook in the late Renaissance which made paradox central to the renewal of self-awareness and awareness of others, they would probably never have reached such heights. They would have retained their status as plausible and vaguely disgusting monsters, banished to the margins of geographical knowledge. Certainly, they would never have assumed the primordial role which, for the West, they did play: both foil and bogeyman, by turns an immovable enemy and – more frightening still – an alter ego.

2

The Cannibal à la mode

ぺ‧ゞ

The complete butcher

How did the cannibal myth travel from its Columbian origins to its apotheosis in the works of Montaigne, Shakespeare, and the Enlightenment philosophers? The journal of Columbus's first voyage was not published, even in part, until long after the events: the discoverer's first two biographers, Bartolomé de Las Casas in 1552 and Fernando, Columbus's illegitimate son, in 1571, made use of it and anthologized certain elements. The rest was lost. Nonetheless, Columbus's discovery of the Cannibals had been very widely publicized through the *De Orbe Novo* of Peter Martyr of Anghiera. The letters relating to the voyages that constitute the first of the eight 'Decades' were published as early as 1511, and were soon pirated and turned into all the principal European languages.

In the first epistle, which narrates the voyage of 1492, the terrors of the unfortunate Taino Indians, who were hunted for food in their native forests, assume almost obsessive proportions: 'The Cannibals take them as small children and castrate them, as we do to capons or pigs which we want to fatten and make tender for our food . . .'[1]

A series of comparisons is used to bring out the horror of anthropophagy, which, as in Columbus's journal, is stripped of its ritual aspect and reduced to a mere matter of nutrition. These early accounts of the Antillean Cannibal bear little resemblance to what was to become, from the late 1550s onwards, standard French wisdom on the subject: the symbolic interpretation of a rite of vengeance, variously transcribed by André Thevet, Jean de Léry and Michel de Montaigne, which has nothing to do with ordinary hunger.[2]

Thus, Peter Martyr, elaborating on Columbus, saw the incursions of the Caribs as a kind of hunt with a human quarry, promptly followed by slaughter or domestication, as required. The need for food seemed a logical explanation of some aspects of the symbolic economy of American anthropophagy. For example, the fact that women were not slaughtered was easily explained by the need for breeding stock. Meat had to be fattened for the table, and that was why young women were not only kept alive, but even 'cared for' and fed by their conquerors: 'They keep them to bear young, as we do hens, sheep, cows and other such beasts, and keep the older women as slaves for their use.'[3]

What passes for actual observation may actually be an imaginative inversion of a hard fact. The Brazilian Cannibals did not keep their female slaves 'as we keep hens to lay eggs':[4] on the contrary, they bestowed their own wives and daughters on the male prisoners, and it was their offspring who were eaten. Since the Indians believed that it was the male alone who had the power to engender, no warrior would have dreamt of eating his own child, even if it were born to a captive mother.

Later on, in France, the king's cosmographer André Thevet poured scorn on such imaginings, which were still being repeated word for word as late as 1570 by his rival, François de Belleforest, a respecter of the oldest 'authorities' on the subject, whom he considered to be the most reliable.[5] The fact that the Caribs attached greater importance to men is sufficient to explain why the women were spared, and why only masculine flesh was consumed at the anthropophagous feast. There is no need to advance the improbable hypothesis of a planned increase in the food supply.

If we compare this first letter of Peter Martyr with Columbus's journal of 1492, which survives only in fragments, we are struck by an odd sort of rationalization, whereby the stuff of legend – the Cannibals, known initially by hearsay and evoked, in all their ferocity, in tales told by the Taínos – is reduced to a scandalous familiarity. In their need to equate the far-distant with the near and familiar, writers projected European culinary habits onto the American Cannibal: because meat was regularly salted at home, their morbid imaginations produced lumps of salted human flesh hanging from the beams of cannibal huts; the familiar spit roast engendered the roasting of human victims over a small fire.[6]

Human forms – apparently sleeping, or horribly headless – roasting on spits like sheep or sucking pigs, appear as early as 1544, (dis)gracing the pages of Sebastian Münster's *Cosmographia universalis*, and reappear later in the margins of his maps, eloquent testimony to the barbarism of the New World. Münster, a German, in fact saw no continuity between the new anthropophagi of America and those assigned by ancient tradition to Asia. He saw the Cannibals of the Antilles or Brazil as near relations of the 'Tauroscythians', 'Agathyrsians' and other 'savage and unruly peoples' who were apt to decorate their chimneys with human heads on poles; or even nearer relatives of the Tartars, who, 'never troubling to use table cloths', roasted their enemies, devoured them 'like starving wolves' and greedily drank their blood. In successive editions of the *Cosmographia*, the same illustrations of butchered bodies on slabs and human trunks turning on spits were used indifferently to illustrate the customs of the legendary Scythians and the equally revolting table manners of the 'gluttonous beasts' who dwelt on West Indian shores.

Figure 2 Top: Cannibals chopping up human flesh. Sebastian Münster, Basel, 1554. Woodcut. Bottom: A man being roasted on a spit. Woodcut, Ibid.

American cannibal cuisine, thus re-created in the European imagination, can be found as early as 1502, in a Portuguese *portulan*. It appears again in the *Carta Marina* of Martin Waldseemüller (1516) and notably in Simon Grynaeus's and Holbein the Younger's *mappa mundi* which embellishes the *Novus Orbis* published at Basel in 1555. The conical hut, topped by a grinning severed head, appears in the right-hand corner alongside a sturdy butcher's table for chopping human flesh, stewpots with a clenched human hand and the inevitable spit, laden with arms and legs, turning over a charcoal fire.[7]

In his *Histoire d'un voyage* (1578), Jean de Léry, who had seen anthropophagi in action in Brazil, protested in vain against the fictitious imagery which associated the sophisticated techniques of the accomplished European butcher with the savagery of the strange Adamite chefs. This phantasmagoria seemed to him worthy of 'Rabelais's tale of Panurge, who escaped from the spit well basted and half-cooked'.[8] And, indeed, in *Pantagruel* the hero's companion, captured by the Turks, is roasted alive by them, 'all larded like a rabbit', and only escapes with his life because his cook providentially dozes off.[9] In fact, Léry had said more or less the opposite: the Indians had laughed incredulously at the sight of a turkey being turned on a spit, saying that it would never cook if they kept waving it around like that.

This warning to ignorant cartographers was to prove a dead letter. Well into the seventeenth century, when the Counter-Reformation was at its height, the Austrian Benedictine Philoponus, in a book about the American peregrinations of missionaries from his order and about their edifying martyrdoms, re-hashed for his own propaganda purposes the whole litany of cannibal horrors from a century earlier. Hurdles laden with roasting children, women being quartered on butchers' slabs or pickled, men roasting on spits: nothing is missing from this pandemonium of anthropophagous horrors, which draws freely on the full range of previous iconographies – preferably Protestant ones – to shift the emotional impact in favour of the Catholic struggle. For this purpose he pillages the *Grands Voyages* of Théodore de Bry, whose text and illustrations were really intended to denounce the cruelties of the Spanish *conquista*. The industrious Philoponus was particularly interested in de Bry's 1599 edition of Bartolomé de Las Casas's 'Brief description of the destruction of the Indies'. The innocent victims of the conquistadors, usually naked and imploring, become victims of idol-worshipping sorcerers or plumed warriors savagely resisting the new arrivals. The inevitable and popular, but outdated and inaccurate, turnspit which appears in Philoponus's crude plates bears witness to the archaic, but efficacious, character of this edifying literature.[10]

The starting-point for this frenzied amplification of American anthropophagy is Peter Martyr, who elaborates on the meagre information provided by Columbus in his very first 'Decade'. He uses sensationalism to stigmatize the barbaric horror implied by the existence of the Cannibal. However, certain traits have disappeared: Martyr has no room for the etymological link with the Grand Khan (really a mythological creation of the Admiral himself), or even for the determined resurgence of the Cynocephali of ancient and medieval legend. The Cannibal, de-mythicized by the loss of legendary origins, seems to have become an object of positive discourse. Peter Martyr, unlike Columbus, is not concerned with deciphering the tracks left on the virgin sands of the New World. His primary concern is not (to borrow a phrase from Tzvetan Todorov) the interpretation of the Other.[11] He was not really interested in the modern Carib as a realization of pre-existing meanings or models.

But what the Cannibals lost on the myths, they gained in evocative power. Detached from a fabulous prehistory, they immediately fed on what is easily identified as repression. Hence, the human joints on spits and the 'freshly severed head of a young man, still damp with blood' which Columbus found on his second voyage in 1493.[12] Hence, also, the ancillary sexuality of these man-eaters, which effectively weds incest to anthropophagy. The impoverishment of the cannibal myth in its Columbian version and its decline into phantasmagoria would at least secure for the theme an incontestable publicity value.

Vespucci and after: the rise of the incestuous Cannibal

De Orbe Novo brought the Cannibal to the notice of humanists throughout Europe. But as soon as the 'Decades' had begun their leisurely progress in 1516, and before they had been published in full (at Alcalá de Henares in 1530), plagiarisms and anthologies were already appearing thick and fast. For example, the *Libretto de tutte le navigazione del Re di Spagna* ('Little book of all the navigations of the King of Spain'), published anonymously at Venice in 1504, reproduced Martyr's first two letters describing Columbus's voyages of 1492 and 1493: the first introduced the name 'Cannibal' and the unpleasant reputation thereto attached; the second told of the visit to Guadeloupe and the discovery of the Caribs' macabre larder containing 'men's flesh boiled with flesh of parrots and birds, some ready on spits for roasting'.[13]

The contents of the *Libretto* were taken over lock, stock and barrel by the *Mondo Novo e Paesi novamente ritrovati da Alberico Vespuzio fiorentino* ('New World and Countries discovered recently by Alberico Vespuzio of Florence') (Vicenza, 1507), the first in what was to be a very long series of Renaissance travel books. The first three parts of this compendium, compiled by Montalboddo, professor of humanities at Vicenza, contained the eastern journeys of Venetian and Portuguese explorers such as Cadamosto and Vasco da Gama; then came the westerly voyages of Columbus (Book IV), Vespucci (Book V) and Cabral and Cortereal (Book VI).[14]

It is worth noting that the 'cannibalistic diptych' of Columbus's first two voyages is placed just before the (controversial) account of Amerigo Vespucci's voyage to Brazil, which was published in Paris as early as 1503, re-issued the following year in Venice with the title *Mundus Novus* and before 1529 went into sixty editions in six different languages.[15] A leading sixteenth-century best seller, *Mundus Novus*, with its mixture of archaism and sensationalism, was perfectly suited to the tastes of its time. In fact, the Vespucci account originally addressed to Lorenzo di Pietro Medici, Florentine ambassador to France, which described the journey of 1501–2 along the coasts of South America to the La Plata estuary and the Falkland Islands,[16] had been interpolated by an anonymous compiler with an unerring feel for publicity.

In the original version of his letter (known as 'the Bartolozzi letter' after its nineteenth-century editor), Vespucci had been content to equate the Brazilian Indians with the Golden Age model: 'they have no law or religious faith whatever, and live according to nature'. This orthodox notion agrees at every point with the ideals of the Florentine humanists, who indeed were not at all surprised to find the mythical humanity of the first ages of the world still alive and thriving across the Atlantic. Vespucci's anonymous reviser thought himself perfectly justified in claiming that the Indians lacked not only religion, laws, rulers and private property, but also the incest taboo.[17] This made the tableau of pristine felicity more colourful, if less consistent.[18] Systematic and repeated infringement of the incest taboo gave some substance to the rather pallid and conventional picture of those distant ancestors unacquainted with labour, anxiety, disease or decrepitude. But it also shifted the balance back towards savagery and away from the tranquillity of Paradise lost. The serene imagery of the Golden Age yielded to the more telling, and inherently medieval, image of the wild man. Authority for this 'hard' primitivism came from Saint Jerome, Brunetto Latini and Antonio Malfante, embroidering the outline supplied by Diodorus Siculus.[19]

Thus re-worked and distorted, the description attributed to

Vespucci of the naked and incestuous Cannibal was given pride of place, though this particular term was not yet employed. Upon the shoulders of these peoples (the Caribs of Guyana and the Tupinambas of coastal Brazil), who were later to be described with fair accuracy by Thevet, Léry and Montaigne, *Mundus Novus* and its derivatives unload a mountain of uninhibited moral misdemeanours. Ignorant of all forms of civil society and religion, they fornicate freely, shamelessly and openly, without respect for the bonds of blood: 'they have as many women as they wish. Son couples with mother, and sister with brother, any man with any woman; any and every time they wish, they divorce from their marriages, and in no thing do they keep order.'[20]

These peoples, as well as enjoying freedom of divorce and the absence of an incest taboo, are voraciously anthropophagous, and here again they ignore all frontiers and taboos. The Brazilians, as imaginatively portrayed by Vespucci's compiler, are hard to recognize as belonging to the Golden Age, as Gilbert Chinard suggests,[21] for 'human flesh is to them a common viand'. The barbarians' liking for this food is so great 'that fathers have been seen to eat their wives and children'. And the pseudo-Vespucci adds, via the pen of his French translator Mathurin du Redouer, that 'I met and spoke with a man who admitted to having eaten more than three hundred human bodies.'[22]

These peoples, with their ferocious appetites and unrestrained sexuality, are the precise opposite of Christian society, as conceived by the Renaissance. For civilized Renaissance societies, the pseudo-Vespucci's Brazil was not so much the rebirth of a pacific and vegetarian Ovidian golden age as a 'world upside-down' – not the least to be envied, for all that it gave free rein even to the most inadmissible and least socially tolerable desires. The fascination of these fables, so much more dubious than Columbus's legends – and for that very reason much more influential – can be traced to the end of the sixteenth century. It lingers, for example, in the glosses which François de Belleforest added in 1570 to the *Histoire universelle du monde* by Joannes Boemus; where the timid appearance of some marginal notes does little to mitigate the riveting brutality of the main observations: 'The Frenchmen who have been there deny that mothers or sisters are abused'; 'Again, the French say that they eat only their enemies'.[23]

Thus, the parallel between Columbus and Vespucci, which Montalboddo's *Paesi* compilation readily invites, ought not to be interpreted as Chinard suggests. The contrast is perhaps less between Medieval Man (Columbus) and Renaissance Man (Vespucci, 'improved' by an indelicate editor) than between two degrees of an ethnocentrism common to both, but on the whole more obvious in the Florentine. It may be said that Vespucci detaches the vision of America from the mythical substratum which is undeniably present in his predecessor, and thus endows it with a sort of secular autonomy. Neither Scripture nor Sibylline prophecy any longer set the parameters of the New World, and Vespucci never shared the providential imaginings of Christopher, the Christ-Bearer. Nonetheless, the tendency thereafter was for the new lands to become a playground for all the tumultuous and fearsome lucubrations of an unbridled libido.

What is important is the bogus continuity which Vicenzo's compilation established between Columbus's *Libretto* and the pseudo-Vespuccian *Mundus Novus*. Columbus had supplied only the (horrific) name of Cannibal; now it was associated with a phantasmagoria linking nakedness and anthropophagy with a truly devouring sexual appetite. Henceforth, the Cannibals were to concentrate in their own person all the greatest crimes of humanity: incest, infanticide, allelophagy. The terrors underpinning this construct placed them at the heart of darkness of the imagination: they embodied both Oedipus, lying with his mother, and Thyestes devouring his own children.

Minds were particularly receptive to this image because it was well suited to certain very particular political and economic considerations. Like the Tainos, the Spanish colonists in the islands were soon subjected to devastating Carib attacks, not to mention the bloody failure of missionary endeavours in the region. In 1501 Isabella the Catholic issued a royal decree declaring that the war against the Caribs was a just war and that prisoners could be sold as slaves.[24] This right of seizure answered only too well to the colonists' need for manpower, and it soon led to worrying levels of abuse. It was only necessary to tie the anthropophagous label to the most peaceable of Indian tribes in order to justify its enslavement, which would inevitably lead to its annihilation.[25] Doubtless, the decree of 1501 and the series of iterations which extended its principles down to the beginning of the seventeenth century restricted this holy war to a relatively small area – some of the Lesser Antilles, Santa Lucia, Dominica, Saint-Vincent and part of the mainland around Cartagena. But in practice, and in spite of the jealous vigilance of royal officialdom, the greedy exactions of the slave traders and *encomienderos* had no bounds.

As it happens, this geographical confusion, very lucrative in the short term but infinitely disastrous in its human and demographic consequences, was at the same time being maintained by

Montalboddo's *Paesi* of 1507. Through the amalgamation of Columbus and Vespucci, a total confusion arose between the Caribs of the Antilles, Guyana and western Venezuela and the equally anthropophagous Tupinambas of the Brazilian coast. By muddling the accounts told by the two explorers, Montalboddo's compilation paved the way for an extension of the 'Cannibal' label over most of South America, from Darien to the La Plata estuary, along the route followed by Magellan and Pigafetta in 1519. We shall see in a later chapter how even at this time, long before Montaigne, Frenchmen were beginning to equate Cannibals with 'Brazilians'.

3

The Cannibal Comes to France

Then [Antiphysis] begat the eavesdropping dissemblers, superstitious pope-mongers, the frantic Pistolets, the demoniacal Calvins, impostors of Geneva, the scrapers of benefices, apparitors with the devil in them, and other grinders and squeezers of livings, herb-stinking hermits, gulligutted dunces of the cowl, church vermin, false zealots, and many more other deformed and ill-favoured monsters, made in spite of nature.

Rabelais, *Le Quart Livre*

The Cannibal as folklore hero

It was in this guise that the Cannibals came to France in early 1517, the same year as the *Paesi* compilation was translated by the lawyer Mathurin du Redouer under the title *Sensuyt le Nouveau Monde et navigations: faictes par Emeric de Vespuce Florentin, des pays et isles nouvellement trouvez, au paravant a nous incongneuz* ('Here follows the New World and Navigations Performed by Amerigo Vespucci of Florence, to the newly discovered lands and islands previously unknown to us'). This was the first work on the discovery of the New World to appear in French. It introduced the American directly in the forbidding guise of the Cannibal, and it was reprinted at least six times within a few months.[1] The 'Canibale', with his cortège of crimes and his arsenal of spits and skewers, had scarcely set a metaphorical foot on land before he was firmly installed in the national imagination.

On 12 January 1533, new style,[2] there appeared, again in French, a compilation of the first three 'Decades' of Peter Martyr, dedicated to Charles, Duke of Angoulême, 'third son of the most Christian King François the first of that name'. The title was *Extraict ou Recueil des Isles nouvellement trouvees en la grand mer Oceane, ou temps du roy Despaigne Fernand et Elizabeth sa femme* ('Extract or Compilation of the Islands Newly Discovered in the Great Sea of Ocean, in the time of Ferdinand King of Spain and Isabella his Wife'), and here, as

is to be expected, we find once again the twin episodes of the
Arawak-hunt and the larder of Guadeloupe. It is significant that
whatever the personality of the compiler (this one was Antoine
Favre) and the overall dimensions of the anthology, the cannibal diptych is always preserved in its entirety. A fearsome reputation, echoing from island to island, is justified by the gruesome portrayal of the
banquet where the guests are also the meal. First the word, then the
object: it was in this immutable order that the Columbian legend of
the Cannibal was transmitted and orchestrated. Sometimes it was
accompanied by Vespucci's embellishments, sometimes not, but the
meaning remained the same.

Thus, when in that same year (1533) the word appeared in
Chronicques du grant Gargantua published anonymously in Lyon, it
was no novelty.[3] It proves, if proof were needed, how popular the
word, which had been widely disseminated in France for some
twenty years, had become, and how it was already firmly attached to
manifestations of a barbarity which was as mythical as it was extreme.
It is no surprise to find that the chief characteristic of the 'Canibales'
in *Gargantua* is their anthropophagy. They kill and eat King
Mioland, father of the fair Badebec; Gargantua, the good giant and
fearless knight, undertakes to avenge the former, and subsequently
marries the latter.[4] Their association with the 'Tartarins', who represent the inhabitants of Tartary rather than 'one of the idols of the
Saracens',[5] is explained by the generally pejorative nature of the passage. It is vain to seek for any geographical logic in this twinning of
'Tartarins' and 'Canibales'. Both are people excluded from the human
race, as much by their barbarous practices as by their distant position
on the fringes of the habitable world. Extremes – Tartars of the
Sunrise and Cannibals of the Sunset – meet in a clash of syllables, and
jointly constitute the living antithesis of real, familiar society.

The same attitude is manifest in Rabelais, from whom the author of
the *Grande Chronicque* may have borrowed the allusion to
Cannibals.[6] The 1532 conclusion to the former's *Pantagruel*, which
promises to locate the hero's future adventures in places as far-flung as
the 'Caspian Mountains', the 'Atlantic sea', the region of the
Cannibals and the Pearl Islands,[7] blithely confuses the western and
eastern bounds of the known world. The Caspian Mountains bor-
dered the legendary kingdom of Prester John, traditionally situated in
India or Ethiopia. The series of descriptions associating the Atlantic
with the defeat of the Cannibals and the southernmost islands of the
Lesser Antilles (Margarita and Cubagua), which were famous for their
pearls, most certainly alludes to the recently discovered Caribbean Sea
and Central America. Moreover, at the end of *Gargantua* the

'Canibale Isles' are again mentioned, in proximity to the 'Pearl Islands', in connection with the splendid clothes of the ladies of Thélème: the narrator assures us that the 'Canibale Isles' export an abundance of 'ingots of gold, raw silk, pearls and precious stones'.[8]

The expression 'Canibale Isles' in this last quotation might even imply a precise geographical location: the Leeward Islands, in the Antilles, where Columbus made his landfall on his second voyage in 1493. In France itself, navigational charts and atlases often made use of this description. In his versified version of the 'Adventurous voyages' of the Portuguese-born navigator Jean Alfonse 'de Saintonge', the poet and bookseller Jehan Mallart gives this description of the Lesser Antilles to the east of Porto Rico: 'Some isles there are which travellers must fear, / These are the islands of the Cannibals.'[9]

Later on the same tag reappears, almost like a refrain, this time attached to Dominica: 'Islands of Cannibals there are here.'[10] However, the menace implied by this fearful presence is no real deterrent, since Mallart immediately goes on to describe the 'great profit' that a voyage there might bring – and he concludes by announcing that he intends to retire there.

But elsewhere in this same versified route map the word tends to be used purely to denote anthropophagy. On Brazil, or more specifically the province of Pernambouc or Fernambourg:

> A rustic, savage people here there be
> Believing nothing save those things they see,
> Or things we give or show to them withal:
> This is the nation of the Cannibal,
> A folk that do their enemies devour.[11]

It seems that the narrowly geographical use of the word very soon came into conflict with the modern meaning. As early as 1544, the *Cosmographie* of Jean-Alfonse de Saintonge applies the originally American term to black Africans: 'This cape of Frenandupau [Fernando-Po, in the Gulf of Guinea] is a great island all peopled with races which are cannibals.'[12] 'These Ambos [people of the Congo] eat them [the 'Magnicongres'] when they can catch them, for they are cannibals.'[13] The first extension of the term is in Antonio Pigafetta's account of Magellan's circumnavigation of the world, as translated by Fabre in 1526: at a latitude of thirty-four 'and a third' degrees south, the discoverers, while in search of fresh water, encountered some 'Canibales, who are men that eat human flesh'.[14] Obviously they could not, in those latitudes, have been Caribs, but man-eating Indians in the broader sense – in this instance, Tupi-Guaranis.

Nonetheless, the narrower geographical meaning endured at least until the end of the century. Where the association with islands is concerned, the 'Canibale Isles' are invariably the Lesser Antilles. This is supported by the evidence of Bruneau de Rivedoux, a French Protestant captain from the Ile de Ré, who plainly means the Lesser Antilles when he describes the voyage of a galleon which left France in September 1572 bound for the 'Canibales'. The vessel, following the route of Columbus's second voyage, reached the Antilles near Dominica, 'which is an Indian land to windward, that is, below the wind'.[15] It then sailed north towards 'Gardeloupe' before reaching Puerto Rico and the Greater Antilles. When the galleon had got as far as 'Jomarique' and Cuba, the crew began to murmur against Captain Maillard and forced him to return northwards to more familiar territory: they had gone much too far beyond 'Gardeloupe' and the 'Canibales'.[16]

The 'Canibale Isles' therefore seem to have been very precisely located, and it would be strange if Rabelais, in putting them near the 'Pearl Islands', which constitute a south-westerly extension of the Antillean archipelago, were to hit by pure chance on this cartographically accurate picture. However, even if the framework of his descriptions of them in *Pantagruel* and *Gargantua* is borrowed from New World geography, they are enriched with a legendary substratum which has no direct connection with the true course of the Great Discoveries. There are pearl fisheries in the Caribbean and the Gulf of Panama, south of the Antilles; and the gold of Hispaniola was indeed one of the reasons behind the ruthless colonization of the island. But silk was unknown to the first inhabitants of the Americas: it evokes, rather, the fabled refinements of the Orient.

Here, Rabelais touches on a complex assemblage of myths, which are also found in Columbus's writings, for example. There, the ferocious Caribs are represented as the guardians of fabulous treasures. Some of their islands are virtually pure gold, or at least their ground contains 'more gold than earth',[17] as the Admiral believed. Columbus's exploits of 1492–3 had quickly become part of folktale. In the morphological schema imposed on the folktale by Vladimir Propp[18] (and the voyage of discovery would lend itself to a similar analysis), the object of the quest is for the hero to perform a succession of tasks, and overcome a series of half-human, half-animal aggressors, so as to obtain possession of an object which will bring him power and wealth. Thus, the hero Columbus's prowess entitles him not only to possess the symbolic object (gold, pearls, precious stones), but also to exterminate (or at least enslave) his adversary, the accursed Carib, who has no right to possess the treasures. The 'Memorandum for Antonio de Torres', which Columbus wrote at the end of his second voyage on 30 January 1494,[19] contains a plan to use the Cannibal Isles as a source of slaves, whose sale would finance further expeditions, always in search of gold. A narrative transformation of a familiar type turns the aggressor into a conscripted and unwilling helper in pursuit of an unending quest.

The Admiral's sordid calculations – on his return he sold hundreds of Carib prisoners in exchange for seeds and beasts of burden – are of course far removed from Rabelais's way of thinking. Nevertheless, the economics of Thélème, the utopia which concludes *Gargantua* and includes the allusion to the isles of the West, are based on a not dissimilar scheme of pillage. The idealized abbey, richly endowed by a munificent prince, imports foodstuffs, silks of Cathay and American gold and pearls free of charge. But it produces nothing in return, since its inhabitants, gentlemen and gentlewomen, live a life of leisure. The 'politics of giving in the last chapters of *Gargantua*'[20] reveal the critical relationship between the concluding utopia of the 'First Book' and the economic realities of the time. The feudal values of gift and counter-gift advocated by the good giant Gargantua had, in reality, been well and truly overthrown by far more complex rules of exchange based on wider markets, the discovery of new sources of precious metals, and the commercial profits offered by ruthless exploitation of new worlds. In this way, and notwithstanding its archaic stance (governed by the medieval monastic model, but in reverse: the only rule is 'Do as thou wilt'), the utopia of Thélème fits neatly into the historical context of the Great Discoveries. Rabelais follows Columbus in 'cannibalizing' the Cannibals and their fabulous treasures.

Rabelais – or the Cynocephalus moralized

Two observations must be made at the outset of our study of the Cannibals in the tales of *Gargantua* and *Pantagruel*. First, in Rabelais, the omnipresent folklore theme of eating and swallowing is not synonymous with cannibalism. The cannibal motif is much more restrained than the eating theme – the uninhibited indulgence of a cosmic appetite, the hyperbolic manifestation of a hunger which takes the entire world as its food and profit. This is why I shall pay no attention to such episodes as the author's journey in Pantagruel's mouth and the grim adventure of the six pilgrims eaten by Gargantua in a salad. Both are inherited from the popular tradition of *Grandes et Inestimables Chroniques*, and derive ultimately from a grotesque travesty of the Journey to the Otherworld.[21]

Second, the occurrences of the word 'Canibales' from *Pantagruel* (1532) to the posthumous *Cinquième Livre* do not always have the same, unchanging referent. The semantic field narrows in 1552 with *Le Quart Livre*, in which the word occurs three times: in the introductory epistle to Odet de Coligny, Cardinal of Châtillon; in Chapter 32, in connection with the portrait of Antiphysis, the allegory of 'Anti-Nature'; and in Chapter 66, during the voyage along the coasts of Ganabin, the fearsome island whose approach strikes terror into all on board and sends Panurge head first into the hold, where he copiously shits himself. These three occurrences alone – and perhaps only the first two – seem to fit the definition in *Briefve Declaration*, that erudite, and sometimes unduly pedantic, glossary found in the appendix to the work and which may not in fact be by Rabelais: 'CANIBALES. A monstrous people in Africa who have faces like dogs and who bark instead of laughing.'[22]

It is a fact that in the first two books the word does not have the distinctly negative connotations which it acquires in the epistle to the Cardinal of Châtillon. It is highly likely that it always implied barbarity and extreme cruelty: the history of the word from Columbus onwards makes this clear. But in association with a West repainted in the colours of the gorgeous East – a necessary filter through which to view the 'new horizons' – those fearsome and fascinating people fitted easily into the world of chivalric romance and wonder tale. Up to this point, Rabelais has made no explicit reference to their insatiable appetite for human flesh, or to the dogs' heads bestowed on them by the fanciful laws of current etymology.

However, the geographical location of these semi-fabulous barbarians is scarcely in doubt. Somewhere near the Pearl Islands (it matters little whether this meant the Pearl Archipelago in the Gulf of Panama, at the entry to the Pacific, as Lazare Sainéan suggests,[23] or the southern end of the Antilles), the American 'Canibales' lived quite happily as symbolic neighbours of the inhabitants of the Caspian Mountains bordering the lands of Prester John, at the other end of the known world.

Thus *Le Quart Livre* subjects the word to a kind of semantic reduction as its geographical horizons are narrowed. There is a return to the false *canis* etymology and to the African roots of the old legends – assuming that we can trust the author of the *Briefve Declaration*. Admittedly, the definition there agrees quite well with the context of the two first occurrences. In the prefatory epistle, the 'Canibales' are at the head of a glum and sinister troop of 'misanthropes and perpetual eavesdroppers' who despise laughter and would have 'Pantagruelism' condemned as a heresy.[24] In the second passage they are among the swarming offspring of Antiphysis, anti-Nature, at the end of the 'Shrovetide' episode, closing the list of 'eavesdropping dissemblers, superstitious pope-mongers, the frantic Pistolets, the demoniacal Calvins, impostors of Geneva, the scrapers of benefices, apparitors with the devil in them, and other grinders and squeezers of livings, herb-stinking hermits, gulligutted dunces of the cowl, church vermin, false zealots, and many more other deformed and ill-favoured monsters, made in spite of nature'.[25] Evidently, their medieval dog-headedness is to be taken as a moral indication: the 'calumnies' of these howling mongrels are an insult to the harmony of Nature and the good. In the original French, the word 'canibale' forms part of a ringing series of assonances: *Ca*lvins, *Ca*phars, *Ca*nnibals. *Ca*-, wrongly taken as a prefix, serves as a kind of sound matrix, the common denominator of the series, and also the first syllable of the key word round which the whole description is structured, though the thing itself is not among Antiphysis' escort: mortal *Ca*lumny.

Ronsard echoes Rabelais, perhaps unintentionally, in the *Continuation du Discours des Miseres de ce temps* (1562): not only does he rhyme 'Cannibales' with 'Calvinales' (in an ironical allusion to 'Calvinist' virtues), he also creates a similar series of fictitious derivations: 'Canada, Callicuth, Cannibales ... Calvinales'.[26] Calvin and his followers are invited to propagate their doctrine in those distant parts, *'Qui n'ont ouy parler de nos Religions'* ('which have never heard tell of our religions') by means of 'some trifling miracle': a convenient way to get rid of a troublesome adversary by challenging him to demonstrate the truth of his doctrine.[27]

Half a century later, the Jesuit François Garasse also enrolled the Cannibals in his fight against the Gallican magistrate Etienne Pasquier, a pugnacious adversary of the Society of Jesus. Turning from a long list of grievances, Garasse calls the deviations of the Protestant churches 'Tragical histories' and 'Cannibal games',[28] to which the Advocate General should turn his attention instead of bothering with the schisms within the Catholic church. Garasse refuses to concede that the Inquisition itself behaves with 'the cruelty of Cannibals'.[29]

To return to *Le Quart Livre de Pantagruel*. In the motley enumeration that closes the description of Antiphysis, Rabelais includes both his personal enemies, Roman Catholics and Genevan Calvinists (coupled together by the system of assonances), and, more generally, an inhuman being which monstrously combines a dog's head with a man's body, a dog's snarl with the image of the Creator. But the 'Canibale', reinstated as the Cynocephalus to fit the polemic, has been moralized, and will be, henceforth, the allegorical vehicle for the author's message.

The definition in the *Briefve Declaration* is surely insufficient on one point: the anthropophagy of these moralized monsters has by no means been discarded. The dog-headed calumniators do not just bark (instead of laughing); they devour their victims. The third occurrence of the word in *Le Quart Livre*, in the Pantagruelists' conversation as they sail the coasts of Ganabin, makes this clear beyond all doubt. The thieves who dwell on this island (a possible allusion to the 'Thieves' Island' in the Marianas, visited by Magellan in 1521) filled voyagers with fear. ' "For may I never stir if they are not worse than the very Cannibals: they would certainly eat us alive. Do not go among them, I pray you," '[30] the terror-stricken Panurge implores his less timorous companions.

Though most of the allusions in this chapter remain obscure,[31] it is certain that the term 'cannibal' retains its figurative value and distinctly pejorative connotation. Panurge thinks that 'it were safer to take a journey to Hell' than to visit the anthropophagi. The proud and scathing rejoinder of the friar Jean des Entommeures, who is always spoiling for a fight and who urges his friends to 'pillage' the islanders without paying for their night's lodging, may be intended to recall the attitude of Columbus and the Spaniards towards the Caribs, doomed to extermination or enslavement, since they could not be acknowledged as peaceful trading partners or docile vassals.

The lowest point reached by the Cannibals in Rabelais is in *Le Cinquième Livre*, in the Land of Satin episode. Here, they figure once more in a list, a catalogue of fabulous peoples created by Hearsay, who 'kept a school for vouching'.[32] The Cannibals are quite at home amongst the geographical marvels and monstrous races dear to Pliny, Solinus, Isidore of Seville and Pierre d'Ailly, in the variegated procession of 'Troglodytes', 'Hymantopodes', 'Blemmies', 'Pygmies' and other 'Aegipans'. None of these will ever be more than a legendary name.

Concluding our journey through Rabelais, we note that the Cannibals have been understood in a great variety of ways. In *Pantagruel* and *Gargantua* the word evokes exotic barbarity and lust, in the wake of the Great Discoveries. In *Le Quart Livre* it becomes an insult directed at the enemies of Pantagruelism; lacking any picturesque content, it seems to emerge from a kind of moralized bestiary. The Cannibals, with their animal grins, represent an attitude that is anti-Nature and anti-human, since (as Rabelais himself famously observed) 'laughter is proper to man'. The needs of allegorical discourse restore these far-off creatures to the dog-headedness of legend: Cynocephali rather than Cannibals, they go back to an unknown origin before the voyages of Columbus and Vespucci. Their legendary country, according to *Briefve Declaration*, is Africa, continent of monsters; or the highlands of Ethiopia or India, if we believe Isidore. At the end of this regression, *Le Cinquième Livre* consummates the rejection of the modern origins of the 'Canibales' and restores them to a place among the most traditional inventions of human memory.

4

Brazil, Land of Cannibals

༼

.... The customs of these Cannibals, a people so famous among our pilots.

André Thevet, *La Cosmographie universelle*

Brazil is an island

Strange to say – and as far as France is concerned this may be a consequence of the developing trade in dye-bark from the Brazilian coasts after the second voyage of Giovanni da Verrazano in 1526–8[1] – the word 'Cannibal' gradually shifted away from the Lesser Antilles towards the mainland of South America and alighted in its northeastern corner – the north-east of present-day Brazil. It is a fact that the Caribs occupied not only the Antilles, where they had settled relatively recently, but also part of the mainland, including Guyana and part of the lower basin of the Orinoco. A region towards the interior of Venezuela had been named 'Caribana' by the discoverers. The poet du Bartas, describing the peopling of the earth by the descendants of the three sons of Noah in the 'second day' of his *La Seconde Semaine*, follows the descendants of Japheth through the solitudes of the New World. As part of this thousand-year spread of mankind over the isthmuses and straits, the 'Caripane' are situated along a line from the Bay of Cumana and the Gulf of Paria to 'Maragnon, in cruel Brazil'.[2] However, the real territory of the Cannibals never coincided with the range generally ascribed to them by French adventurers from the 1550s onwards, which was to extend eastwards as far as Cape São Agostinho.

The geographical shift of the word is perceptible in two of the documents relating to the entry of Henri II into Rouen on 1 October 1550. This solemn entry went down in the annals of the Norman capital for the 'Brazilian' pageant, which was performed before the Court in a meadow beside the Seine. Fifty Tupinamba Indians, in their habitual nakedness, and two hundred and fifty prostitutes and sailors, similarly clad, mimed scenes of savage life: hunting, fishing, walking, amorous dalliance in a hammock, gathering dye-bark, warfare and the burning of an enemy village. The spectacle ended with a battle between a French ship and a Portuguese caravel, which was soon shot to pieces, plundered and set on fire, with the assistance of the savages and to the great joy of the audience.[3]

In a collection of miniatures entitled 'The Joyous Entry of Henri II into Rouen', now in Rouen municipal library, there is a watercolour showing the King and his cortège on a bridge, with, on one side, the troupe of naked Indian warriors disporting themselves in the groves of the Faubourg Saint-Sever, and, on the other, the duel between the French and Portuguese ships on the Seine. The naval combat is accompanied by a mythological escort, 'The Triumph of the River': mermaids, seahorses and other monsters of the deep surround Neptune in his floating chariot. Opposite the miniature is a verse commentary celebrating the sovereignty of the King of France over the four continents. Not only do the Portuguese flee and the country of Guinea tremble at the great name of Henri, but also: 'Thy power to the cannibals extends: / Faithless to others, they remain our friends, / And in those islands we may safely dwell.'[4]

The word 'Cannibals', for a people whose reputation for warlike savagery is well established, seems here (by a slippage such as we have noted elsewhere) to denote the Lesser Antilles. But it could equally well mean Brazil, which many early sixteenth-century maps showed as an island or archipelago. For example, the pilot Jean Alfonse and the rhymester Jehan Mallart thought that the Maranhâo, or 'river Maron', flowed from south to north and reached up-river to the sources of the Rio de la Plata, forming an almost continuous ribbon of water separating Brazil from the west of the continent and the Andes.[5] This archaic conception of a detached Brazil, very common on Portuguese and Genoese charts and globes at the beginning of the century, is still to be met with in the *mappemonde* of Paolo Forlani and Ferrando Bertelli, the *Universale Descrittione*, published in 1565. The same vertical division is assumed in André Thevet's *Histoire de deux voyages*, written at the end of the 1580s, but now it is the Amazon (or 'Orelane', from the name of its discoverer, Orellana) which flows along the meridian that divided the Spanish possessions from the Portuguese.[6] Turning Brazil into an island by means of these conjoined rivers had the advantage of creating a natural frontier between the rival empires, separated by the Treaty of Tordesillas (7 July 1494) which drew an arbitrary line from pole to pole.

As a footnote to this discussion, we may mention the house in Rouen called 'the House of the Isle of Brazil', which has carved panels, probably dating from the middle of the sixteenth century,[7] showing 'brazier wood' (*pau brasil*) being cut by Herculean Indians, carried to the coast by porters and loaded onto ships anchored off-shore. This indicates that the islands stigmatized as 'faithless' by the author of 'The Joyous Entry' may not be the Lesser Antilles, but fragments of the Brazilian littoral, which was known only in part and was not continuously settled, from the north-east to the south of the country, until long after the time of the Great Discoveries.

The geographical ambiguity of the word is dispelled when we consider the prose commentary on the same Rouen festivities of 1550. This is a booklet published in the following year by Robert le Hoy and Robert and Jehan du Gord, with the title *C'est la deduction du sumptueux ordre plaisantz spectacles et magnifiques theatres dresses* ('The deduction of the sumptuous order, pleasant spectacles and magnificent theatricals'). It explicitly associates 'the country of Brazil' with the country of the 'canyballes' to denote the place supposedly represented in the exotic pageant offered to Henri II and his court.[8] Several of the king's subjects who 'had long dwelt' in those distant parts – and the vague 'several' seems to mean quite a large number – will confirm in all good faith that this 'perfect simulacrum of the truth' is accurate. Now the 'figure of the Brazilians' (the title of one of the engravings in the book)[9] shows continental Tupinamba Indians. Thus, in all probability the phrase 'country of Brazil, and cannibals' refers to two regions contiguous with each other, corresponding to two different areas of modern Brazil.

Southwards, on the Tropic of Capricorn, the 'country of Brazil' proper is the stretch of Atlantic coast where the famous *pau brasil* grew, the 'brazier wood' which yielded a red dye, soon adopted by the textile industry of Rouen and its rural hinterland. The trading stations most frequently visited by Norman sailors, even after the collapse of the France Antarctique venture in March 1560, were Cabo Frio (Gallicized as 'Cap de Frie') and the bay of Rio de Janeiro ('Genèvre'), where Villegagnon had set up his shortlived colony in November 1555. As for the 'country of the Cannibals', which was also inhabited by Tupinamba and Potiguara Indians, it lay further to the north, from Cape São Agostinho (Saint-Augustin) to the Equator, and was, if we are to believe Thevet and Léry,[10] a repulsive region on which French sailors, though elsewhere on good terms with the coastal tribes, were reluctant to set foot. This division is confirmed by cartographical evidence. The *Cosmographie universelle* (1556) of Captain Guillaume Le Testu, a nautical atlas in the Portuguese tradition dedicated to Admiral Gaspard de Coligny, makes the same distinction between Indians 'upstream' and 'downstream': 'near the equinoctial they are cunning and evil'; 'those who are further downstream from the equinoctial are approachable'.[11] The complex interplay of alliances and rivalries among Indian federations explains this fundamental divergence in the relationships between Europeans and tribes which often belonged to quite similar ethnic groups and spoke the same language.

In the land of the *androphagi*

The pejorative view of Cannibals as being, by definition, faithless must not be extended to Brazilian anthropophagi as a whole, of whom some were trading partners or even highly 'approachable com-mensals'. In the work of André Thevet it is associated with the geo-graphical division that we have just described. His intention to classify the native peoples is clear in *Les Singularitez de la France Antarctique*, published in 1557. This work, which follows the for-tunes of Villegagnon's settlement on 'Coligny Island' at the entrance to Rio de Janeiro bay, is richly illustrated and based on firsthand evi-dence; the poets Jean Dorat and Etienne Jodelle competed to supply the introductory verses. It was the first original study of the New World to appear in French. The most important part of the book, the central Chapters 24–60, is the most original and the best informed on questions of ethnography: it deals almost exclusively with the Tamoios, a subgroup of the Tupinamba Indians living on the coast between the 'Bay of Kings' (Angra dos Reis) to the west and the 'Cap de Frie' (Cabo Frio). Thevet calls this people and their neighbouring tribes, all of whom speak the Tupi language and practise anthro-pophagy, 'Amériques', using the word to denote both the country and its inhabitants. But the Cannibals are, by reason of the spatial dichotomy described above, banished further north, beyond Cape Sâo Agostinho as far as the 'Marignan river', meaning the deeply indented estuary of the Maranhâo, which in the seventeenth century saw the foundation of Saint-Louis (now Sâo Luis), capital of the shortlived colony of France Equinoxiale.[12] Thevet shrinks or enlarges the geographical area thus delineated, as his context requires: it becomes, for example, the region between the Spanish and Portuguese American possessions, a sort of buffer zone between the spheres of action of two competing imperialisms.[13] At any time the Cannibals, who are 'the most cruel and inhuman people' in all America, and who 'ordinarily eat human flesh as we would eat mut-ton',[14] are an absolute frontier. This allows Thevet to depict the colo-nial no man's land as the place where military and geographical reconnaissance from either side always runs into the sand.

It follows that the north of André Thevet's Brazil is radically

Figure 3 The friendly anthropophagus: 'Portrait of King Quoniambec'. André Thevet, 1575. Woodcut. Paris: Bibliothèque Nationale.

opposed to the south. In the horrid zone of equatorial forest, not far from the no less redoubtable Amazons (who accept male advances only once a year and kill their male children), Thevet's Cannibals, direct descendants of Vespucci's legends, can be found on the same map as the 'Americans our friends': the Tamoios, allies of the French, who live below the tropics and who are described on the basis of detailed research. This information was gathered from 'dragomen' or interpreters who had been living among the coastal tribes for decades, sometimes as well-integrated savages.[15]

Thevet's geographical separation between 'good' and 'bad' Indians also appears to be an inevitable consequence of his use of sources. *Les Singularitez* is in fact the outcome of a patient montage made by the scribe Mathurin Héret, a competent Hellenist who ghosted parts of the writing. Alongside firsthand information on the Indians of Rio de Janeiro, Héret drew on the *Novus Orbis* of Simon Grynaeus to fill in the gaps in his picture of the Americas.[16] Because his sources are so varied, Thevet's picture lacks coherence. It is partially, but not wholly, the same as Vespucci's. Chapters such as 'Of America in general' (27), 'Of the religion of the Americas' (28) and 'Of the Cannibals' (61) owe a good deal to Vespucci. Schematized treatment, ready-made judgements and the acceptance of their most tenacious legends are clear indications of borrowing from the earlier tradition. The easiest way to resolve the manifest contradictions was simply to set down the various pieces side by side on the chessboard of the world.

In Book XXII, Chapter 2 of his *Cosmographie universelle* (1575), entitled 'Observation and pursuit of the land of the CANNIBALS', Thevet does not hesitate to contradict the initial impressions of the great explorers, starting with Columbus and Vespucci, so as to preserve the improbable 'cannibal' territory which he has roughly carved out between the bay of 'Marignan' and Cape Sâo Agostinho.[17] In other words, the Cannibals, confined to the mainland between the Maranhâo and the famous Bahia de Todos os Santos, are excluded from most of the regions which they actually occupied: the Lesser Antilles towards Hispaniola ('L'Espaignolle') where Columbus had anticipated finding them on his first voyage; and Guyana and Venezuela as far as the borders of present-day Colombia, then known as Castille d'Or ('Golden Castile'), along the coasts visited by Vespucci in 1499–1500. By pronouncing this cosmographical *doxa* Thevet is openly and deliberately contradicting the earliest evidence on the New World. However, he is also placing himself within another tradition, more recent and closer to home (since it had been formed in the harbours of Normandy and Saintonge), according to which the term 'cannibal' no longer applied so much to the Lesser

Figure 4 The unfriendly cannibal: 'Portrait of a Cannibal King.' André Thevet, 1575. Woodcut. Paris: Bibliothèque Nationale.

Antilles as to the north-eastern coastlands of Brazil. The threshold of this doom-laden region was the present Cape Sâo Agostinho, feared as much for its squalls, which were followed by interminable flat calms,[18] as for its hostile inhabitants. This was where ships from Europe made their South American landfall, after the double 'flight' across the Atlantic before the trade winds, following the south-westward route to the dye-wood coast.

Thevet's endeavour is, therefore, to halt the cartographical drift of the word 'cannibal' by, correlatively, limiting the meaning of the term. It is allowed to retain its original emotive connotations. By distinguishing so carefully between 'anthropophagi' and 'cannibals', he endows the latter with an inexplicably increased load of horror, and, in the process, he virtually whitewashes the ritual anthropophagy of the 'Americans our friends'. The latter are seeking vengeance (a tooth for a tooth?) and their behaviour is thus uncouth, perhaps, but still recognizably human; whereas the Cannibals proper have a perverse and bestial taste for human flesh. Later, we shall see the importance of this difference of intent in the context of the debate on the origins of cannibalism which goes right through the age of classicism.[19] The conclusion (to borrow the word which the pilot Toussaint de Bessard applied to the Tupi of Cabo Frio, who ate only prisoners of war and their male offspring) is that not all *androphagi* are cannibals.[20]

Later in the same chapter, Thevet pursues his attempt to narrow the semantic field of 'cannibal' by abandoning humanist nostalgia and ruthlessly excluding all bogus oriental or African origins. The word ceases to evoke the Ethiopia of Prester John and the fabulous East Indies:

> Thus shall you truly particularize these countries. Otherwise the Cannibals would extend their territories into Ethiopia, and to the depths of the East Indies, if all those who ate human flesh bore the name of Cannibals. But just as the new discoverers of my time have erred by calling that country, India, because of the similarity of customs between one Climate and the other, so they have erred knowingly, giving the name of Cannibals, to those who feed cruelly on the flesh of men.[21]

With a curious mix of arbitrariness and rigour, Thevet, cosmographer to the last of the Valois, seeks to dictate the course of onomastics. At the very least, we may find some interest in his desire to restrict the use of a term which had apparently become entirely synonymous with 'anthropophagous races'. Thevet sees this lexical abuse as a consequence of the East–West confusion which led to the assumption that America was part of East Asia. Just as Columbus and his successors confused helm and bowsprit, ancient India and the New World, so the Cannibals were taken to be one of the fabulous peoples described by Pliny and the geographers of Antiquity. But in the last case the error was the other way round: there was a backlash, which caused the unknown term to be applied to the traditional lands of the East. The word 'cannibal' had sailed eastward along the route of the conquistadors, emigrating from the Antilles and Brazil towards Africa and India.

It seems that, by 1575, when Thevet was finishing his *Cosmographie universelle* and giving the word its correct etymology, it was no longer necessary to refute the learned derivation from *canis*. 'Cannibal' was generally used simply to mean 'anthropophagus', and the dog-headed men had long since vanished into the mists of erudite legend.

PART II
In Search of the Honourable Cannibal

It appears that vengeance is the sole seasoning for a dish that humanity would spurn.

Abbé Raynal, *Histoire des deux Indes*

5

The First Ethnographer of the Tupinamba Indians

Plus qu'un Scythe inhumain
Tu vis le Canibale
Qui chair et sang humain
Engloutit et avalle.*

Guy Le Fèvre de la Boderie,
Ode à Mons. Thevet. Cosmographe du Roy

Montaigne, 'Of Cannibals' and the cannibal tradition

In or around March 1580 the printer Simon Millanges of Bordeaux brought out the first edition of Montaigne's *Essays*. It contained a recently written chapter entitled 'Of Cannibals', which was devoted to the inhabitants of 'this other world which has been discovered in our time'.[1] It was the only chapter in the two books of *Essays* published to date which was entirely given over to the peoples brought to light by the discovery of the New World in 1492.

Thus, it was only a few years after Thevet undertook to disentangle the complex skein of beliefs wound about the term 'cannibal' that Montaigne took up the word, with a success that has become proverbial. Montaigne confines it to South America, and Brazil in particular – this belief, at least, had taken root since Thevet – but he was not much concerned to retain the geographical divisions, at once precise and arbitrary, which Thevet had instituted. Montaigne does not contrast the accursed Cannibals and the good 'Amériques': on the contrary, he merges them. Montaigne's Cannibals precisely resemble the Tamoios described twenty years earlier by Thevet, and more recently by Jean de Léry. What Montaigne tells us at the beginning of the chapter puts this beyond doubt: the information he is to give us relates not to America in general, but 'the place where Villegagnon made his landing, which he called France Antarctique'. This does not, of course, deter him from ignoring the spatial restriction later in the chapter, when he pronounces a more or less general eulogy.

The Cannibals, then, appear in Chapter I, 31 of the *Essays* – but only in the title. The essay itself never mentions those redoubtable inhabitants of the New World by name, and does not favour them with the pejorative description of 'barbarians' or 'savages', preferring to clothe them in an all-enveloping periphrasis, such as 'this nation', 'these nations', 'a nation'. Mostly, they are sufficiently distinguished by the third person plural: 'they live in a very pleasing and well-tempered region'; 'they are settled along the sea coast'; 'they have great abundance of fish and flesh which have no resemblance to our own'.[2] This implies that the use of the word in the title is intended to astonish.[3] The 'conjoining' of word and thing is effected by paradox. The sensational title, heavy with the most ferocious and dubious connotations, heralds an unexpected eulogy. Montaigne consciously plays on the disjunction between the word 'cannibal' and the contents of a chapter which is devoted to something else entirely. Instead of the hackneyed nightmares, repeated from Columbus and Vespucci to Rabelais – and which Thevet confines within narrow geographical boundaries – we have the paradisical vision of a society many aspects of which are in harmony with Nature, and which is expanding freely over an entire continent, the largest of all.

Such a transformation could not have been accomplished without a well-established literary tradition: it would be wrong to ignore the conceptual framework into which the chapter fits. The 'sociological revolution' through which observer and observed, native and ethnographer, change places was a current procedure which had been frequently used before Montaigne.[4] The first book of *La République des Turcs*, by the Venetian Guillaume Postel (1560), unreservedly eulogized the virtue and honour of the Ottomans, though they were inveterate enemies of Christendom. The little interview in Rouen which ends 'Of Cannibals', in which the newly disembarked American passes judgement on the European, has a rather close analogue in the Venetian fiction, in which the Turk, surprised by the contrast between rich and poor on the wharves of Venice, practises what he preaches by giving alms secretly and discreetly, exactly as recommended in the New Testament.[5]

There are also some direct borrowings from the already lengthy tradition of travellers to the New World. Thus, the orthodox attack on 'cosmographers' towards the beginning of the essay is closely based on the Preface to the *Histoire d'un voyage faict en la terre du Brésil*, in which Jean de Léry lays into his predecessor and rival, the Franciscan André Thevet, who, after his lengthy voyages to the Levant and Brazil, had been elevated to the status of king's 'cosmographer' (i.e. geographer). Léry accuses Thevet of 'filling and augmenting his idle tales' by undertaking to describe the whole world, even as far as the 'realm of the moon'.[6] Léry declares that he himself speaks 'not about all of America in general, but only of the place where I lived for about a year'.[7] Léry's *Histoire d'un voyage* explicitly offers itself to the reader as the kind of 'particular narration' proffered by Montaigne. Its author perfectly fulfils – in anticipation, as it were – the modest and severe aims of the 'topographer'. This gives Montaigne's pious wish the appearance of a feint which is intended to conceal the extent of his borrowings: first, from Thevet (predigested by Léry), whose *Les Singularitez de la France Antarctique* (1557) is invariably at the heart of any report on Brazil; second, from Léry himself, whose moralizing reflections on comparative cannibalism in Europe and America are the direct source of one of the most famous passages in the essay. The very silences and energetic denials in 'Of Cannibals' place it naturally within a tradition closely connected with topography.

Some time ago Gilbert Chinard was both pleased and saddened to unexpectedly put his finger on the still more shameless plagiarism of three passages towards the beginning of the essay, concerning Atlantis and the colonies of Carthage, which are lifted bodily from Urbain Chauveton's commentary on the *Histoire nouvelle du Nouveau Monde* by Girolamo Benzoni (1579). Chinard duly and sweepingly deplored the regrettable 'feeling of *déjà vu*' brought on by the chapter as a whole.[8]

Even if the text of 'Of Cannibals' is so easy to recognize and does betray so many reminiscences – or outright plagiarisms – this is no obstacle to critical appreciation. The borrowings do little to diminish Montaigne's originality, which lies in the colourful multiplicity of themes, the interlaced materials which so enrich and complicate the reader's response. The 'astonishing orderliness' which some readers have claimed to find in the essay[9] may well be one's first impression, but the superficial clarity and coherence of a discourse which, unusually for Montaigne, contains relatively few digressions fail to withstand a more careful reading. And if one compares this dense composite writing with its sources one begins to wonder what interpretation can ultimately be placed upon it.[10]

Thus it is wrong to consider this chapter of the *Essays* as a kind of textual meteorite, falling from the heaven of ideas upon the land of humanism: we must restore the literary and scientific substratum by which it was engendered and nurtured. We will begin with Thevet, who, though rejected by some later generations, is the cornerstone of all anthropological discussion of the subject.[11]

André Thevet and Tupinamba ritual cannibalism

Thevet tells us that cannibalism is a form of revenge, and this explanation was accepted by most of his contemporaries. But, in fact, 'to avenge oneself with one's teeth', to borrow a happy turn of phrase from Thevet himself,[12] has little to do with the blind appetite of the ogre, or even the *allouvi* who devours his own kindred for lack of other food. Thevet applies the expression to the Tupinamba Indians' habit of eating lice and other vermin, but it could equally well be used

(a)

Figure 5 Cannibal cookery among the Tupinamba Indians of Brazil. While Hans Staden (b) and Théodore de Bry (c) both show the butchering of dead prisoners, André Thevet (a) adds more details: the prisoners are disembowelled and their limbs are grilled on a *boucan* or barbecue. The bowels and head are put on to boil in a huge earthenware cauldron (c). Children carrying a severed head appear in two of the pictures, bringing the moral motif of 'vanity' into this macabre sequence. The bearded figure watching in horror in De Bry's picture (c) is none other than Hans Staden himself: an arquebusier from Hesse who entered Portuguese service and spent over a year as prisoner of anthropophagous Indians, who eventually spared him when they learned of his gifts as a healer and prophet.
(a) André Thevet, *Les Singularitez de la France Antarctique* (Paris, 1557), fol. 77 recto. Woodcut. Paris: Bibliothèque Nationale.
(b) Hans Staden, *Warhaftige Historia und Beschreibung eyner Landtschafft der Wilden, Nacketen, Grimmigen Menschfresser, Leuthen in der Newenwelt America gelegen* (Marburg: A. Kolbe, 1557). Woodcut. London: British Library.
(c) Théodore de Bry, *Dritte Buch Americae* (Frankfurt, 1593), p. 86. Engraving.

(b)

(c)

of their habit of eating prisoners of war. Such readiness with one's teeth implies an eager impulsiveness which is not altogether compatible with Christian charity. But whatever repugnance Thevet, as observer, may feel for such practices, which he frequently describes as 'bestial',[13] he has to admit that these are fully human activities, part of a code of conduct, endowed with meaning.

Thevet continued to enrich and nuance his picture of the anthropophagous Indian over almost half a century. There are, in fact, three successive strata in his Brazilian writings. *Les Singularitez de la France Antarctique*, which was published while Villegagnon's colonial enterprise was still in progress, consists of selections from a larger corpus of material which was to be progressively exploited in the later works: the *Cosmographie universelle* of 1575 (Book XXI of which, entirely devoted to the Tupinamba Indians, was almost immediately challenged by Jean de Léry), and, in particular, his two last works, which remained unpublished: *L'Histoire d'André Thevet ... de deux voyages par luy faits aux Indes Australes et Occidentales*, and the *Grand Insulaire et Pilotage*. They contain, in an obviously confused and unfinished state, all the information he possessed on the subject.[14]

Les Singularitez (1557) is thus a sort of digest, a quick and agreeable read. The cannibalism of the Tupinambas is dealt with in one brief and incisive chapter, whose moderate degree of cruelty is intensified by two woodcuts. One, which might be an imitation of a picture by Hans Staden, shows a prisoner bound by a rope around his waist, defying his enemy even as the executioner's club is about to land on him (see Figure 5a). The other, mannerist, even sensational, shows two men being literally butchered: their heads are severed and their limbs roughly chopped off to be 'roasted' on a barbecue (*boucan*) which is visible in the background.[15] A young woman, with long, unbound hair, energetically unravels the intestines of a gutted, decapitated corpse, while two chubby infants play with the severed head, whose features are as impassive as those of a marble statue. The detail of this macabre 'vanity', as laughing children play with the horrors of death, was to be imitated later by Théodore de Bry.[16] Through the window of the hut, which is European in style, projects a pole, bearing, like a trophy, another grinning human head, shaven like the first two but with a ring of hair at the back. Smoke billows from under the *boucan*: a man is blowing on the fire so vigorously that it threatens to burn both barbecue and meat.

There are many fantastic elements in this, on the whole, traditional composition. The nude butchers with their cleavers, the head on a pike projecting from a window, recall the engravings in Sebastian

Münster's *Cosmographia universalis*, in which Tauroscythians, Tartars, Cannibals and other barbarian peoples from the far corners of the world readily interchange their respective attributes.[17] The children playing ball with a human head were to inspire the macabre stage-set portrayed by Théodore de Bry in the second volume of his *America* (see Figure 5c). The motif readily lent itself to moral allegory. Only the strangely monastic-seeming tonsure of the Indians stems from almost unmodified observation.

The commentary, however, is more original. When he is not borrowing from Vespucci (and thereby including firsthand observations on the Tamoios of Rio de Janeiro, but also introducing a hotchpotch of the approximate and the extraordinary and a collection of off-the-peg judgements on those 'marvellously strange and savage people, faithless and lawless, with no religion and no civility, but living as beasts without reason'), Thevet's description is remarkably restrained. The wholesale warfare waged by the 'Americas our friends', 'by both land and sea', marks the first appearance of anthropophagy in connection with the Tupinambas.[18] It is also the most sensational and the most repugnant. The combatants do not wait to clinch their victory before eating their adversaries: 'If they are not strong enough to carry him away, then at least, if they can before he is rescued, they will cut off his arms and legs; and before leaving him they will eat him, or at least, each will carry off some piece of him, either large or small.'[19]

This *in vivo* cannibalism, thus unceremoniously performed on the field of battle, betrays a certain hastiness and contrasts with the calculated slowness of preparations for the feast which is held when the savages return home. However, Thevet does not confine himself to criticizing 'the unjustified cause' of their wars, or the more than bestial brutality of their behaviour. He connects the violence directly with vengeance, and thus makes it assimilable to earlier or more exotic, and of course non-Christian, models: 'Of old, the Turks, Moors and Arabs did almost after this fashion ... and moreover they used almost the same weapons as our Savages.'

At an earlier stage Thevet compared the exchange of insults between the two sides before the battle with the customs of the ancient Greeks and Latins. What was more, these brutal customs could accommodate an allegorical reading. The anthropophagous Indians, who had allied themselves with the French, were doing no more than put into practice what the latter thought or said when they wanted to express a strong dislike of someone else: 'of whom we still say in the proverb, "I should like to have eaten of his heart." '[20]

By emphasizing the affinity between the savage's way of acting and the civilized people's way of speaking, Thevet suggests that both belong to the great human family. He throws a bridge between words and actions which his successors, starting with Léry and Montaigne, will not hesitate to borrow in order to relativize the Indians' ostensible barbarity and stigmatize, all the more vigorously, the uncharitable conduct of self-styled Christians.

Here, the allegorization of cannibalism is still in the embryonic stage, a mere sketch. Thevet is too pragmatic to be satisfied with figurative meanings and too curious to abandon the search for 'singularities' in favour of moral considerations: he returns promptly to the rituals of anthropophagy, which he describes quite minutely in the following chapter. The prisoner is brought back in triumph to the village and is given favoured treatment: he is fed on 'the best viands that may be found' and fattened up 'like a moulting capon', an expression which seems to owe something to Vespucci. He is given a wife, often the daughter of his captor, who will serve him 'in his bed or otherwise'. He is allowed freedom of movement, at least up to the eve of the slaughter when he is put in irons, a custom probably borrowed from the Europeans. Throughout the weeks – sometimes years – of an almost comfortable captivity, the prisoner has only the necklaces of shells like 'paternosters', which he wears round his neck and one of which is removed each new moon, to remind him of the approach of the fatal day. Apart from this calendrical necklace (sometimes replaced by a knotted cord reminiscent of an Inca *quipu*), there is nothing in his way of life to distinguish him from his conquerors.[21]

The night before the slaughter is spent in drinking and rejoicing, in which he himself takes part by boasting of his exploits against his ephemeral conquerors and prophesying the vengeance which will so soon devour them in their turn. This heroic defiance, which was to impress Montaigne, is accompanied by a profound contempt for death. If there is an offer to ransom the prisoner, he rejects it with disdain. If he saved his life in that way he would become a slave. The cycle of vendetta would be broken, and his relatives and friends would have no occasion or duty to avenge his death.

Meanwhile, the ceremony is prepared. The prisoner's chief captor calls together the dignitaries of the tribe for a solemn *cahouin*. They drink like Germans, each striving to down the largest number of pots of millet beer fermented by women's spittle. The victim, tightly bound with cotton cords held by two acolytes standing a good distance away, continues to defy the assembly of 'ten or twelve thousand' who will soon be feeding on his flesh, divided into infinitesimal portions. Then, without unnecessary suffering, he is simply 'knocked on the head like a sucking-pig'. Léry, embroidering on Thevet, compares the 'scalding' of this newly slaughtered human meat with the boiling water which 'the cooks on our side' sprinkle on a 'sucking pig ready for roasting' in order to remove the bristles.[22] The visitor from Europe finds a disconcerting familiarity in the very act which ought most to scandalize him. The cooking of human flesh in the Americas turns out to be closely related to the peasant cooking of Morvan or the Bourbonnais, where Léry spent his childhood. It could even be said that a simulacrum of anthropophagy haunted the kitchens of old Europe. At the 'pork festival', the slaughter (already mentioned) and consumption of the pig were comically assimilated to a transgression of the taboo against cannibalism: the animal, whose throat was cut and which was washed in hot water, then eaten, was referred to as the 'gentleman in a silken suit'.[23] Thevet and Léry only had to turn the traditional identification on its head in order to describe – and by implication, to excuse – the actual cannibalism of the Tupinambas.

Thevet admits that this first draft of the cannibal scenario omits, for the sake of concision, 'several ceremonies' attendant on the last moments of the prisoner. The preparation of the body for cooking is conducted with the same refinement: 'The body thus cut up, and cooked after their fashion, will be distributed among them all: however numerous they may be, each has his portion.' There is a passing allusion to the 'moderate grief' displayed by the dead man's wife before she joins in the general rejoicing. There is little detail about the ritual distribution of the body according to the age and sex of the guests: women receive the entrails, the head is stuck on a pole. The missing details are filled in by the *Cosmographie universelle* of 1575: the women eat not only the viscera of the victim but also his 'shameful parts'. Suckling infants are 'washed' in his blood.[24]

Les Singularitez pursues, from chapter to chapter, the analogy between elements that are spatially and temporally distant. This diptych structure invariably requires not only a description of exotic customs, but also a comparison with antiquity – and anthropophagy is no exception to the rule. For an example of 'such excessive cruelty' we have to go back to the siege of Jerusalem by Titus, when 'after they had eaten everything else', starvation 'compelled mothers to kill their infants, and eat them'.[25] Thevet is generalizing from one celebrated incident in Flavius Josephus' *Jewish War*, which is also quoted by Léry. Thevet adds the mythical Anthropophagi mentioned by Herodotus and Pliny: Scythian peoples who fed on human flesh and who are made to look like remote ancestors of the Brazilians. The evocation of ritual anthropophagy ends with a chapter giving a wider view of the psychology of New World inhabitants: 'That these Savages are marvellously vindictive.'[26] Thevet supplies proof in the form of two exemplary anecdotes. The first concerns a Portuguese who was pitifully murdered and devoured, without the customary pomp, because instead of resolutely facing his executioners he had implored them 'in the humblest and mildest words he could find' to spare his life. The second, which goes to prove the Indians' inveterate devotion to vengeance, tells of a 'Tabajare' who was duly 'baptised, brought up, and married in Rouen'. Returning to Brazil on a ship out of Normandy, he landed in the territory of his enemies. Learning that he was on board, they waited until the crew had gone ashore, crept on board the ship, flung themselves upon the unfortunate man and hacked him to pieces. Thevet gives him a martyr's end: in his last hour he 'protested to them the faith of *Jesus Christ*, one God in three persons and a single essence'. But, unimpressed by such theological niceties, they proceeded with their deadly work. For once, they did not eat their victim.[27]

Thus, vengeance appears to be the keystone of Thevet's description of Tupinamba cannibalism, at least in its first version. The clarity of the design soon becomes confused, however. In the *Cosmographie* the anthropophagous violence is indeed explained largely by the vindictive character of the Indians. But, as new material is introduced into the description, the interpretation becomes more complex. The prelude to the victim's slaughter is considerably enlarged. The triumphal escorting home of the prisoner after the battle, which, Thevet tells us, is a pretext for 'fanfares, games, cries and shouts' is now used to bring out the association between the sacrifice and the commemoration of the dead. First, the captive is led to the tombs 'of their deceased fathers and mothers', 'as if he were a victim to be sacrificed in their memory'.[28] Then, clad in plumes from shoulder to thigh, he marches into the village at the head of the procession, 'with such a fine appearance and such a swaggering gait that he seems to be the chief of the assembly'.[29] Henceforward, he enjoys a degree of freedom and is 'incorporated' into the victorious group before it devours him. He is taken to the house of the newly dead man, and is given his bows and arrows – and sometimes his widow also, which is intended as a consolation to her.[30] Finally, the destined executioner takes a new name, a practice which is supposed to avert the wrath of the victim.[31]

Thevet's inclusion of these new details suggests an interpretation which goes beyond mere vengeance. The capture of a prisoner by the tribe serves as a reparation. Through the period up to his death, the captive acts as a substitute. He exactly fills the place of the dead man, just like the passing stranger whom the women welcome with cries and tears in the rite of tearful greeting.[32] His active presence – he goes fishing and hunting, helps clear the forest and till the soil, participates wholeheartedly in festivities and lives lovingly with his spouse, who may even give him children – makes up for the loss previously suffered by the group. Thus, the community receives a fresh infusion of energy, and eventually regains its lost wholeness by ingesting the flesh of the victim, down to the most insignificant morsel. The children born to him in his captivity suffer the same fate, since they are 'children of the enemy' and inspire no confidence in their maternal relations.[33]

The *Cosmographie* goes beyond the eye-for-an-eye, tooth-for-a-tooth doctrine of *Les Singularitez* and hints at a more subtle explanation: a series of indications which may converge on religion. The cannibalistic contract is no longer made between individuals, or groups, who are hostile to each other and yet akin. It may include a vertical dimension which regulates the relationship of humanity to the gods, drawing the former towards a higher realm.

Thevet may be suggesting this hypothesis, but he does not make it plain. In fact, the first missionaries of the New World were sometimes confusedly aware, by analogy with the Christian mysteries, of the similarity between this ritual anthropophagy and the sacrament of the Eucharist. Thus, Father José de Acosta used the word 'host' to refer to the victims of Aztec sacrifices, which, as is well known, were associated with anthropophagous practices. He was probably thinking of the etymology *hostia, quasi ab hoste*.[34] The victim was always taken from the enemy. In both Mexico and Brazil it was only prisoners of war who were sacrificed. It may well be thought, however, that the use of 'host' in such a context was not altogether innocent. To Acosta's Catholic readers the word would infallibly suggest the modern meaning: the Eucharistic bread, which became Christ's body at the celebration of the Mass.

A century and a half after Acosta, another Jesuit, Father Joseph-François Lafitau, wrote an essay on comparative anthropology, in one chapter of which he attempted to reinterpret the Tupinamba ritual largely on the basis of a close reading of Thevet's *Cosmographie*. The fourth volume of *Mœurs des Sauvages Ameriquains comparées aux mœurs des premiers temps* ('Customs of the American savages compared to the customs of earliest times') deals successively with the 'execution of slaves' in North and South America.[35] Lafitau is vulnerable to the demon of analogy and stresses resemblances rather than differences, putting the sadistic games which the Iroquois play with their victims for days on end on a par with the cannibalism of the Tupinambas of Brazil, which seems magnanimous by comparison; and he extends the Tupinamba model to the whole of South America. He is well aware that the execution of their prisoners has a sacrificial character: 'I say that he will be offered as a sacrifice; for this terrible feast is celebrated with so much pomp and ceremony that it quite resembles an act of Religion.'[36]

But Lafitau fails to grasp the nature of that sacrifice. Either through censorship (which is probable) or through carelessness (which is possible), or through excessive trust in the pictorial evidence derived from Staden and Thevet via Théodore de Bry, Lafitau becomes quite blind. This is what he says of the 'slave' (in fact he was not really a slave) who is about to be sacrificed: 'A fire is lighted before him two paces away, which seems to me to be like the Divinity to which he is to be sacrificed.'[37] This is a strange remark explained perhaps by the importance which Lafitau ascribes throughout his essay to 'Pyrolatry' or 'the worship of the sacred Fire', which he believes to be the common denominator of all the religions of America.[38] In this would-be global reconstruction of religious practice in the New World, it is clear that the solar cults of the Aztecs and the Incas have been of decisive influence. The Virgins of the Sun, rather hastily equated with the Vestals who guarded the holy fire in ancient Rome, cast their legendary aura via the Amazons of the equatorial jungle, even to the shores of Brazil. In reality, the Tupinambas confined themselves to making the prisoner stand directly before the fire on which he was to be cooked, which was lighted just as the club was raised over his head. This piece of stage-management was intended to provoke a last shudder of fright – but the prisoner, in his ambivalent role of victim and collaborator, would do his best not to give one. It is hard to see how the Brazilians could have taken this cooking fire for a solar fire thirsting for human blood and worthy of their worship.

In spite of these divagations, the comparative analysis is pursued with rigour. Lafitau does not scruple to connect the writings of the Huguenot Jean de Léry – the 'Ministre de Leri'[39] – with Catholic reports on the subject. However, for all its minuteness, the conclusion of the chapter seems very disappointing. Lafitau makes no clear choice between the two canonical explanations of cannibalism: 'Whether it be an appetite for human flesh, or rage and fury against their Enemies, there is none who does not eat . . .' This unanimity of anthropophagous enjoyment more or less compels a comparison with the greatest Christian sacrament, but Lafitau does not make it, and goes on: 'and who does not show that he finds its taste very refined and delicate'.[40] The hermeneutic impulse is scarcely hinted at before it relapses into the banality of accepted interpretation. Cannibalism is nothing but an alimentary perversion, which is in fact found among 'almost all the Barbarian Nations of America'.[41]

In contrast, Thevet's ideas are saved by their disorder. Faced with the disquieting affinity of ritual anthropophagy to the Eucharistic mystery, he reacts with a pulsillanimity which, as we have seen, was normal in Catholic circles. A Protestant such as Jean de Léry could show a strongly polemical audacity when dealing with the same subject. He used the genuine cannibalism of the Tupinambas to discredit, by assimilation, the 'papist' dogma of transubstantiation. For Catholics not only ate real people when they got the chance – the Wars of Religion had furnished a number of examples – they also ate God at the sacrifice of the Mass.[42]

But there was another sacrifice to which the cannibal ritual could legitimately be compared: baptism, a rite of rebirth and warrant of eternity – or, as a contemporary anthropologist has said with reference to the Arawete Indians, 'a means of access to the divine'.[43] It is, of course, a baptism of blood. The warrior who has taken the prisoner takes a new name at the cannibal ceremony. The sacrificer, who may be a different person, also changes his identity after accomplishing the murder. And we have seen how little children were anointed with the victim's blood. Charlevoix, a Jesuit priest, citing his fellow Jesuit Ruiz de Montoya, said that the Guarani of Paraguay 'had a kind of Baptism' connected with the slaughter of the prisoner. On the appointed day he was slain with considerable formality: as soon as he was dead, 'they all came up to touch the Corpse with their hands, or hit it with sticks, and gave a name to all the Children who hitherto had had none'.[44] The ceremony ended with the consumption of the victim's flesh: every family took a share of it home and made a broth, 'of which each person swallowed a spoonful'. Mothers with suckling infants would put a little of the broth in their mouths.

Whatever explanation is accepted – rite of vengeance, Eucharist or baptism – it is a fact that Thevet leaves all avenues of explanation open. Some twenty years after his *Cosmographie*, he returned to the subject one last time. This third version of the Brazilian story includes another batch of details, and the narrative becomes yet more entangled. *Histoire de deux voyages aux Indes Australes et Occidentales* is a draft manuscript dating from 1587–8, which has come down to us in two distinct versions.[45] Here, Thevet is at least free from the editorial constraints which had governed *Les Singularitez*, and, to a lesser extent, his *Cosmographie* of 1575. It seems that he was no longer afflicted with the 'slaves' whose task consisted not just of endless copying, but also of selecting from a hyperabundance of documentation, embellishing it with borrowings from the best authors and putting the huge mass of material into some sort of order.[46] He was now able to deliver an entire load of raw information, probably gathered in the course of his voyage to Brazil, from interpreters who had acclimatized to life among the savages.

We learn, for example, that in addition to the exo-cannibalism of the Tupinambas, who devoured only enemies taken in war, there were other nations in Brazil who practised endo-cannibalism. Thus, the Tapuia or 'Tapouys', inland from Bahia, disdained the flesh of their prisoners, whose corpses they left to dry in the sun or threw into a river; but they ate their own dead relatives to spare them the indignity of rotting in the earth.[47] The circumstantial description of a ritual massacre in the village of Margariampin, in the Rio Grande do Norte, reports at even greater length on the ceremonies preceding the execution. Thevet traces the successive stages in the mock duel engaged in by the prisoners, who were provided with 'cones of juniper' as projectiles, slings, and blunted arrows with which they tried to strike their vanquishers. Still accompanied by their guards, and by women who supplied them with ammunition, they were allowed to run about the village, where they invariably injured and beat up all those whom they met.[48]

The wailing of the old women, whom Thevet disarmingly calls 'sweet Proserpinas' and who surround the captive during the funeral wake; the fifteen-year-old girl who is given him for his last night on earth;[49] 'his poor wife' crouching beneath the hammock where the ephemeral lovers lie: these particularities give the ethnographic tableau a vivid impression of truth. The smallest details of material civilization are now reported, from the making of the 'Maussorrent' or *musurana*, the long cotton cord which was put round the captive's neck, to the painting of the club, which had a specially plumed handle and of which both the flat and the sharp side were smeared with gum.[50] Thevet comments here that the women, using eggshell, would draw the same geometrical 'compartments' on the club as on the face which it was intended to smite. This gave material expression to the symbolic identity of murderer and victim.[51] As for the careful distribution of parts of the body among the revellers, according to sex and age, it is now described remorselessly, even down to the most indigestible details: 'The blood-sausage and tripe are given to the young men, and all the quarry [that is to say, the heart, liver and lungs] to the young women.'[52]

If a myth is to be understood as the sum of its variants (Claude Lévi-Strauss's definition),[53] it may be said that Thevet's ethnographical writings, which accumulate without abridgement and juxtapose without coherence, are themselves a kind of mythic creation, the fruit of a 'savage mind'. The amateur construction is nowhere more in evidence than in the final version of Thevet's description of Tupinamba ritual anthropophagy. It is here, also, that he pays most attention to Tupinamba cosmogony: several chapters of the *Cosmographie* and the *Histoire de deux voyages* are devoted to the myth of the Twins, the brothers and sworn enemies Ariconte and Tamendonare.[54] There is a strong impression that the mythic material, which becomes more and more pervasive in his work, influenced even its organization and style. Instead of a linear narrative, we have a collection of loosely connected data. The result is that the cannibal sacrifice is hugely inflated, into a liturgy lasting three or even five days.[55] Is this the 'cannibal tragedy' of the Indians, as it really took place – over a nicely gradated five acts?[56] Or is it the fortuitous outcome of a sum total of unsorted evidence? To that question, Thevet's method, which rejects nothing and leaves no stone unturned, provides no answer.

6

Jean de Léry, or the Cannibal Obsession

A universal symbol

Jean de Léry (1534–1613) began life as a shoemaker, but became a pastor in the church of Geneva after his return to Europe from Brazil, where he went when he was just twenty-one. After the discord which arose in 1557 between the Chevalier de Villegagnon and the Huguenots who had come to join his colony, Léry returned to France, arriving in January 1558. It was not until twenty years later that he published (in Geneva) his *Histoire d'un voyage faict en la terre du Bresil*. Thus, he could approach his experiences with the benefit of hindsight, something not found in Thevet. At such a distance the vision could be filtered and set in order – and also schematized. Those parts of Thevet's narrative which had already been published (*Les Singularitez* in 1557 and *Cosmographie universelle* in 1575) were used by Léry as preliminary sketches for his own work. Léry wrote against the Catholic cosmographer, but also after him (in both the chronological and imitative sense). He was able to extract the essential details from his predecessor's haphazard portrait: accurate and minute ethnographical information, and an indulgent and almost positive portrayal of Tupinamba cannibalism.

Thevet's merit was to have offered a wide range of possible interpretations of Brazilian cannibalism, and an abundant, though disorderly, supply of useful materials relating to myth and ritual. Léry's is the opposite virtue of classification and clarification, but he also impoverished, to some extent, the stock of information available to him. All in all, his portrayal of ritual anthropophagy is thinner than that given by Thevet in the various re-workings of his material.[1] But while he added very little to the documentary evidence, Léry considerably enriched the interpretation and symbolic exploitation of that material. He turns the Cannibal into a universal key, a symbol which can account for the most glaring moral and social evils on either side of the Atlantic, and even for the horrors of recent history.[2]

There are two main axes to Léry's re-reading of Tupinamba cannibalism: first, he systematizes the 'vengeance' interpretation; second, he allegorizes the act of eating, emptying it (so to speak) of its carnal substance and drawing it 'towards a higher meaning'.

Léry accepts the solution which had seemed inescapable to Thevet, namely that cannibalism means vengeance, and gives the classic formulation of it. The Tupinambas eat for vengeance, not for food 'as far as one can judge'.[3] This paradigm appears to exclude all others. The sensory pleasure, though undeniable, is secondary: 'Although all of them confess human flesh to be wonderfully good and delicate', they devour it 'more out of vengeance than for the taste'.[4]

At this stage Léry, like Thevet before him, is compelled to distinguish between good and bad cannibalism. He spares the anthropophagi of Rio de Janeiro, but condemns their adversaries, the ferocious Ouetacas who live by a more northerly shore, at a latitude of some twenty degrees south. He says they are incapable of cooking their meat and as voracious as wild beasts; moreover, they speak an incomprehensible language. Unlike other Indians, they wear their hair 'long and hanging down to the buttocks', refuse to trade with their neighbours and will not barter with voyagers from Europe. They hunt stags and deer, and 'like dogs and wolves' they eat their prey raw.[5] Léry takes no trouble to hide his disgust and revulsion: indeed, he makes them plain through a series of typological oppositions, of which the last, and most decisive, is that between the raw and the cooked.[6] The presence or absence of the cooking-fire dictates the pertinence and supposed function of the cannibalism. The Ouetacas are considered as homophagous vampires: they eat their own kind for food. The Tupinambas cook their meat: they are taking vengeance.

Cooking banishes the spectre of the Barbarian; it repels, from within the sphere defined by cannibalistic practice, the divergence between nature and culture, human reason and unreasoning bestial rage. Whereas Tupinamba cuisine arouses European interest – and sometimes even European appetite – by its complexity and the strange metamorphoses to which it subjects its ingredient of human flesh, the homophagy of Léry's Ouetacas, or of Thevet's 'Cannibals',[7] blurs the distinction between savage mankind and the most repugnant animality.

Setting aside for the moment Montaigne's paradox, which unifies the *corpus cannibale* into a single entity, let us look at the variegated landscape of Brazil, as seen by Thevet and Léry at this early stage in the science of Otherness. By reason of the contrast between the Good Savage of Guanabara, who is so ready to welcome Frenchmen that he will accept them as sword-brothers and companions, and the Cannibal who is hostile to the passing stranger and incapable of cooking his meat, the sphere of American cannibalism breaks in two.

On the one side we have the complexity of a ritual, and the impressive arsenal of culinary skills, rendered familiar through detailed description, which were accredited to the honest Tupinambas. Being 'neither monstrous nor prodigious with respect to us' (as Léry remarks),[8] they lacked only the enlightenment of Christian revelation to become equal to the Europeans. On the other side looms (for lack of accurate information) the menacing shadow of the Cannibals as seen by Vespucci and Thevet, or of Léry's Ouetacas, a cynosure of all imaginable barbarity. Compared with the jovial figure of the Tupinamba, who keeps open house and welcomes the European to his table, the former are like exotic avatars of a folktale werewolf or ogre. If it were possible to find a spark of humanity in them – but is it? – they would be under the influence of Saturn, the fearsome god who devoured his own children.

But the truth was that the bad Cannibals were to be found not only outside the group of good anthropophagi (which would make them easy to isolate), but also at the heart of it. One need only to think of the old women who 'have an amazing appetite for human flesh' and greedily licked up the fat that trickled down the wooden supports of the *boucan*.[9] Léry, in agreement with the most pitiless judges of his time, was a warm supporter of witch-hunts, on both sides of the Atlantic – in the Burgundian villages where he preached, as much as in Brazil, where he had spent a year's leisure in his adventurous youth. In an addition to the chapter on savage religion, made in 1585, he quotes at length from Jean Bodin's *Démonomanie*, a witch-finder's manual, and boldly asserts that Brazilian women and French witches are 'guided by the same spirit of Satan'. Neither the remoteness of the place nor the 'long sea passage' were any obstacle to 'the father of lies' who could easily fly over the boundless ocean and 'work, on this side and that, in those people who are delivered up to him by the just judgement of God'.[10] This highly pessimistic remark does not appear in the first revision of Léry's *Histoire d'un voyage*, which is aglow with nostalgia; it is one of a series of additions, all made at the same time, which considerably darken the mood of the work. As we shall see, the portrayal of anthropophagy, which is steadily enriched from edition to edition, contributes heavily to *Histoire d'un voyage*'s inclination towards apocalyptic prophecy.

In reality, the problem is not so simple. Cannibalism is not susceptible to rationalization, even on the basis of sentiments or attitudes as firmly rooted in the aristocratic and popular mind as the thirst for vengeance and the code of honour. There is always something left over: an unassimilable horror, a condensation of the unspeakable which attracts the most lively repulsion.

The second aspect of Léry's treatment of cannibalism is allegorization. Anthropophagy is not a mere fact. It can signify beyond itself: cruelty, usury, an absence of all charity. The key to this modulation of meaning is the way in which Calvinist theologians interpreted the Eucharist.[11] At the beginning of *Histoire d'un voyage*, Léry tells us that the words of Christ at the Last Supper cannot be taken literally, but must be understood figuratively. When Jesus said, 'This is my body, this is my blood', he meant the disciples to understand that 'This signifies my body, my blood...'[12] Therefore, the bread and wine undergo no metamorphosis, as the Catholics maintain: these 'God-eaters' are the victims of a sensual illusion, and are guilty of idolatry. But Christ was simply using a linguistic technique which is quite common in everyday language, what in rhetoric is called a trope. A trope works by transferring meaning from the thing signified – the body, the blood – to the thing signifying – the bread and wine: it is a kind of metonymy, a figure based on contiguity, whereby we might use 'flag' to refer to an army, 'laurels' for a victory, an 'olive-branch' for peace. In other words, Christ expressed himself through allegory, as we all do every day without realizing it. (Monsieur Jourdain, the hero of Molière's *Le Bourgeois Gentilhomme*, who was so delighted to find he had been speaking prose all his life, might have been equally pleased to find he had been speaking in tropes.)

Léry uses all the arguments current in his faction, which were repeated *ad nauseam* throughout the Wars of Religion. He was adept at rhetorical readings of the Bible: in the language of the time, he was a 'tropist', a lover of tropes. The Eucharistic controversy is crucial to *Histoire d'un voyage*. In 1557, in Brazil, there was a sort of generalized repetition of the debates which were to focus the attention of the Colloquy of Poissy, in the autumn of 1561, and which, after the failure of this attempted reconciliation, were to unleash the Wars of Religion. Villegagnon, a knight of Malta and leader of the Brazilian expedition, defended the dogma of the real corporeal presence of Christ in the bread and wine of the Last Supper against the Calvinists, even though he had summoned them on purpose from Geneva: 'The words "This is my Body; this is my Blood" cannot be taken otherwise than to mean that the Body and the Blood of Jesus Christ are contained therein.'[13]

In the other corner, the energetic Pierre Richer, leader of the Genevan mission and pastor of the Reformed Church, was scandalized by this materialism and ranked his adversary with the Ouetacas, the worst kind of anthropophagi, who did not even cook their food. Indeed, Léry concludes, Villegagnon and his infamous side-kick, the

Lutheran Jean Cointa, an erstwhile discalced Carmelite, wanted 'not only to eat the flesh of Jesus Christ grossly, rather than spiritually, but – what was worse – like the savages called *Ou-ëtacas*, they wished to chew and swallow it raw'. Obviously, such a regression from cooking-fire to animality was incompatible with the holiest mystery of Christianity.

It now becomes clear that Léry has taken this metonymic interpretation, drawn from the Calvinist dogma of the Eucharist, and applied it wholesale. When prisoners are sacrificed in the Indian villages of Brazil, the same thing happens as in the churches of the new, Reformed religion: when the faithful are gathered around the Holy Table and the bread and the cup pass from hand to hand, the blood is not blood, but a sign; the flesh is not food, but a metonymy for food. Thereby, the anthropophagy of the Tupinambas becomes, if not acceptable, at least comprehensible. Just as the Calvinist Eucharist signifies, but does not repeat, Christ's gift to the believer, so Tupinamba cannibalism expresses extreme vengeance. Hence, it tends to lose its actual substance. It might be easy to reduce the frugal elements of the Christian mystery, the unleavened bread and communion wine, to signs; it was not quite easy with the carnal nourishment of the Tupinamba rite. The fact that the Indians' ritual repast could be interpreted as a process of signification did not mean that it was not actually consumed. Despite Léry's views, at that moment the sign coexisted with the thing, however repugnant that thing might be to a Reformed conscience.[14]

To prevent his readers from turning in disgust from what happens in Brazil, Léry suggests a comparison with Europe, where still worse crimes are committed every day. But, unexpectedly, he does not immediately refer to the cases of actual cannibalism that had been witnessed during the Wars of Religion. The first parallel that occurs to him between the anthropophagy of the Old and New Worlds is usury: usurers suck the blood and marrow of 'many widows, orphans and other poor people, whose throats it would be better to cut once and for all, than to make them linger in misery' – and thus effectively eat them alive. The Jews are not mentioned, but the passage recognizably includes an old anti-Semitic cliché whereby the loathed Jew was accused of two equally damnable crimes, usury and anthropophagy.[15] The most celebrated example of these two inseparable and subtly interconnected crimes is the character of Shylock in *The Merchant of Venice*, who, unable to recover his lost loan, demands a pound of flesh from next the heart of the borrower. Léry quotes the prophet Micah to licence this shift from the real to the symbolic: 'And that is why the Prophet says that such men flay the skin of God's people, eat their flesh, break their bones and chop them in pieces as for the pot, and as flesh within the cauldron.'[16]

Once again, cannibalism represents something other than itself. It is a moveable sign, a signifier which can cover the most varied signifieds. Indeed, in the successive enlargements of *Histoire d'un voyage* Léry never tires of adding fresh illustrations.

In order to 'justify our Brazilians, or at least abhor them less', Léry produces a long string of examples, in which the cannibalism of the 'Jews at the time of Trajan'[17] is followed by 'the execrable cruelties of Amurat and Mechmet' as recorded by Chalcondylus;[18] by those of Vlad III, surnamed Dracula;[19] and by the horrors of the Wars of Religion, previously detailed in the *Histoire ecclesiastique françoise* of Theodore Beza.[20] The list ends with a 'cannibal triptych' in which the litany of horrors already evoked is fitted into a tripartite stage-set showing Brazilian, Turkish and French butcheries, each with a lavish exhibition of mutilated bodies and scraps of human flesh.[21] This tragic theatre is displayed with Senecan ghoulishness from 1585 onwards. But it is still further embellished in the fourth edition of 1599, with the addition of the 'more than abominable cruelties of the Spaniards', as reported by the Dominican Bartolomé de las Casas: at this point it

Figure 6 Cannibalism as allegory. Martin de Vos and J.-B. Vrints, 'The oppressor of the widow and orphan is crueller than these'. Flanders, *c.*1580.

becomes a foreign body encysted in *Histoire d'un voyage*, a chapter in its own right.

Léry's avoidance strategy is particularly striking here. Instead of telling us of the Cannibals of Brazil and detailing their bloody rites, he presents us with all the violence which history has to show. But the feint does not succeed, or at least its result is paradoxical. Cannibalism, which was nowhere in particular, now seems to be everywhere. It no longer has a place of its own. In the next century the Protestant minister Charles de Rochefort, an enthusiastic reader of Léry, was to apply the same conclusions to the Caribs of the Lesser Antilles: 'By these examples, it seems clear enough that our Cannibals, are no more *Cannibals*, meaning *Eaters of men*, although they particularly bear that name, than many other Savage Nations'.[22]

Léry had already pushed this reasoning to its uttermost limit. Cannibalism is not where one would expect to find it, among the most barbarous of barbarians; but it is everywhere else, even among self-styled Christians, even inside the Protestant community itself. Léry, nearing the end of a tumultuous life, was speaking from bitter experience.

Sancerre, or the return of the repressed

We must now return to the author's biography, for its influence on his work is continuous and decisive. He was haunted by cannibalism throughout his life, and the theme haunts his writings. At the age of twenty-one the focus was on his sojourn in Brazil and the discovery of Tupinamba ritual cannibalism, which Léry probably saw with his own eyes. Sixteen years later, in 1573, the Cannibal returned in the guise of a family from the French provincial town of Sancerre, who ate their dead child in the last weeks of a siege whose horrors re-enacted, on a smaller scale, those of Titus' siege of Jerusalem. The trauma of this second experience is superimposed on the first. It makes Léry sick, which never happened during his wanderings among the cruel Brazilians. Let each judge the spectacle for himself:

> ... having seen the bone, and the top of the skull of this poor girl picked clean, and gnawed, the ears eaten off, having seen also the tongue cooked, as thick as a finger, which they were making ready to eat when they were surprised; the two thighs, legs and feet in a cauldron with vinegar, spices and salt, ready to be cooked and put over the fire: the two shoulders, arms and hands clasping each other, with the chest cloven open, made ready to eat, I was so afraid and taken aback, that my stomach heaved.[23]

Léry, a horrified witness of the crime, immediately rejects the excuse of necessity and concludes that the partakers of this repast were inspired by Satan. It was an old woman in the household, Philippes de la Feüille, who brought about this 'more than barbarous act', by insisting to the husband 'that it would be a pity to put this flesh to rot in the ground, and moreover, that the liver was very good for curing his swelling'.[24] Thus skilfully tempted by this ageing latter-day Eve, the husband tasted the forbidden fruit. He then tempted his wife, who had been absent up to that moment. Returning from a shopping expedition, the mother discovered the macabre cookery and, in spite of some understandable misgivings, eventually joined in the meal. To describe this inverted Fall, Léry borrows the sparse narrative style of Genesis: 'and he having given it to her she took, and ate of it also'. The old woman, who died the next day in prison, was condemned to be burned as a witch, and the father and mother guilty of this 'barbarous and more than bestial cruelty' were condemned along with her.

To justify this rigorous sentence, Léry reports a case of anthropophagy from near Abbeville during the Hundred Years War, involving a peasant woman, a child-stealer and ogress. Her judges had also shown themselves to be inflexible, despite the famine which was raging at the time, and the old woman had similarly been condemned to be burned alive. Léry's approval is unconditional: 'Which, I think, none will think ill of: rather, all will say that she deserved a harsher punishment, if one could have been thought of.'[25]

At Sancerre, and at Abbeville a century and a half earlier, the most important thing was to avert any possible contagion. Old Philippes de la Feüille might have had imitators, as was shown by a 'certain person afflicted with hunger' to whom Léry gave an indignant answer. This scrupulous believer had asked his pastor 'if he would do ill, and offend God, if in this extreme necessity he ate of the buttock of a man who had been killed, which seemed to him very good meat'. Léry pitilessly consigns this lustful soul to its own remorse, citing the example of the beasts, especially wolves, 'who, it is said, do not eat one another'.[26]

This frightening narrative has much to teach us. First, it should be noted that it is one of Léry's earliest writings. Even before inserting the description of the famine in his first published book, *Histoire memorable de la ville de Sancerre* (1574), Léry had composed something very close to the final version on the spot, the 'Sommaire discours de la famine...', along with an epistle dated 20 August and addressed to Monseigneur Claude de la Châtre, the victorious captain of the siege.[27] Thus, the cannibalistic episode in Sancerre was hurriedly put down on paper in the month immediately following the siege. There is every reason to believe that this haste was the result of a profound trauma. Apart from the diplomatic motives which induced Léry to tell the vanquisher the horrible secret concealed in the besieged town, his step in the direction of the enemy betrays an urgent need to confess. As much as, or more than, the desire to win the favour of a magnanimous adversary, this haste betokens an eagerness to relieve his conscience of an intolerable burden. The burning of the three cannibals was not enough. The rite of purgation had to be completed. After sacrificing the guilty ones – scapegoats of a city chastised by God – the unspeakable had to be spoken before the exorcism could be complete. Léry became the ambassador of a horrorstruck city: his 'Sommaire discours' relieved the entire community of a verbal taboo.

There is no doubt that the fear was collective. To overcome it, the exorcism unfolded in three movements. The judicial enquiry disclosed the awful past of the accused, Monsieur and Madame Potard. They were voracious drunkards who were cruel to their children, and had begun by living in sin before 'going off to be wedded at the papist church'. Ten years before the crime was committed, they had already been excommunicated for contumacy and cut off from the Reformed Church. Their death sentence was, in a way, a confirmation of that initial exclusion. They were ideal scapegoats. Since the Church had expelled them a long time ago, it was not really contaminated by the vileness of their 'prodigious, barbarous and inhuman' crime.[28] The catharsis of the stake was the fiery culmination of a process of rejection. The third and final stage was Léry's narrative, which arose from and summarized the enquiry, and brought to light not only the crimes of adultery, concubinage and anthropophagy, but also that of homicide – for Monsieur Potard had once murdered a man for his clothes. (The man had been suspected of espionage, but had just been released by the Council.) This supplementary information was proof that the accused was most certainly a damned soul – the fire was, if anything, too good for him.

The exorcism, necessary to the spiritual health of the community, was necessary also to Léry personally. By telling the story of this abominable crime and sending a copy to the all-powerful Claude de la Châtre, Governor of Berry, Léry hoped to obtain a safe conduct – which, in fact, he did. By putting the thing into words, he objectified and distanced it, and that was a real deliverance. He was able to flee the accursed town without interference and continue his pastoral ministry elsewhere.[29] At a deeper level, by narrating the famine he was able to come to terms with himself and bring to light the obsession with cannibalism which ran through his life, and would also run through his work. It was then that Brazil became prominent once again, and Brazil was not as alien as might have been thought to the Burgundian town in the throes of the Wars of Religion.

The first link between Sancerre and Brazil is one of opposition. Whereas the cannibalism of the Tupinambas seems to lend itself to interpretation on a higher level, the anthropophagy of Sancerre is apparently inexcusable. Far from being part of any social or religious symbolism, it was diametrically opposed to the Christian religion, and perhaps even more to the Reformed conscience, which revolted from the idea of sacrifice and shedding of blood.[30] Nevertheless, the two forms of transgression have one thing in common: the presence in both of old women greedy for human flesh. Philippes de la Feüille, the instigator of the Potard crime, has a counterpart in the 'savages with hanging breasts' who busy themselves scraping the fat from the *boucan* and licking it off their fingers. This is a recognizable folklore archetype, whose manifestations range from the myth of Hecuba, whose dog-like howls transformed her into a bitch, to the many variants of 'Little Red Riding Hood' in which the grandmother and the wolf are one and the same. In the manuscript version of the 'Sommaire discours' Léry had suggested a medical explanation for this phenomenon: 'And I believe that old age desires and seeks more <+> as well as human flesh, as if old people sought to renew themselves.'[31]

This sentence was cut out of the text published in 1574. It appears that Léry was anxious to suppress any kind of extenuating circumstance. The witch of Sancerre, like her counterparts in Rio de Janeiro, could expect no mercy from her judges, and would receive none from the supreme Judge on the Latter Day. Her case savoured not of medicine, but of demonology. This pronounced misogyny also helps to explain the unequal treatment of cannibalism on 'this side and that' of the Atlantic. In Sancerre, the anthropophagy was primarily women's business. The husband, however criminal he might have been on his own account, served merely as a messenger between the aged Philippes de la Feüille and the grieving but conniving mother. When he offered forbidden food to his wife, he was only repeating the original invitation. As at the beginning of time and human history, the Tempter was female. In Brazil, on the other hand, the economy of vengeance cannibalism seemed to be essentially masculine. It was a point of honour, a highly virile sentiment, which impelled the cycle of warlike and alimentary violence: 'they eat the prisoners which they take in war'[32] – and that was all, or nearly all. On the stage of this anthropophagous spectacular, women had only walk-on parts, or so Léry would have us believe. They dragged the ritual down to a lower level, towards the flesh and purely animal appetites, whereas the haughty speech of the prisoner, defying his vanquisher on the brink of death, raised it to the symbolic level.[33]

This is why, in the last analysis, the cannibalism of Sancerre is literally unassimilable. It makes Léry sick with disgust. The anthropophagy of the Tupinambas becomes almost acceptable by comparison. During a scene which we shall consider in a moment, Léry came within an ace of conversion to these table manners, which, however strange and barbaric, had the merit of fostering a warm male camaraderie.

Léry passed the last two months of 1557 among the tribes allied to the French, and during this time he shared in every aspect of Tupinamba life – except cannibalism. One evening he came home to find a *cahouinage* in full swing in a village where a prisoner had just been slaughtered. At the height of the feasting and carousing, Léry, tired from his journey, fell into an uneasy sleep filled with nightmares. Suddenly – 'a proper occasion for fear' – a savage brandished over his hammock a human foot 'cooked and *boucané*.'[34] Léry was terrified, not understanding that this was an invitation to join in the

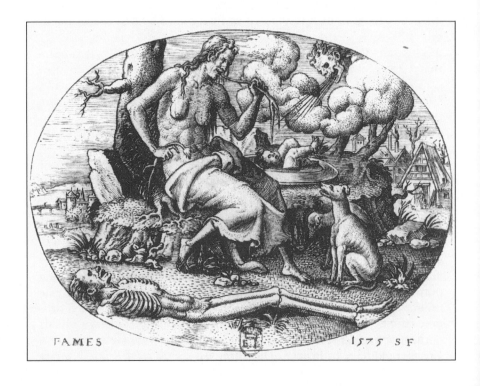

FAMES   1575 S F

INVIDIA · S · F ·

Figure 7 The old woman eating a child may represent either Hunger or Envy. These two allegories, etchings by the Protestant artist Etienne Delaune, date from 1575 and are thus slightly later than the siege of Sancerre during which a mother and father, egged on by an old woman in their household, were driven by famine to eat their daughter 'aged about three' (July 1573). Paris: Bibliothèque Nationale.

joyous festivities. Losing all desire to sleep, he sat shuddering in his chair until dawn. The next day the misunderstanding was revealed amidst peals of laughter from the Cannibals, and the apparent menace was explained as a gesture of hospitality.

The episode, which begins like a bad dream and ends with a lesson in cannibal manners, facetiously conveyed, seems like the decisive stage in an initiation. The conclusions are drawn a few months later, when Léry returns to France. The ship was blown off course and supplies became exhausted, so that the passengers began to steal murderous looks at one another, famine having given them 'evil thoughts regarding that barbarous act'.[35] After reaching the Breton coast, the captain revealed that he had determined to sacrifice one of his passengers the next day so as to feed his crew. Léry, far from being scandalized or retrospectively frightened at the notion, treated it as a joke: in any case, he was so thin that his flesh would have been quite uneatable! He drew the same moral from the incident as he might have drawn from the Cannibals of Guanabara.

Thus, Léry conquered his fear and came to terms with his private dread. He had succeeded in confounding the 'terror'[36] attached to the taboo on anthropophagy. But the exorcism only really worked 'on the other side', in the dreamlike Brazil far removed in space and time, where conflicts were resolved in words of honour and friendship, and flesh melted into language. One could not stay there for ever. Returning from the country of Cannibals, reality – obsessive, proliferating, stubborn reality – was still with him. Indeed, it was everywhere, even in the most peaceful corners of provincial France: from Sancerre, to Sens, to Auxerre.

The price of this reduction of thing to meaning and cuisine to symbol was indeed a heavy one. The result, as we have seen, was to extend the theatre of cruelties to the entire universe. A world which had become one vast killing field was inevitably doomed to catastrophe. Chapter XV of the 1580 edition of *Histoire d'un voyage* begins by evoking the figurative cannibalism of usurers and exploiters of the poor, but then falls into the all-too-real anthropophagy of civil wars. At about the same time as the St Bartholomew massacre, a person known as 'Coeur de Roy', who 'professed the Reformed Faith in the city of Auxerre', supplied grim proof of this. In a gruesome jest, his executioners did their best to make his punishment fit his name – heart-of-a-king. In a blatant denial of the nominalist conception of the Eucharist defended by Léry and his co-religionists, the 'king's heart' was plucked out, chopped in pieces, auctioned off, cooked on a grill and finally eaten with much enjoyment.[37]

What end could be found to this incessant return of the repressed? The only solution was to break away from the Christian vision of history. As we shall see later, Montaigne no longer conceives the matter in terms of either sacrifice or redemption, and the end of history ceases to loom over the horizon of the loose and chaotic weft of visible events. Allegory will triumph when the irrational hope of deliverance, along with the spectre of hunger and bloodshed, is passed over in tactful silence. The respite, which was undoubtedly to be a temporary one, was to be marked by the brief reign of the honourable cannibal.

If Léry did no more, he did pave the way for this lull in the manipulation of cannibal danger, by taking a fear which he well knew to be deeply rooted in his own society and religious culture, and removing it to a far-distant and savage land.[38]

7

The Melancholy Cannibal

The ogre and the amorous lady

If we are to understand the mildness of French voyagers' reactions to the ritual anthropophagy of their Brazilian Indian allies, we must take a look at Europe. While it is true that the New World throws a very revealing light on the customs of the Old, the latter offers its own interpretative model and draws its own line to subdivide the uses of the body. And reactions to some actual cases in early modern Europe had already evinced a degree of tolerance toward cannibalism.[1] The vigour with which the transgression was reproved depended on the meaning which might or might not be attributed to it. At one extreme it could be accepted, in so far as it could be integrated into a social symbolism relating to a *crime passionnel* or to the code of honour – a feudal survival at the 'moral heart of the Great Century',[2] 'tamed' by the ritual of vendetta. Though it represented a threat of destruction to society, it also appeared as the extremist manifestation of a moral view which had long been dominant, and which up to the dawn of the seventeenth century was an aspect of the governance of the old social elite, the *noblesse d'épée*.

Let us start from a more humble viewpoint, however, and look at two early seventeenth-century pamphlets which echo much earlier models and allow us to trace an opposition between 'good' and 'bad' uses of cannibalism at the heart of European culture.[3] Both are would-be exemplary tales which claim to derive from the most up-to-the-minute judicial reportage. As well as their immediate context – the execution of the guilty, justice duly done for the crime of anthropophagy, the day, the hour, the town, the large audience of potential or fictitious witnesses – the two pamphlets draw on a substantial folkloric tradition which, since the Middle Ages, had nourished folktales, novels, lays and proverbs.[4] These stories, of which one is (as we shall see) described as 'prodigious', while the other is 'horrible and frightful', actually conform to ready-made narrative and ideological models which were part of the consciousness of both the anonymous narrators and their public.

The meaning and the lesson of the first of these anecdotes are made wholly clear in the title: *Histoire prodigieuse d'une jeune Damoiselle de Dole, en la Franche Conté, laquelle fit manger le foye de son enfant à un jeune Gentilhomme qui avoit violé sa pudicité sous ombre d'un mariage pretendu: ensemble comme elle le fit cruellement mourir, et se remit entre les mains de la Justice pour estre punie exemplairement: le Samedy 19. jour de Novembre, 1608. Avec l'Arrest de la Cour de Parlement prononcé contre elle.* ('Prodigious history of a young Lady of Dole, in the Franche Comté, who gave the liver of her child to eat to a young Gentleman who had violated her honour under the pretence of marriage: and how she put him cruelly to death, and gave herself into the hands of Justice for exemplary punishment: on Saturday the 19 day of November, 1608. With the Sentence pronounced on her by the Court of Parliament').[5] An edifying tale, then, with a moral. The sequence of disorderly conduct – clandestine marriage, infanticide, induced cannibalism and the murder of the seducer – ends with a legal sentence, which is rigorously carried out. However, despite the horror of her crime, the heroine of the pamphlet is shown in rather a favourable light. She may have killed her child and fed its liver to the man who had abandoned her, but this was the vengeance of a person scorned in love. We are told that as she prepared to serve the fatal feast to her wicked seducer, Cécile 'barked' that the hour of vengeance was nigh.[6] But this wolfish rage and hunger for human flesh are not in the least bestial: they reveal no perverse appetites. Their value is essentially symbolic. The cannibalistic offence is the exact pendant to the initial crime of adultery. The text makes this explicit: 'Cécile ... took her child which she had had brought secretly for this purpose, killed it, took out its liver and prepared it as a hash so that it might return to the place whence it had its origin.'[7]

The meal served up to the seducer, de la Chambre, creates a circle of connections which both begins and ends with him. The seed, which he so wrongly and inconsiderately spilled, comes back to him in the form of a hashed child's liver: the fruit of his loins returns to them. Cécile's deliberate intention is to match like with like: she vicariously accomplishes an act of 'alimentary incest'.[8]

This enforced return to the origin, short-circuiting the carnal sequence, obviously flies in the face of nature, and thereby recalls the similar circuit made by the 'wolf-woman' who ate her own child, as described in *Les Tragiques* of Agrippa d'Aubigné: 'Your blood returns to the place where you sucked milk, / Against Nature it returns to the breast that suckled you: / That breast, which fed you, shall be your sepulchre.'[9]

But, whereas the Protestant poet sees this cycle as the ultimate scandal, both a sign and an announcement of God's wrath against mankind, the macabre feast prepared by Cécile for her faithless lover is seen as the logical and almost natural consequence of his treachery. Through a sort of symmetry, the crime of cannibalism is required – in the same way that blood is supposed to cry for vengeance – by the original offence of the clandestine marriage. It is the latter crime only which provokes indignation from the author of the tale. That, indeed, is the moral of the story: just before she was beheaded by the executioner in the presence of the entire populace of Dole, all of them moved to tears, Cécile addressed the required harangue to the 'girls' among the audience, in which she herself drew the moral of her misfortune. She condemned the practice of clandestine marriage and added 'that one should never receive the nuptial benediction in secret'. After delivering herself of this 'notable lesson', the heroine died with fortitude.

Thus, Cécile appears as a martyr: her only error was to put her trust in a stranger without gaining the blessing of the Church and without telling her parents. It is no surprise to find, at the end of the pamphlet, a restatement of the conservative values so often peddled in chap-book literature. What is most striking is that this edifying tale, with its stale and sententious moral, features – without either criticism or blame, indeed with approval – the practice of cannibalism. In fact, the theme of cannibalism as love-vengeance had become a topos of the tragic errors provoked by passion. Several medieval tales give eloquent expression to the motif. In the 'Lay of Ignauré', written in the early thirteenth century, the private parts and heart of a young lover of twelve ladies are fed to the latter by their cuckolded husbands, who thus take exemplary collective vengeance on the seducer.[10] The same pattern features in the 'Romance of the Châtelain de Coucy and the lady of Fayel':[11] the latter unknowingly and appreciatively devours the heart of her lover (killed on the Crusades), which has been secretly cooked by her jealous and cruel husband. Two well-known stories from Boccaccio's *Decameron* (Fourth Day, no. 9; Fifth Day, no. 8) repeat, with some variations, this traditional theme of the heart which is eaten, or given to somebody else to eat, as an act of love-vengeance.[12]

In every case, the recourse to cannibalism may be understood as reparation for a sexual misdemeanour, usually adultery. Eating the body – or, synecdochically, the heart or liver – of the beloved symbolically re-enacts the illicit sexual relationship, but also neutralizes it by simple absorption. The symmetry between the sexual excess, which requires correction, and the cannibalistic excess, which corrects it, is particularly evident in the 'Lay of Ignauré', in which the heart, seat of the passions, is accompanied by the offender's phallus, cut up and stewed to nourish the twelve inconstant fair ones. As they eat it, they enjoy, for the last time, the flesh of the beloved. The carnal relationship is renewed through the mouth and belly, and immediately destroyed: a dead body encounters other bodies, which are themselves on the verge of death. Discovering the horror of their meal and unable to expel the cherished, but now repugnant, flesh, the twelve ladies starve themselves to death. Thus, the act of cannibalism finally reabsorbs the unacceptable adultery.

In the cases we have examined, cannibalism is not 'the disquieting image of an intolerable excess'.[13] It follows a very strict judicial logic. In the mutual demise of eater and eaten, the cannibalistic punishment fixes a liaison which should never have arisen in the first place: the liver of the son in the stomach of the guilty father; the heart and phallus of the lover in the bodies of the faithless wives. It illustrates a kind of primitive justice which is not exactly 'an eye for an eye and a tooth for a tooth', but which does show a metaphorical symmetry between the crime and its punishment. Even if the agents of cannibalism – whether the cannibals themselves or those preparing the horrid meal for someone else – seem to be inspired by a thirst for vengeance, they are not out of their minds. Their acts, however 'prodigious', follow a ritual which is seen to be totally coherent and absolutely necessary.

Alongside this vengeance cannibalism, which ultimately re-establishes an order (or at least some sort of equilibrium) that has been briefly compromised by amorous passion, we also find other forms of anthropophagy, which cannot be reduced to social symbolism and which are therefore thrown back into the realm of demonology and madness. The second pamphlet is a perfect illustration of this. It is the *Histoire horrible et effroyable d'un homme plus qu'enragé, qui a esgorgé et mangé sept enfans, dans la ville de Chaalons en Champagne* ('Horrible and frightful history of a man smitten by worse than madness, who slit the throats of seven children and ate them, in the town of Chaalons in Champagne'), published together with the 'memorable execution which followed' in Paris in 1619. Just like the first, this pamphlet, which is inspired by a contemporary incident, draws on an old stock of mythical motifs.[14] The monster of Châlons is simply an updated avatar of the fairytale ogre. Both kill children by slitting their throats, and mince them up before eating them. Moreover, the story follows the iterative structure of the popular tale, for the ogre commits the same crime seven times over in exactly the same way: he invites a group of seven children to a party at his house, and 'of the seven that there were, he would detain one, and let the other six go'. The group would be reconstituted the next day by the addition of a new arrival, because 'following their nature', young children 'lead and take one another everywhere to amuse themselves together'.[15] The story continues until number seven is reached. Then the grieving parents arrive, closely followed by the judges and the executioner. It all ends with the avenging fire, in the midst of which the ogre emits a last dying snigger.

Though it is codified by a long legendary tradition, it is clear that the behaviour of the cannibal of Champagne is wholly inadmissible. This is the fundamental difference between him and the young lady of Franche-Comté who murdered her own child in her despair at having been rejected in love. The enormity of his crime puts the ogre beyond the reach of any symbolic redemption. His crime – the consumption of seven children, minced up one after the other on the seven days of the week – hurls him beyond the reach of normality. His act provokes an unprecedented imbalance; it represents no kind of compensation and seriously threatens the body social by subjecting it to an irrecoverable loss. The ogre's 'furious rage'[16] opens a bottomless pit in the heart of the micro-society of Châlons.

The ogre is condemned to the stake (Cécile of Dole was spared this and was merely decapitated), and he is quite incapable of pronouncing any edifying last words. At once the fire seizes on his bowels, the instrument of his repeated crimes. He then begins to grasp handfuls of burning sticks and throw them over the audience. At last he expires amidst 'horrible cries and yells, like a man dying insane'.[17] The ogre of Châlons, whose identity is never revealed – does he even have a name? – is abominable through and through. His spectacular and disquieting death-agony exactly resembles that of a man possessed. The criminal remains a danger to the social order up to his last gasp. It is only when his ashes have been scattered to the winds 'as the sentence required' that the malefic presence contained within him finally ceases to be active. Indeed, his cannibalistic violence can be neutralized by nothing less than the fire of the stake, which corresponds to, and is absorbed in, the cooking-fire; and by the ash-laden wind which finally dissipates the 'horrible and frightful history'. Thus closes the gaping rent which the evil deeds of the werewolf have torn in the social fabric.

Of course, these two examples are not the only cases of actual cannibalism in early modern Europe. They are probably not even the most eloquent witnesses to a theme which is etched on the collective imagination, from popular songs and tales (such as the numerous variants on 'Little Red Riding-Hood'[18] in which the little girl colludes with the wolf to devour the grandmother) to Boccaccio's novellas and the 'Tragical Histories' of Bandello, in which the paths of vengeance lead into the mouth of a hungry dog.[19] But such as they are, this pair of antithetical pamphlets, which are so clearly attached to a long tradition, bring out two main trends in attitudes towards the cannibal taboo. This taboo appears to be absolute when its transgressor evinces a supposedly bestial appetite – an unnatural urge which impels an individual to eat the flesh of fellow humans. The taste for human flesh is viewed as an intolerable perversion, and the criminal must be exorcised, or, more radically, consumed in the purifying fire of the stake.

On the other hand, when the symbolic intention outweighs the raw horror of the act, as in vengeance cannibalism, the inherent significance of the practice divorces it from brute animality. This makes the cannibal act less 'blameful' and integrates it into a value system – heroism, passionate love, implacable and desperate vengeance – which is to some extent common both to the Tupinambas of Rio de Janeiro and to the tardy devotees of a bastardized form of courtly love. This brings us back to the human domain of custom, and in Montaigne's essay on the subject (I, 23), cannibalism has a lofty place among the strange practices which distinguish this 'Queen and Empress of all the World'.[20]

Jean Bodin and the sadness of the Cannibal

The fury of vengeance is the exact antipodes of ogreish bestiality, and this remains true even in the geographical expression of the word. On his world map, Jean Bodin placed one of them in the South and the other in the North,[21] in two diametrically opposed climatic zones. The Scythians of the North represent the bestial appetite for human flesh: since the days of Herodotus, Solinus and Pomponius Mela they had been the incarnation of absolute barbarity. These peoples, who lurked with their chariots in the northern fringes of the inhabited world, drank the hot blood of their enemies and readily fed on human flesh – according to somewhat unreliable witnesses.[22] To this classical model of exceptionally brutal alimentary practices Bodin adds the 'strange cruelties' of the 'King of Muscovy', who had inherited both Scythian territory and Scythian barbarity, and, more especially, the misdeeds of 'Dracula duke of Transylvania', which, as we have already mentioned, also interested Léry.[23] These diverse examples tended to show that 'the less reason and judgement men have, the closer they approach to the nature of brute beasts'.[24]

Such, according to Bodin, is the condition of the peoples of the North, who, though of robust constitution, are not distinguished for sharpness of wit, or even for reason itself, which is supposedly common to all men. They are of sanguine temperament, as is to be expected, considering the dry, cold climate in which they live and which confines their natural heat to the interior of their bodies,[25] and their customs are similar in cruelty to those of the bears and wolves which hunt in the same territory. The bloodthirsty rage which inspires these barbarous peoples, sometimes impelling them to devour one another, must be the lowest degree of anthropophagous perversion.

At the other end of the chain, living in the opposite clime, the southerners are cruel in an equal but opposite way. They also practise cannibal cruelty, but they are driven to it not by their bellies, but by their passions. Their blood is not greedy for the blood of others, as is that of the northerners: they obey the impulses of black bile (melancholia), of which they harbour excessive amounts. This bile is 'engendered by the humours burned by the scorching heat',[26] and settles as dregs at the base of their bodies, dooming them to implacable passions. This is recognizably the anatomy of the melancholic, who is naturally inclined to activeness of mind, may have moments of genius, but also seeks the most refined vengeance. This means that the southerner's appetite for vengeance should not be confused with the wolfish rage of the scythian. From either a spatial or a psychological viewpoint, the one is the antipodes of the other. The most complete expression of southern rage is the tragic fury repeatedly illustrated in the drama of Ancient Greece: Ajax, Medea, Thyestes and Agave are all melancholic heroes who kill, rend asunder or devour the object of their mad passion.[27]

Bodin, through an audacious hyperbole, extends to whole peoples the clinical characteristics of the great tragic figures: first to Greece, begetter of those exemplary rages, then to Italy and Spain, nations noted for their intellectual and artistic achievements, but also for the extreme vengefulness of their character. As contemporary French chroniclers were never tired of repeating, cases of abominable tortures (that roasting of the living flesh of which so many refinements were developed as the century progressed), and even cannibal feasting *per se*, were no rarity among those peoples, highly civilized as they were widely reputed to be.[28]

Here, it should be remembered that this psychological profile, which today may seem strange as applied to the peoples of the South, was based on some tenacious assumptions. When Bodin published *Methodus* in 1566, and ten years later, when he embroidered on his celebrated climatic theory in *Six Livres*, many of his fellow Frenchmen were convinced that the cultural and political influence of

Spain and Italy was becoming more and more pervasive, and were roundly criticizing it: current xenophobia was building on stereotypes developed through centuries of experience.

The vengeful cruelty of the Spaniard had become a commonplace after the conquest of the New World and the wars in the Low Countries. We have heard Léry's remarks about the 'more than abominable cruelties of the Spaniards' in the later editions of his *Histoire d'un voyage faict en la terre du Bresil.* The corollary of the Great Discovery was the 'destruction of the Indies', in the course of which (if we are to believe Bartolomé de Las Casas) the conquistadors practised enforced cannibalism on a colossal scale: for example, in Guatemala the new master of the country forced the subject peoples to devour one another wholesale, since it saved him the bother of feeding them and enabled him to put them to work, while confiscating all their food resources for his own profit.[29] And the savage repression of the Lutherans in the Netherlands and the Franche-Comté included several scenes of ritual anthropophagy. This was an obligatory motif for Protestant propagandists, and it also appears in the writings of political historians such as Jacques-Auguste de Thou, who excoriated 'the insolence of the Spanish soldiery',[30] and Pierre de L'Estoile, who, describing the sack of Antwerp in November 1576, declared that 'the victorious Spaniard is customarily insolent, and so cruel and disrespectful that he spares no effort to be avenged upon his enemy'.[31]

It was, however, the Italians who lifted vengeance to the highest degree of horror and gave it a distinctly culinary turn. The gravest accusations were concentrated upon this nation, as France was engulfed in civil war: 'on the tenth of September [1563] the enemy camp arrived at Gien and its environs, where infinite cruelties were committed, so much so that certain Italians having cut a living child in two from hatred of Religion also ate of its liver'.[32]

Whether true or invented, this anecdote, from the *Histoire ecclesiastique des Eglises reformées* compiled by Theodore Beza, clearly bears witness to the quasi-Satanic aura which emanated from the Italians. The ritual consumption of the innocent victim's liver – the liver being the seat of life and the soul – may be compared to the infamous practices attributed by Huguenot pamphleteers (including d'Aubigné) to Catherine de' Medici and her entourage of Florentine wizards and sorcerers. These anecdotes, a caricatural expression of the refusal to accept a foreign elite whose interference in the affairs of the kingdom had assumed scandalous proportions, proliferated throughout the queen mother's personal rule. They give the impression that the customs and practices of this immigrant aristocracy, which was progressively imposing its values, fashions and speech on the French Court, were utterly and completely barbaric.[33]

The same militant anti-Italianism is displayed by the printer and Protestant humanist Henri Estienne in his *Apologie pour Hérodote*, which was published in the same year (1566) as Bodin's *Methodus ad facilem historiarum cognitionem*. He reports examples 'of the cruelty of our age', among them the following anecdote borrowed from Portano: 'Certain Italians ... having taken one of the family with whom they had a quarrel, incontinently chopped him into small pieces, and having drawn forth his liver, roasted it on burning coals; and afterwards each ate his portion of it with great joy, with diverse solemnities such as sprinkling the blood and profaning the corpse.'[34] Later in the same chapter, which makes continual references to Thyestes (the mythical hero who devoured his own children),[35] Estienne cites, from memory, the *exemplum* of the Châtelain de Coucy and the lady of Fayel. There follow several telling cases of extraordinary vengeances taken from the 'Tragical Histories' of Matteo Bandello, the protagonists of which are always either a Spaniard, 'a lady of Milan', or a vengeful Italian. The most striking aspect of this string of anecdotes handed down from previous centuries is that they are now clad in Italian garb or a Spanish ruff. It seems that traditional expressions of the horror of cannibalism are being exiled beyond French frontiers. It is a kind of exorcism at other countries' expense: the Thyestes myth, which must have been deeply embedded in contemporary French culture under both popular and scholarly guises, is sent elsewhere, to the sun-scorched southern fringes of the realm, or among the carnivorous fevers of the black bile.

The southern horizon is thus common to the political theories of Jean Bodin and the religious polemics of his time. But whereas Estienne, Beza and their ilk make no distinction between codified ritual and mere bloodthirstiness, between vengeance and wolfish barbarity, Bodin restores the full distance between South and North, hot and cold, civility (however cruel) and crass brutality: 'We may thus observe the different cruelty of the peoples of the North, and of the South; in that the former perform it with brutal impetuousity, and like beasts without reason; and the latter, like foxes, employ all their wits to satisfy their vengeance.'[36]

Thus, the bestial stupidity of the northerners contrasts with the foxy cunning of the southerners. The carnal and sanguinary appetite of the former contrasts with the latter's anxiety to satiate a thirst for vengeance which is moral rather than physical. The fact that mouth and stomach are employed for the purpose is of small importance: it is the intelligence of the quest and the subtlety of the means which make the difference between one group and the other.

Completing his systematization of climates and humours, Bodin adds to the Mediterranean peoples (the typical southerners) the savage 'Brazilians [who] are not content to eat their enemies, unless they also bathe their little children in their blood'.[37] The melancholy Cannibal has extremely violent passions, and consequently 'he uses his wits to avenge his grievances'. Thus, the Tupinambas, whose anthropophagous customs Bodin had learned from Thevet, are the most striking example of intellectual and cannibalistic melancholia. To Bodin, as later to Montaigne, the Tupinamba Cannibal is diametrically opposed to the Scythian, both in the spatial realm of geography and in the hierarchy of alimentary values. The two are separated by half the surface of the earth, and by that distance which forever separates the beast from humanity, which is endowed with reason and passions.

The step-by-step horizontal succession of climatic zones from the Equator to the Poles, from the torrid regions to the subpolar margins, in which every form of madness and alimentary perversion must find its own place, represents an easy-to-read system of classification, and also the setting for a hierarchy. The South is superior to the North to the precise degree that humanity is superior to animals: 'It is very clear that fury seizes upon Southerners more easily than on Northerners, just as madness attacks men more easily than beasts.'[38]

Bestial rage, inspired by an excess of blood, is at the bottom of the human and the climatic scale. The 'wolfish' individual, who, driven by extreme hunger, flings himself upon his fellow man, is more of a wolf than a man: a werewolf.[39] And the cases of cannibalism among the destitute which were reported during the Wars of Religion were considered perverse and inexcusable. In the last chapter we saw how Jean de Léry, who was an eye-witness to the famine at Sancerre and the cannibalistic incident which brought it to an end, instantly rejected the hypothesis of necessity and was inclined to attribute the affair to Satanic influence.[40]

Moreover, this form of cannibalism might very well prove to be infectious: once the taboo had been transgressed on the urgings of extreme need, the consequence might be allelophagy unlimited, as human beings devoured one another. It was in order to eliminate such a dreadful danger that offenders were sent to the stake, as at Sancerre in July 1573, and in times of famine during the earlier Hundred Years War. The sacrifice of the criminals served as a deterrent: it saved the community from self-destruction.

The opposite extreme to bestial, hunger-driven rage is the cannibal fury of the melancholic, which had been accepted since antiquity as an appurtenance of nobility. Being an attribute of passionate temperaments, it especially affected individuals who had been driven beyond ordinary bounds by their excessive sufferings and strength of feeling. The very fact that these sufferers from melancholy are found chiefly among the warrior aristocracy, the heroes, means that their brand of fury is restricted to a few isolated cases and presents small danger to the rest of the social order – except, of course, to the nations of the South and of Africa, where, as Bodin remarks, 'the number of furious persons is almost infinite'.[41]

And there is another difference. Fury, or its cannibal variant, does not advance as blindly as 'the evil rage of hunger'. 'Furious' persons usually select from the sacrificed body the portions which they intend to eat: the liver, heart, phallus, all organs bearing a heavy symbolic load, which exist in order to satisfy an appetite more 'metaphorical' than bestial. This proclaims the fact that 'furious' cannibalism is a substitute. It is the indirect, metaphorical, exacerbated expression of a passion which sees the act of eating as a sort of symbolic compensation. The voracity of the mouth palliates the cravings of the heart. Thus, cannibal fury does not derogate in the least from the morality of punctilious honour: indeed, it is one of its most extreme manifestations. Here, Christian morality, which enjoins pardon for offences, clashes with another, essentially aristocratic morality, which sets more store by vengeance – an eye for an eye, a tooth for a tooth. This is the reason why authors from Thevet to Montaigne are inclined to excuse the honour cannibalism of the Brazilians.[42] It is the same impulse which explains, even when it cannot justify, the strange alimentary practices which passion can arouse even in the Old Continent, if pamphlets and hearthside tales are to be believed.

All in all, Bodin's system, whose originality lies in the snapshot vision which he offers across the climatic scale of the various levels of madness, and of its alimentary expression, exposes the hierarchy which is implicit in pamphlets, folktales, novellas, and the miscellanies which were popular during the Renaissance.[43] They always distinguish between 'fury' and 'rage', in both intensity and quality.

This antagonism between the respective alimentary aberrations of North and South seems designed ultimately to highlight the exclusive privileges which Bodin thinks are due to the happy medium: the peoples of the temperate regions, and first of all the French, know almost nothing of either wolfish rage or cannibal fury, and consider both to be equally barbaric: 'Now the median peoples cannot see, or even hear of, such cruelties without horror.'[44]

These 'median' nations, which occupy the zone between the thirtieth and sixtieth parallels, are governed by anger, which subordinates both Nordic brutality and cruel southern ingenuity to its own whims and caprices. They cannot fix on a single attitude, and this saves them from both brutishness and despair. These in-between people represent the alimentary norm to which the rest of humanity ought to adhere. Choler, situated midway between blood and black bile, desires none but lawful foods. The devastating and contradictory influences emanating from the voracious North and the cruel South neutralize each other there, and so define the very nature of civility.

However, even if one accepts this third term as arbitrator of the conflict, there is still an imbalance between the two extremes. In the domain of table manners, the South governs the North – which implies that true barbarism exists on only one side of the median climate. The vengeance that drives the Cannibals who dwell in the hot countries can never be fully excused from the viewpoint of evangelical morality; but at least their perversion savours unambiguously of a practice and a symbolic load which are fully human.

It might be said that the robust and hungry northerners mark the last lurking place of the repressed, on the threshold of unknown lands: in so far as they are the incarnation of a hunger which denies any form of social existence, they seem to be the direct heirs of those 'insolent' giants who, 'in despite of the heavenly spirits', ruled before the Flood.[45] Like them, they 'eat and devour men' and 'give themselves up to all such impieties', but now that they have been repelled to the highest latitudes, Scythians of the Old World or Patagonians of the New, they are no longer in a position to cause any anxiety to omnivorous, 'median' humanity, save in the interstices of nightmare.

To conclude the present diptych we need only refer to the opinion of Pierre de Dampmartin, the popularizer *par excellence* of the ideas of his learned contemporaries. In his treatise *De la connoissance et merveilles du monde et de l'homme* ('On the Knowledge and Marvels of the World and of Mankind') (1585) he compares 'brutish' cruelty with vengeance which 'is justified by resentment of an offence'.[46] The parallel soon modulates into enthusiastic praise of vengeance, a virtue 'natural' to well-born men, which is contrasted with cruelty, 'the bloodthirsty enemy of all humanity'. This unnatural cruelty reaches its highest pitch in the tyrants who act towards innocents 'as if they were Lions or Bears seeking to devour their bodies'.[47] It is for this reason that the two passions are fundamentally opposed, even in their most extreme manifestation of anthropophagy: 'Vengeance has been considered as natural, even praiseworthy, by some, but cruelty never.'[48]

This reads like a first sketch, or crude copy, of Montaigne's position: hatred of cruelty,[49] but a readiness to excuse vengeance, which, if it serves the cause of honour and beauty, is not really as barbarous as it seems.

8

The Spitting Cannibal

～∶～

I fear me our eyes be greater than our bellies, and that we have more curiosity than capacity.

The Cannibals and savage people do not so much offend me with roasting and eating of dead bodies, as those which torment and persecute the living.

Montaigne, Essays

Montaigne, or the paradox of 'Cannibals'

'Of Cannibals' emphasizes the opposition of art and nature in such a way as to demonstrate the superiority of the latter. This emerges from its attractive, and distinctly favourable, picture of Brazilian Cannibal society, which had already been described in very similar terms by Hans Staden, André Thevet and Jean de Léry. This apology for the virtuous and anthropophagous Indian, in whom live again the heroic virtues of Leonidas or Iscolas, produces a relativization of cultures which evinces what Hugo Friedrich calls 'clear-sighted scepticism': it is summed up in Montaigne's celebrated formula, 'men call that barbarism, which is not common to them'.[1]

But beyond this general observation, interpretations of the essay have differed. What is the exact value of this surprising paean of praise to naked anthropophagi? Must Montaigne be taken literally, or must the essay be read as humorous and ironical? Is the chapter 'biased', as suggested by Alphonse Dupront, offering a 'paradox of words rather than things? Is it possible to agree with Raymond Lebègue, who accuses the author of 'abusing our naivety' and writing the chapter for effect, without any 'profound conviction'?[2]

It seems to me that the embarrassment of critics who seek to reduce the immediate intentions of the essay to a literary bluff, an inconsequential rhetorical and philosophical game, betrays a profound uneasiness about the taboos that are lifted or circumvented by Montaigne in one of his most daring moods: cannibalism, polygamy, nakedness.[3] The best way to avoid insulting Montaigne's posthumous prestige is to make out that he is being playful, and to refuse to take seriously his 'systematic glorification of Natives' even in their most undesirable alimentary and sexual practices. A similar desire to extenuate Montaigne may lead the critic to cast doubt on the tortures which he mentions in passing, and which are amply documented in Renaissance sources.[4]

The notion of 'paradox' may be a useful analytical tool, but only if it is understood according to the most rigorous rhetorical definition. 'Of Cannibals' does indeed have features of literary paradox, but neither more nor less than Erasmus' *Praise of Folly*. Here and there an apparently humorous remark may point to a profound truth. The comic overtones, which are felt, in particular, at the conclusion of the essay, are intended to put the reader in a questioning frame of mind. When Montaigne pretends to be finally indignant about, or at least moderate in his praise of, the Cannibals, he is really insinuating the opposite conclusion: 'All that is not very ill; but what of that? They wear no kind of breeches or hosen.'[5]

The Brazilian – here, the Tupinikin of Rio de Janeiro, whose image and ferocious prowess had already been revealed by Thevet and Léry – is now raised to the rank of an ideal. To Montaigne, this is tantamount to a reincarnation of the Gymnosophist, the 'naked philosopher' of India whose prelapsarian simplicity compelled admiration from the Ancient Greeks. In far-off Brazil, this is the realm of dreams rather than of real experience:

> it is a nation ... that hath no kind of traffic, no knowledge of Letters, no intelligence of numbers, no name of magistrate, nor of politic superiority; no use of service, of riches, or of poverty; no contracts, no successions, no dividences, no occupation but idle; no respect of kindred, but common, no apparel but natural, no manuring of lands, no use of wine, corn, or metal. The very words that import lying, falsehood, treason, dissimulation, covetousness, envy, detraction, and pardon, were never heard of among them.[6]

This string of negatives allegorizes the Brazilian savages and separates them from their own ethnographic reality: in reality they did practise agriculture, engaged in barter, recognized an extremely complex system of kinship, etc. Thus the Indians reach, or rather 'exceed', 'all the pictures wherewith licentious Poesy hath proudly imbellished the golden age'.

The first literary topos to employ a comparable series of negatives was indeed the Golden Age. Montaigne takes up the litany from the first book of Ovid's *Metamorphoses* and Ronsard's *Complainte contre Fortune*. The Golden Age, an age of ease and abundance, is defined by the absence of everything that characterizes civilized life: art, technology, clothes, law and custom, all human inventions which

generate labour and constraint. In a letter, which was probably completed after the *Essays* and seems to borrow from them, the magistrate
Etienne Pasquier adopts this series of absences, which is in fact a
cliché of exoticism: 'As for their political administration, they have
no magistrates, no towns, no kind of republic, save that they are
divided into families according to their kinship and relations ...' But
he comes to the opposite conclusion from Montaigne: these peoples,
whose 'uncouth customs' reveal them as entirely 'novel', are
brusquely returned to the void whence they came. Pasquier's solidly
ethnocentric and bourgeois consciousness triumphs over the dizzying
abyss of paradox.[7]

    To this first mythic model Montaigne appends a second, which is,
in a way, its opposite: the ideal republic, the masterpiece of rational
construction, offspring of the most considered wisdom. Like the
poets, however, the philosophers of antiquity and their political fictions, however ingenious, lag far behind the example of the
Cannibals. Alas for the divine Plato and the Spartan lawgiver
Lycurgus: 'the conception and desire of philosophy' are attained and
surpassed by the carefree inhabitants of Brazil.

    One of the most probable sources for this chapter by Montaigne is
La Pazzia, an anonymous pamphlet published in Venice in 1554 and
translated into French in or before 1566 under the title *Les Louanges
de LA FOLIE* ('In Praise of Folly').[8] In this 'very pleasing Treatise in
form of a Paradox', which is evidently inspired by Erasmus and uses
the same procedure as the *Encomium Moriae* (*Praise of Folly*), there is
a long discussion of the 'people newly discovered in the West Indies',
who 'without laws, without letters, and with no sages' lived the hap-
piest life in the world. They despised gold and 'precious jewels' and
knew 'neither avarice, nor ambition, nor any other art at all'. Taking
their food 'from the fruits which the ground produces without artifice', they 'had as in the Republic of Plato, all things in common, even
to the women and little children: the which from their birth they
nourished and brought up in common as their own'.[9] As a result of
this community education, fraternal harmony reigned and everyone
was part of one big happy family: 'Whereby such little children
(acknowledging all men as their fathers without distinction) void of
hate and passion, lived in perpetual love and charity: as in the happy
era which was called the golden age of old Saturn.'

    This meticulous agreement with Plato does not deter the writer
from cocking a final snook at the Athenian philosopher, who wished
philosophers to be kings – or, if that was impossible, to make kings
into philosophers. The conclusion openly defies his authority: 'To
that I will answer no: but that the peoples could not be more

unhappy, nor in a greater calamity, than if they were to fall into the hands of such false philosophers and over-wise men.'[10] Evidence for this is the coming of the Spaniards, who, 'with their excess of learning, their very harsh and unendurable laws and edicts', filled the once blessed country full of 'a hundred thousand evils, annoyances and labours'.

If Montaigne had access to this text – which is probable – he would certainly have realized that it was heavily ironical. He mitigates this irony, but his own text retains the imprint of its daring original. It is now the Cannibal who teaches the philosopher a lesson: 'It is a nation, would I answer Plato, that hath no kind of traffic ...' Plato would be surprised, to say the least, to find that a society could defy his imagination and 'be maintained with so little art and humane combination'.[11] Here, experience administers a brusque correction to the learned and complex architecture of the *Republic*. As for the verdict of recent history, it agreed with that of the anonymous Venetian: in the conquest of America, artifice had triumphed over nature, but this had brought nothing but misfortune to the peoples of the New World.

Famine or banquet?

Let us go straight to the heart of the problem: the cannibal act itself, which is immediately evoked by Montaigne's title and represents the main dish on his Brazilian menu; the cannibal act, which still embarrasses many modern commentators. It is true that Montaigne devotes no more than two or three pages, out of the dozen or so which constitute 'Of Cannibals', to the act itself. But that is precisely the difficulty, if difficulty there be. By playing cunningly with the taboo, by setting it at the heart of his reflections on Otherness, Montaigne seeks to attract the attention of readers to this strange half-desire, half-repulsion which men feel for the flesh of their fellows: a desire/repulsion which underlies, in the most fundamental way, the mythic thinking of the West.

The crucial problem is how to say the unsayable by suggesting a schema which may seek to explain, but must for that very reason be reductive. Reduced to its alleged causes, the fact of cannibalism loses its immediate violence and its invincible horror. Instead of provoking revulsion and nausea and representing an unendurable scandal (which is what it ought to represent to any European observer), cannibalism becomes an object of study, a subject of reflection and writing. From the very beginning – and the essay itself is a demonstration of this –

the task is to find a way of speaking about a 'vituperable' and barbaric fact and thereby not only understand, but also exorcise it. Amazingly, many critics have seen Montaigne's analysis as no more than an affirmation of triumphant relativism – whence the astonishingly modern ring of his teaching – and not as a successful attempt at exorcism, for which he adopts alternately the tone of the moralist, the ethnographer and the humorist.

To account for Brazilian cannibalism Montaigne had access to two solutions developed by earlier writers: the practice could either be dismissed as a 'custom' (what we should now call an aspect of culture) – and the chapter entitled 'Of Custom, and how a received law should not readily be changed' (I, 23) deals copiously with this – or it could be transformed from a transgression into a consequence of natural constraint – famine, siege, over-population, etc. In his essay, Montaigne raises both possibilities in succession, but makes no clear-cut transition from the one to the other.

After the cannibalism of the Brazilian Tupinambas, who eat their enemies not as food, 'as some imagine', but 'to represent an extreme, and inexpiable revenge', Montaigne brings in the Gauls besieged by Caesar in Alesia, who 'resolved to sustain the famine of the siege, with the bodies of old men, women, and other persons unserviceable and unfit to fight.'[12] Montaigne's allusion to this famous episode in the conquest of Gaul does nothing to explain what in Brazil is an everyday practice, in time of either peace or war, whose ends are purely symbolic. On the contrary, it makes it more obscure by adducing what is a very precise counter-example. In the Gaulish *oppidum*, starving people fed on the bodies of the most vulnerable and useless: women, children, old men unable to fight. In Brazil, the appetite for vengeance feeds on the vigour of strong young men endowed with all the warrior virtues. In entrenched Alesia, anthropophagy was endogenous to the group: the besieged were forced to devour their own kin; in Brazil it is clearly exogenous, since they eat only enemies taken in war.

The fact is that Montaigne, showing none of the rigour suspected here by some of his commentators, is defending his Cannibals by using, turn and turn about, arguments borrowed from two distinct and well-nigh incompatible theories. Using the tactics of extenuation, he first profits from the advantages offered by the first thesis (honour-based warrior custom); then, without warning and unperturbed by the slight disjointedness which results, he turns, in his quest for rhetorical effect, to the second tradition (starvation or medical procedure). In the same way, he refers to the medicinal uses of mummies, a fashionable element in the sixteenth-century pharmacopoeia, and quotes Chrysippus and Zeno, 'arch-philosophers of the Stoic sect' to the effect that 'it was no hurt at all, in time of need, and to what end soever, to make use of our carrion bodies'.

If Montaigne is being deliberately playful in this essay, and manipulating the reader's mind with consummate skill, it is surely by means of this subtle shift from one example to the other: from Brazil to Alesia via Chrysippus and the mummy. By means of this imperceptible slide from one argument to its opposite – both of which form opportune elements in a demonstration which is continually pushing things to the limit – 'Of Cannibals' becomes an essay in the most literal sense of the word, an experiment, both playful and rigorous, in the exercise of a shocking degree of freedom. This links it with the genre of 'declamation', an exercise in oratorical elaboration on a given theme which rhetoricians recommended as part of the training of an orator. The acrobatics are all the more perilous in that they play on the most tenacious and essential taboos of Christianity: nakedness, polygamy, cannibalism. The essay ends with a sudden somersault, the mordant remark about the 'breeches' which the Cannibals do not wear; but it also includes personal recriminations against nagging wives, and a skilfully blended dose of medical, sociological and moral reasoning which never follows the line of least logical resistance.[13]

All in all, Montaigne clearly prefers the first of his two cannibal hypotheses, and he seems to have mentioned the second only as a reminder, so as finally to carry his hearers' conviction by storm. It is, then, 'to represent an extreme, and inexpiable revenge' that the Tupinambas so eagerly devour their enemies, and not to feed on them like the besieged people of Numancia or those most barbaric of barbarians, the Scythians of Herodotus.[14] Their 'noble and generous warfare', as subsequently described, confirms this unequivocal preference. It would be hard to understand this evocation of a war which is concerned neither with territorial borders nor with the enslavement of bodies otherwise than as a typical example of honour cannibalism. The issue of these ferocious battles is purely moral. It has nothing to do with the seizure of any kind of material goods – fertile lands which the Indians have no need to plough, riches of which they have none, leisured bodies unsuited to any exercise other than hunting, love-making and war. The Cannibals take no slaves, and if they sometimes transgress their natural bounds – the 'mountains' which they cross in order to assail their neighbours – it is only to return victorious 'into their own country, where they [do not] want any necessary thing'. Their prisoners will live as free men, hunting and fishing in company with their vanquishers, living with a woman of the tribe, and the advantages of finally roasting them will be symbolic rather

than material. This disinterested warfare takes the form of a prome-
nade interrupted by swift and bloody skirmishes. It is the opposite of
the 'slow and pitiless sieges' later evoked by d'Aubigné,[15] such as that
of Alesia or, in the sixteenth century itself, that of Sancerre, which
included an anthropophagous episode of quite exceptional horror.
The self-giving of the Cannibal contrasts with the implacable use, or
usury, of the besieged, starved and tortured bodies of old Europe.

The continent of Cannibals

If we consider the defined space within which cannibal practices are
engaged, we notice that even there, Alesia and Brazil represent antithetical terms. A closed, insular space – the besieged town – contrasts
with 'that other world', 'an endless country' where there ought to be
no problems of subsistence. The island and the continent constitute a
two-sided paradigm in which cannibalism must be imagined in two
diametrically opposed ways: on the one hand, the enclosed space containing an incestuous and devouring hunger, active within the tight
circle of the city walls; on the other, an open country, with no discov-
erable boundaries, which sets cannibalism against a background of
primitive abundance and natural fertility (Montaigne emphasizes this)
and reveals it as a luxury, a superfluous practice.

This question of whether cannibalism was or was not a natural
necessity was to be one of the fundamental justifications for Western
condemnation of so-called 'primitive' societies. It was only when
cannibalism had been well and truly 'de-symbolized' and reduced to
its outward appearance of bestiality that the anthropophagous peoples could justifiably be exterminated, reduced to the same level as the
human quarry which they themselves hunted in order to survive. But
as long as cannibalism remained on the side of 'luxury' and 'glory' it
could be understood as a value, and, perhaps, 'assimilated' by the
Europeans.

The framework of cannibalism is crucial in this respect. Depending
on the size of the space in which it acts, its meaning can change
entirely. Restricted to the island, it is explained by the natural constraints of topography, and scarcely ever rises above the level of material, carnal appetite. Amplified to a whole continent abounding in
every kind of plant and animal, its value inevitably moves on to the
symbolic plane.

Montaigne, in fact, goes for the most extreme, and therefore most
favourable, hypothesis. America is the largest and richest of the four
continents.[16] It is an 'endless country' which stretches from pole to

pole. Therefore, the siege explanation can no longer be invoked. The stage is too vast for the re-enactment of a scene such as those seen in Alesia, Numancia or Sancerre. The cannibalism of the Cannibals is a gratuitous act whose ostentatious refinement serves mainly to show up the stoical 'generosity' of the warrior prisoners, their sovereign detachment from the things of this world and their calm indifference to death.

Léry, who had seen both in his lifetime, had been acutely conscious of the full distance between the European model, based on penury and promiscuity, and the American paradigm, which (he thought) was a matter of noble sentiments and broad horizons. While Brazilian cuisine seemed to him highly excusable, the exceptional case of anthropophagy in Sancerre in 1573 made him fear lest divine vengeance should fall upon the community and, he thought, justified an exceptional punishment, burning at the stake. It was at the exact antipodes of the starveling and incidental anthropophagy of European towns during the Wars of Religion that he found, on American territory, the cannibalistic generosity of a duel in the open field, which did not repel him in the least.

Conversely, as soon as it was discovered that America – South America at least – was an island, however huge, with limited food resources and practically devoid of herd animals,[17] the hypothesis that cannibalism was concerned with food was to triumph. After that the Cannibals could no longer be exalted for the glory of their arms and their warlike virtues. They became unhappy slaves of necessity, the incarnation of degenerate Nature. That was the first step upon the road which led eventually to the declarations of nineteenth-century racists, who saw the remaining anthropophagi of the Pacific islands as the last remnants of a subhuman race, doomed to nothing less than extinction by both their hostile environment and their aberrant 'superstitions'. The novelist and geographer Jules Verne blithely pronounced just such a verdict through the mouth of the absent-minded Paganel in *Les Enfants du Capitaine Grant* (*The Children of Captain Grant*).[18]

It should, by now, be clear that such a hypothesis would have been inconceivable in the Christian Europe of the Renaissance. Except to a narrow circle of medical men, some of whom might have extended their Hippocratic determinism so far, it would have been inconceivable that cannibalism might be a natural need, any more than the term could have applied to incest or homicide; all of them were human perversions inspired by Satan. Evil could not come from Nature, which was the creation of God.

Under these conditions Montaigne's hypothesis does not seem at all difficult, and his apology for the virtuous Cannibal presents no danger whatever. It is value-related, solidly mounted on the plinth of a paradisical continent, and implicitly excludes any strict causal link between Nature and an act which belongs to the widest definition of culture. Thus, Montaigne is finally able to save both the New World, in all its native goodness, and the Cannibal, whose appetites are moralized and endowed with a fully human meaning.

Montaigne considers that the 'Nature of the New Indies'[19] is fundamentally good, and it is not the fault of that Nature if her children devour one another. A corollary of this is that the natural generosity of the 'endless' continent is echoed in the 'generosity' of an approach to warfare which involves no self-interested calculation. It is a notable contrast to the 'avarice' of the first conquistadors. The Portuguese who made alliances with their former adversaries taught them another way to kill people, infinitely more cruel than simply eating them: 'which was, to bury them up to the middle, and against the upper part of the body to shoot arrows, and then being almost dead, to hang them up'.[20] These inventive torturers are the forerunners of the more numerous and destructive hordes stigmatized in Montaigne's 'Of Coaches'. He believes that indigenous warfare knew nothing of such refined cruelties. The natives were also immune to the logic of profit and plunder, and therefore perfectly 'virtuous'. Like the environment in which they lived, the naked warriors of Brazil gave without counting the cost. Their idea of fighting was based on fair single combat, which could easily turn into a sporting contest – of 'valour' and magnanimity as much as physical strength. Thus the self-giving of the warrior, which extended even to his muscles and veins when he became his enemy's prisoner, seems as whole-hearted and willing as Nature's yielding of her fruits.

Cannibalism of words

How, from this viewpoint, was one to understand the Cannibals' appetite for the flesh of their fellow men? By adducing the Scythian parallel at an early stage, Montaigne denies that it was prompted by a need for food. The flesh of the prisoner who is to be devoured is in no way a food, but a sign. It is this sign that the vanquishers absorb into themselves. Eating the body of another person does not provide nourishment or strength, or put on flesh; in the last analysis it is a purely verbal transmission: 'They require no other ransom of their prisoners, but an acknowledgement and confession that they are vanquished.'[21]

It is very significant that the bodily duel, carried to the point of murder and 'shedding of blood', soon gives way to a purely verbal contest between victor and vanquished. The threats of death, the description of the butchery to which they will soon be subjected, 'with mangling and slicing of their members, and with the feast that shall be kept at their charge', are countered by defiance, insults and accusations of cowardice. Whereas Thevet, and even Léry, devoted whole chapters of patient and minute exposition to the preparations for the banquet, the murder of the prisoner and the distribution of the smallest 'scraps' of his flesh (and thereby prepared a feast for modern ethnographers), Montaigne marks a deliberate pause. Instead of giving a circumstantial narrative, he writes a few restrained lines: 'which done, they roast, and then eat him in common, and send some slices of him to such of their friends as are absent'.[22]

In this way he avoids the most uncomfortable aspect: the human flesh, which is both repugnant and good to eat and which might stand in the way of a clear understanding of cannibal words. They are the heart of the matter for Montaigne, and to reach it, and regain the limpid rationality of discourse, the butchered and roasted flesh must be passed over as quickly as possible. The corpse is, it seems, nothing but a lure or distraction: it stands for something else. Get round the body and the road to freedom is open – in words. These words will be proud and warlike: the cannibal act represents an extreme revenge. Without dwelling on what happens after the murder, Montaigne returns to the honourable act of defiance, the exchange of insults, the war-song composed by the prisoner before he dies. The reader almost forgets that the Cannibal's mouth has teeth.

Montaigne's Cannibals are really rather odd specimens: their behaviour is exceedingly curious. They speak more than they eat, and give out more than they take in.

Moreover, according to Montaigne, who knew his contemporary travellers' tales and their illustrations, the victims were pictured 'spitting in their executioners' faces, and making mows at them'.[23] And, indeed, engravings illustrating contemporary accounts by Thevet, Staden and Léry show the prisoner bound with a rope around his waist: as the feathered and painted club is about to descend on his head, he defies his assembled executioners (who keep at a safe distance) by both hand and mouth.[24] This is a truly singular Cannibal, who grimaces, shouts and spits at the very moment of death!

The reason is not far to seek: the Cannibals are not really spitting at their traditional adversaries, the ferocious Margajats of Rio de Janeiro Bay, but at Montaigne's contemporaries, the cruel and greedy Europeans who had been systematically plundering the recently

(a)

(b)

(c)

Figure 8 The cannibal prisoner defies his captors, as portrayed by (a) Hans Staden, who was himself held prisoner by the Tupinikin Indians and feared for his life. The captive, bound with a rope round his waist, shrinks under the club which is about to descend on him. But, in the later engravings by Thevet (b) and Léry (c), the gesture of fear has turned into an attitude of defiance. The prisoner, on the brink of death, faces up to his executioner, threatening him by pointing skywards with his finger. He predicts that vengeance will soon fall upon his tormentor, and spits in his face. In 'Of Cannibals' (1580), Montaigne praises this 'triumphal loss'.
(a) Hans Staden, *Warhaftige Historia und Beschreibung eyner Landtschafft der Wilden, Nacketen, Grimmigen Menschfresser, Leuthen in der Newenwelt America gelegen* (Marburg: A. Kolbe, 1557). Woodcut. London: British Library.
(b) 'The slaying of the prisoner in a public place'. André Thevet, 1575. Woodcut.
(c) Jean de Léry, *Histoire d'un voyage faict en la terre du Bresil*, 2nd edition (1580). Woodcut.

discovered New World for the last three-quarters of a century. This was to become clear a little later, in 1588, when the third edition of the *Essays* was published. At that time Montaigne, adding a third book to the first two, completed his description of America by including a tableau of the brilliant civilizations of Mexico and Peru, brutally struck down by the blind cupidity of the conquistadors. The New World depicted in 'Of Coaches' springs visibly from the Brazil portrayed in 'Of Cannibals'. 'Mechanical victories' – commonplace, vulgar victories – is the scornful description given by Montaigne to those easy triumphs over naked peoples who knew nothing of iron or gunpowder. And all this – provinces laid waste, empires in ruins, peoples enslaved and millions dead – was merely for the sake of 'the traffic in Pearls and Pepper'.[25]

But if we look a little closer, the same accusation is already implicit in 'Of Cannibals'. The 'Brazilian dialogue' which ends this earlier essay is a direct echo of the *Discours de la servitude volontaire* by Montaigne's friend Etienne de La Boétie. In fact, Montaigne does not speak in his own voice. True to the principles of *declamatio*, he delegates his speeches to others who can express themselves with perfect freedom. Just as, in Erasmus' paradoxical encomium, it is Folly who speaks (*Stultitia loquitur*), so in 'Of Cannibals' the Cannibals themselves have the last word. It scarcely matters that they are really mouthpieces for Montaigne or for his brother-in-law. It is enough that they speak loud and clear, without restraint or censorship, and that the reader cannot help but listen.

The three Brazilians who arrived in Rouen, where Montaigne met them in the autumn of 1562, face their European interlocutors with a few home truths. Instead of admiring 'the form of a fair City', as they are invited to do, they are astonished to find that an adolescent king with a poor complexion and unhealthy appearance – this being the twelve-year-old Charles IX – can issue orders to his Swiss guards.[26] How can a wave of a hand from such a feeble creature compel the homage of so many strong men, who would be far better suited to command than he is? The surprise felt by the ambassadors of the New World before these 'tall men with long beards, strong and well armed', who 'submit themselves to obey a beardless child', recalls the oratorical indignation of La Boétie's *Contr'Un*: what an 'unhappy vice' it is to see 'an infinite number of persons' submitting to the tyranny 'not of a Hercules or Samson, but of one poor specimen of a man, often the most cowardly and effeminate in the whole nation!'[27]

In the land of the Cannibals, the King shows his superiority mainly by being the first into battle – which shows the infinite wisdom of that people. Save in such extreme circumstances, when he must risk his life to save the community, the King loses all kind of prerogative. The implied conclusion is that Europeans, who fear death and choose the weakest of their number to lead them – 'who', La Boétie adds, 'is quite unable to serve the least of women in the vilest capacity' – have the minds of slaves. Worse still, they propose to extend this slave regime to others than themselves. Most certainly, the free men of the New World have no respect for those who have chosen to sell themselves unconditionally to a tyrant.

They are equally scandalized by the inequality they see in the streets. They are so struck by it that they fear (or wish – it is not clear which) that the beggars and the poor, 'hunger-starven, and bare with need and poverty', who grovel at the rich men's gates may 'take the others by the throat, or set fire on their houses'.[28] The 'triumphal loss'[29] of the Cannibal dying in the midst of his enemies, but dominating them with high courage and scorn, and the incendiary prophecy made by one of his brethren to the curious and fascinated Europeans in the midst of one of their finest cities, are expressed in the same kind of vengeful and devastating words which are the victim's rejoinder to his actual, or merely potential, executioner. The great vanquisher of history may well turn out, in the end, to be the vanquished. Such is the European, whose civil society, racked by antagonism between rich and poor, is in danger of collapse.

The chapter 'Of Coaches', in Book III of the *Essays*, pursues this inversion to the limits. The pretext is a description of the *requerimiento*, a strange and scandalous ritual whereby the Spaniards solemnly enjoin the Indians to submit to the 'King of Castile, the greatest King of the habitable earth', and to the Pope, who had given him the principality of all the Indies.[30] When this necessary summons had been served, the conquerors were legally entitled to massacre or enslave the hostile, or merely unbelieving, populace. This 'accustomed remonstrance', formally communicated to the Indians in the presence of a notary, is described at length by Montaigne, who brings out all its absurdity. It is the central panel of the sequence of American tableaux which constitute the last third of the chapter. The word passes from the conquistadors, who present it with arrogance, to their interlocutors, and is immediately captured by these naked and defenceless 'children', who teach them a lesson of exceptionally forceful eloquence: 'happily they might be quiet and well-meaning, but their countenance showed them to be otherwise: as concerning their King, since he seemed to beg, he showed to be poor and needy ...'

The supposed barbarian is delivering judgement on the European. The same 'sociological revolution' (to borrow a phrase from Roger Caillois[31]) is at work in both essays. In 'Of Coaches', the *requerimiento* is the fulcrum around which eyes and voice both pivot. Montaigne, borrowing the description of this caricature of a legal ritual word for word from the 'General History of the West Indies' by the Spaniard Francisco López de Gomara, takes a passage which was originally intended as an apology for the tormentors and turns it on its head, so that it speaks, instead, for the victims. 'These narrations we have out of their own books: for they do not only avouch, but vauntingly publish them.'[32]

Montaigne is a cunning reader. He draws from the unknowing and shameless Gomara the means of restoring to the Indians their power of speech.

In 'Of Cannibals' cannibalism is seen in essentially linguistic terms, as we have seen. The exchange between eaters and eaten boils down to a to and fro of words: gift and counter-gift, question and answer. 'These muscles, this flesh and these veins' which you are about to eat, says the Cannibal, spitting at his ephemeral vanquishers, 'are your own' – for they themselves will soon be caught in the wheel of sacrifice and become victims of the very violence which they have themselves unleashed.[33]

These are no empty threats, whether they are addressed to Indian enemies, to the Court visiting Rouen or to the vengeful Spaniard. They hint at a possible reversal of the situation. Hence the impact of paradox in 'Of Cannibals'. In 'Of Coaches' the potential reversal is signified by the sight of 'the heads of certain men sticking upon stakes about their City'[34] which the high-hearted inhabitants exhibit to the Spaniards to moderate their pride. It must be admitted that, in this case, the real conclusion is postponed to the end of, indeed to outside, history. Immediately after the ritual submission, a deluge of calamities falls upon the unhappy New World, which is aged before its time by the brutal bloodthirstiness of the conquistadors. The sobriety of the narrative – four long pages almost free from comment – strengthens the cumulative effect of the catastrophe. The excess of horrors, described with remorseless objectivity, produces the impression of a world out of joint, and this is driven home by a key image on the last page of the essay: the Inca falling from his chair of state in Cajamarca on 16 November 1532, on the fateful evening of his meeting with Pizarro. This patently unjust imbalance ought to presage a moral reversal, the triumph of victim over executioner. But the reversal of fortune remains eternally potential, compromised by the sheer scale of the massacre:

> Look how as many of his porters as were slain, to make him fall (for all their endeavour was to take him alive) so many others, in order and as it were avi[dly], took and underwent presently the place of the dead: so that he could never be brought down or made to fall, what slaughter so ever was made of those kind of people, until such time as a horseman furiously ran to take him by some part of his body, and so pulled him to the ground.[35]

Clearly the parallel agonies of Atahualpa, the Inca who was put to death immediately after receiving baptism, and Cuauhtemoc, the Aztec emperor who succeeded Montezuma and who was 'half-roasted' in the hope of obtaining 'some odd piece or vessel of gold',[36] frequently echo the agony of the cannibal prisoner who 'triumphs' at the moment of death. Their ends are eloquent, worthy of the great-hearted princes which they had proved themselves to be. They speak through their deaths, denouncing the iniquity of the manner of their dying and prophesying vengeance, blood for blood. When the treasures thus extorted are swallowed in the sea, and the tormentors 'consumed by intestine wars and civil broils, wherewith themselves have devoured one another',[37] the wheel of violence rolls once more from victim to executioner. Again, oral voracity serves to turn violence back on itself, using the reversible image of the eater–eaten. The earlier 'Of Cannibals' had condemned the roasting of living flesh, as practised by officers of the law on the bodies of their victims and by the Portuguese of Brazil on their defeated adversaries. The conquistadors who burned Atahualpa and abominably roasted Cuauhtemoc are eaten in their turn, engulfed by the waves or devoured by their comrades, falling victim to the enforced allelophagy which they themselves decreed.

No longer, however, can vengeance be taken man-to-man, in a sort of single combat between victim and executioner. It demands recourse to a transcendent third term. For the first time in Montaigne's American diptych he mentions God, who 'hath meritoriously permitted, that many of their great pillages, and ill-gotten goods, have either been swallowed up by the revenging Seas in transporting them or consumed by the intestine wars ...' It must be acknowledged, however, that this is a feeble and unconvincing riposte to the destruction of the Indies.

The pugnacious avidity of the West, its hunger for wealth and gold: all the impact of the conquest is expressed in terms of a generalized cannibalism – a mercantile cannibalism from which every tone of magnanimity has now been expunged. For the cannibalism in 'Of Coaches' is not merely a continuation of the cannibalism in 'Of Cannibals': it is a perversion of it. As plunder becomes the rule and the tyranny of the strongest replaces the generous rivalry of self-giving, all hope of revenge begins to fade. Between the *Essays* of 1580 and those of 1588, between Brazil and Mexico, the lesson of history has taken a decidedly pessimistic tone.

Cannibal brethren

In the triumphal agony of the Brazilian Cannibal, the terms of the exchange had a certain mutuality: same blood, same muscles, same use of signs by both eater and eaten. As long as it maintains the virtue (in the broadest sense of the word) of the voracious combatants, cannibalism preserves a sort of linguistic circulation which renews the bonds uniting the great human family, from man to man and from mouth to mouth: 'Those that are much about one age, do generally enter-call one another brethren, and such as are younger, they call children, and the aged are esteemed as fathers to all the rest.'[38]

This portrayal of a fraternal society follows a patriarchal model which is familiar in the context of regressive utopia. It is also a traditional element in the praise of friendship – that friendship which is celebrated by Montaigne in one of the most heartfelt of the *Essays*[39] and which is also central to La Boétie's political utopia. Indeed, according to the propositions in *Contr'Un*, friendship is the sister of liberty and is as natural, as essential to mankind as is the latter. It is friendship that holds together the republic which emerges after the ruin of the One, the cowardly and loathed tyrant. Among the Cannibals, too, friendship is the basis of an elective kinship. In their society, as in the Sparta of Lycurgus – the real, existing utopia, which inspired the dreams of Socrates, Plato and Plutarch – the emulation of virtue binds the whole group together as firmly as a blood relationship. But the Cannibals surpass their remote and ancient predecessors in that they have attained the unanimity which Nature intended, wishing 'not so much to unite us as to make us one'.[40] The unity of the Cannibal republic is confirmed by anthropophagy, a continual recycling of flesh and speech. Paradoxically, conflict promotes concord, and cannibalism functions as an active symbol. It strengthens the sinews of the body social through the worship of dead warriors and the universal admiration for 'invincible greatness of heart'.

By conferring heroic virtues on the South American Indians, Montaigne, like his many predecessors, is signalling that he sees them as the direct heirs of the heroes of antiquity. It is therefore no surprise to find extended parallels between the peoples of the New World and the illustrious Greek and Roman captains lauded by Plutarch. Even in Thevet, Brazil already features as a latter-day Sparta. Thus the 'demi-giant' Quoniambec, 'garlanded with the most exquisite rarities', is heir to the manly virtues of Leonidas.[41] Even their very insults have a certain nobility and show the same greatheartedness as we find in the heroes of Homer.

To conclude: in Montaigne, the whole subject of Brazilian cannibalism is shifted on to the level of discourse. The prisoner's flesh resolves itself into words: defiance, insult or song of death and revenge. This yields not only the true meaning, but also the true purpose of the cannibal exchange.[42] The Brazilian Cannibal is raised to the status of an orator and philosopher, a free and fraternal citizen of a back-to-nature utopia: as such, he no longer provokes horror. By gracing him with an abundance of words, Montaigne completes the rehabilitation begun by Léry. He has successfully cleansed anthropophagy from the stigma of the flesh.

PART III
Cannibals by Constraint

9

Cardano, or the Rule of Necessity

ᜦ

Hatred as necessity

In the last chapter we saw how Montaigne took one model and pushed it to the limit: cannibalism based on vengeance and the most punctilious code of honour, taken over lock, stock and barrel from Léry, Thevet and others. This model, which stresses the sign in preference to its gory enactment, turns up at the same period in the most varied corners of literary expression: besides the folktales, chapbooks, novels and 'tragical histories' which we have already discussed, there was also drama, for Seneca's *Thyestes* and its avatars enjoyed considerable success.[1] From Giraldi Cinzio's *Orbecche-Oronte* to the plays of Antoine Favre and Monléon, baroque tragedy takes considerable delight in this myth, in which vengeance follows the path of incestuous anthropophagy.[2] Let us not be misled by appearances here. When, in his tragedy of the 'Gordians and Maximins' (1589), Antoine Favre shows the father, Maximin, hungry for vengeance on his supposedly treacherous son – 'May my mouth engulf in raging morsels / The flesh of his face, and swallow the pupil / Of his savaged eyes ...'[3] – or when Pierre Mainfray, in a Senecan play, couples eating and vengeance in the mouth of his bloodthirsty tyrant – 'I swear / That ere long, in pursuance of my revenge, / I will privily serve you your own son'[4] – the metaphor is probably meant to be taken in the full and literal sense. But this enactment of a figurative 'appetite for vengeance' never, even in the ultimate horror of perpetration, effaces the underlying symbolism. The hunger is never reduced to animal appetite, and the spectacular impact of the macabre feasts, which are so uninhibitedly played before the audience, is really intended to demonstrate the superabundance of meaning which they carry. These baroque paroxysms of (literally) devouring hatred or jealousy have no other function than to give redundant expression to an excess of passion, and to denounce the evils of tyranny in which the unbridled appetite of one man defies all divine and human law.

However, the fact that this model explanation for cannibalism –

wolfish rage subordinated to vengefulness – was the dominant one at the time (and Montaigne was, in fact, espousing a substantial majority viewpoint) does not mean that the opposite view was not also in evidence. The second model, which subordinates the sign to the object and reduces the ritual to an expression of bestial hunger, was spelt out in 1557 by the physician and mathematician Girolamo Cardano. The reduction of cannibalism to necessity appears in a chapter of his *De rerum varietate* ('On the variety of things') which is entitled, not without irony, 'Gentium ritus' ('The rites of peoples') – for the 'rite' is nothing but the deceptive solemnity which is sometimes employed in order to satisfy an unspeakable hunger.[5]

In fact, Cardano uses more devious means to de-symbolize cannibalism. He begins with the commonplace suggestion that *odium*, hatred of one's enemies, is the most obvious explanation of American anthropophagy. Travellers' tales are unanimous about this: the Cannibals themselves readily explain the ferocious resentment they feel towards their fellow men. Such hatred explains, if it does not jus-

Figure 9 The cannibal unclad. Antoine Jacquard, *Les Divers Pourtraicts et figures faictes sus les meurs des habitans du Nouveau Monde* (Poitiers, *c.*1615–20). Paris: Bibliothèque Nationale.

tify, the worst excesses of alimentary violence. And the Caribs, not content merely to devour enemies taken in war, do not shrink from eating children whom they have begotten upon their slaves. They are infamous enough to rip their own offspring from the womb and devour it, and then eat the mother as well. 'This', adds Cardano, 'is a thing which horrifies us even in brute beasts.'[6] Nonetheless, the learned academic from Bologna is not exactly struck dumb with horror at the crime, for he returns to it twice in the course of this description.[7]

The difference from the Montaigne tradition is immediately obvious. Here, cannibalism assumes the solemnity of a theatre of sadism for which there are no taboos. Anthropophagy accompanies infanticide, and amorous dalliance lapses into an orgy of blood. The bonds of kinship, as well as those of blood, are scandalously transgressed for the sake of a stupid and bestial appetite, which alternates between sex and hunger: the victorious warrior fornicates with his female captives before devouring them along with their adulterous offspring. It is

clear that Cardano cares little for ethnographical accuracy. He proclaims at the outset that he intends to treat the West Indies as a single whole, and blithely proceeds to confuse the sacrificial rites of the Aztecs, who tore the hearts from living victims and flung them, raw and quivering, upon the altar, with the vengeance cannibalism of the Tupinambas, as described by Thevet, Léry and Montaigne. Societies, territories and practices which should be entirely separate are stirred into the same spicy and subtly titillating mix. Cardano, far from moralizing on these alleged customs, throws them on a disorderly heap which offers no foothold for symbolism. Searching through this pile of sacrificial corpses and victims, all willingly fattened up like porkers for the feast (*ut sues aluntur ad saginam*), to be mutilated, butchered and eaten, it is impossible to recognize what truly relates to Carib vengeance and what to Mexican religious practices – which, as everyone knows, were exceptionally complex and cruel.

Montaigne, on the other hand, took great care to specify which rites belonged to which peoples, who might be living hundreds of leagues apart. His 'Of Cannibals' deals only with Villegagnon's Brazil, though it is synecdochically extended to cover the whole continent. This is the phenomenon dubbed 'tupinambization' by the anthropologist William Sturtevant: the process, widespread in sixteenth-century geographical literature, of extending the ethnic and cultural traits of the Tupinamba Indians to all the peoples of the New World.[8] Montaigne's tupinambization is, however, discreet, involving only the youthfulness and the innocent state of nudity which characterize America in general.

Despite this simplifying idealization, Montaigne distributes praise and blame on geographical principles, with the result that the blame is strictly circumscribed. He also selects his ethnographical material with some care. In 'Of Coaches' he comes to the defence of peoples – particularly the Aztecs and the Incas – who have been oppressed and destroyed by the conquistadors. The requirements of this speech for the defence induce Montaigne to remove all references to the religion – bloodthirsty and cruel, refined and demonstrative – of the Aztecs. This matter is relegated to another chapter heading at the end of the essay 'Of Moderation' (I, 30): it gives rather an ironic twist to that title.[9] It may be that Aztecs, Caribs and Tupi-Guarani rest on a common foundation of 'the new countries discovered in our days yet uncorrupted, and virgins, in regard of ours'.[10] But the bulimic religion discovered in Mexico by Hernán Cortés, which yearly sacrificed fifty thousand men to the gods, seems to be thematically opposed to the agonistic and logomachic cannibalism of the Brazilians. The nobility of character evinced by the latter retains some link with 'natural laws'. Their banquets may not obey the necessity of Nature, but they do reflect her generous profusion. The Mexicans, more civilized and therefore more corrupt, are on the side of art, which is perverse. Their religion requires the feeding of innocent blood to imaginary divinities amidst rituals that are refined to the point of madness. Montaigne's strategy now becomes clear: it amounts to separating things which had become linked, or even confused, in the minds of his contemporaries.

Cardano, however, makes no distinction between the Aztecs' sacrificial volcano – the pyramid streaming with sunlight and blood[11] – and the chivalrous combats of the Indians on the Brazilian mainland, free men who fought and devoured one another in the open, against a backdrop of gardens and forests. Moreover, as we shall see, his concept of American Nature is the complete opposite of that *locus amœnus* which Montaigne, not without nostalgia, depicts for us.

Cardano, indifferent to the specific characteristics of the various rituals, is no more attentive to their internal organization than to their purpose. When, in the course of an Aztec sacrifice, the hearts of the victims were plucked from their bodies, it was not with the intention of eating them: they were first struck against the altar stone so as to project the blood towards the sun, which was magically regenerated thereby.[12] The association of cannibalism with the rite was secondary: the corpse of the sacrificed victim, which had slumped to the foot of the pyramid, was retrieved, skinned and butchered for use in solemn feasts – or, in the case of slaves, as a lucrative sideline. Aztec anthropophagy was essentially domestic and must be considered as a corollary of the sacrifice, not its main purpose.

Modern anthropologists might not agree with Montaigne here. The distance between the ritual cannibalism of the Tupinambas, the happy cannibals of essay I, 31, and the human sacrifice of the Aztecs is not, in fact, very great. Both evince the same elaborate attention to appearances and the same ritual solemnity. There are also some surprising convergences: the singular consideration accorded to the potential victim; the mystical relationship between captive and captor; the gift of a wife to the prisoner and the erotic prelude to the sacrifice; the obsessive, indeed mind-dulling, dancing just before the murder, which puts the victim in a paradoxical state of mingled excitement and stupor; the simulated duel at the moment of death, which can sometimes turn into an actual combat; the ostentatious conviviality of the cannibal feast; finally, and most important, the analogous idea that the sacrifice could restore energy and initiate a collective, social and cosmic regeneration.[13] However that may be, Montaigne's errors of interpretation – or rather, his prejudices – are of little importance.

It is abundantly clear that he uses them consciously to confer some meaning on the apparent barbarity. Moreover, he is famous for his fidelity to his dead friend Etienne de La Boétie, of whom he is the conscientious heir, on both the personal, memorialistic side and the political and doctrinal one. This very naturally inclines him to redirect the lesson of *Contr'Un* with America in mind. That is why he prefers the republic of the Cannibals to the tyranny which he sees in the theocratic state of the Aztecs – that new and utterly repellent avatar of 'voluntary servitude'. The essential difference between one and the other is the 'virtue' of a freely accepted sacrifice. Hence the secret and inverted kinship between the economics of Aztec sacrifice and the unbearable yoke of the conquistadors: both Mexicans and Spaniards demand absolute obedience to their respective emperors, and they prefer enslavement to human brotherhood, fear to friendship. They are more like cruel gods than true men, feeding literally or figuratively on flesh and blood. That is the force of the anecdote which concludes 'Of Moderation', in which Cortés, after one of his victories, receives the Indian ambassadors:

> The messengers presented him with three kinds of presents, in this manner: 'Lord, if thou be a fierce God, that lovest to feed on flesh and blood, here we give slaves, eat them, and we will bring thee more: if thou be a gently-mild God, here is incense and feathers; but if thou be a man, take these birds and fruits, that here we present and offer unto thee.'[14]

Montaigne is alive to the beauty of gesture: the triumphant exhibition of moral munificence is also aesthetically pleasing. Not so Cardano, who makes no attempt to understand the aims of the rite, only its material consequences. By reducing religion to alimentation, he embarks on a deconstruction of the symbol. The results will become apparent as we proceed.

As for fathers who devour their children, and their mistresses immediately after childbirth, and who are described with such prolixity by Cardano, they are in fact an inversion of a feature well established by sixteenth-century travellers, an inversion already to be found in Peter Martyr of Anghiera and the *Mundus Novus* as rewritten under the influence of Vespucci. It had been seen, especially among the Tupinambas of Brazil, that warriors taken in battle were given a wife who served them throughout their captivity, which could last not just for 'two or three months', as Montaigne suggests, but for several years. They might have children by her, and these children would also be killed and eaten, either at birth or when they had become 'a little bigger'.[15] French and Portuguese travellers unanimously attest to the existence of this custom, which conforms to the overall symbolism of the Cannibals. The reason for these serial murders given by Thevet and Léry (Montaigne sins by omission here) explicitly contradicts Cardano's version: the Indians believed that the power of procreation resided in the father alone.[16] Therefore, a Cannibal would be unlikely to devour his own son or daughter, which would amount to eating his own flesh, a monstrous autophagy. But there was nothing to stop the mother from eating the offspring of casual intercourse with a captive, assuming that she felt so inclined: she had done no more than shelter and nourish the seed of her enemy.[17] Moreover, Thevet tells us that female prisoners, if there were any, were never presented with a husband, but spent their captivity in a state of strict celibacy until they were ritually consumed.[18] In this way, no father could eat his own children, and it was very unlikely that he would taste the flesh of his mistress. Such an encounter of paternal mouth and filial flesh would be rather more repugnant to Indian thinking than to Cardano's – for Cardano is evidently savouring the piquancy of such a scene.

It is unlikely that Cardano is making any of this up. When he inverts the true ethnographical pattern, he is following respected sources such as the *De Orbe Novo* of Peter Martyr and the *Mundus Novus* of pseudo-Vespucci. In so doing he appears to be yielding, quite unresistingly, to a typically western and masculine fantasy: an abusive father-lover who devours his slave-wife and the offspring of their fornication. The sexual connotations of this unbalanced transformation of American reality are so obvious that one hesitates to attribute them solely to Cardano's pious respect for his sources. Nor is it very surprising to find Cardano, at the late date of 1557, reverting to the first European representations of the American Cannibal: naked, shaggy, armed with a butcher's chopper and animated with a sexual and alimentary appetite untrammelled by any boundary or taboo. Similarly, François de Belleforest, in his French adaptation of Joannes Boemus's 'Universal History of the World' (1570), stirs incest, infanticide and cannibalism into the spiciest of pot-pourris.[19]

The cardinal fact to be extracted from all this is Cardano's deliberate contempt for ritual, and for American society as a whole. The only thing which is important to him is the relationship between man and his natural environment, and it is from this strictly medical and ecological viewpoint that his analysis appears to be innovatory, even revolutionary. He is at the opposite pole from the *Essays*. He looks not at things, but at causes.[20]

What, then, is at the fountain-head of cannibalism? The answer must be hatred. Montaigne, for his part, stressed the lively force of vengeance and warlike prowess among the Cannibals. Consequently, he cautioned 'lest a man should think that this is done by a simple, and servile, or awful duty unto their custom'.[21] Cardano, on the other hand, maintains that hatred swiftly declined into a mechanical habit (*odium initium dedit consuetudini*) and a silly rule, which, fortunately, is now yielding before the spread of Christianity. From start to finish the liberty of Montaigne's Cannibals, whose virgin minds have as yet received no imprint, no inscription of the arbitrary letters of the law, contrasts with the brutish servility of Cardano's 'Caribs'. The former act from greatness of soul and courage; the latter appear to be enslaved, through stupidity (*stultitia*), to habit and necessity. This brings us to the climax of Cardano's demonstration: '*Ergo hunc ritum induxit odium (ut dixi) et bellum ac necessitas*' ('Therefore, hatred induced this ritual (as I said), together with war and necessity').[22] The first two terms – hatred and war – are in a way annihilated by the power of the third, necessity. It is necessity, not custom, that produces Cannibals. Hatred and war (the former conditions the latter) are, at most, nothing more than auxiliaries, or circumstantial avatars, of an imperious requirement, which (as Cardano goes on to explain) proceeds from Nature herself.

Indeed, this ostensibly discreet and anodyne addition, *ac necessitas*, casts doubt on the first suggested cause – *odium*, hatred – which was generally accepted by contemporary writers. Consequently, there may be reason to fear that Christianity alone will not persuade the Indians to abandon their alimentary habits. While hatred and a blind lust for vengeance are deplorable and may be combated by an acquaintance with the Christian religion, as Thevet maintained,[23] necessity cannot be so easily circumvented. Moreover, if natural necessity does indeed constrain men to devour one another, is it reasonable to argue that this allelophagy goes against Divine Providence? What religious exhortations can properly be addressed to peoples who are reduced by confinement and indigence to such extremities? Cardano's hypothesis, taken to its logical extreme, appears well and truly scandalous. It might come from an 'atheist' who denied that men had free will. Or from a mind which is objective to the point of cynicism; which is quite ready to sacrifice half of humanity on the altar of causal reasoning.

The continent of hunger

Cardano, anticipating these burning and most dangerous questions, is quick to suggest solutions to such a miserable state of affairs. Pre-

Columbian America was woefully short of red meat: 'There was no quadruped there whose flesh was agreeable to the taste: neither pigs nor cattle, nor sheep, goats, deer, horses or donkeys.'[24] It was this extraordinary lack which originally forced the inhabitants of the West Indians to eat one another. So the remedy was simple: America must import, 'along with the Christian religion and fear of the laws', these indispensable flocks and herds which the Cannibals so sorely needed. The faith would be propagated alongside the sheep, pigs, goats and cattle which had already begun to people the vast wastes of the New World. If famine and paganism were suppressed at a stroke, that ought to end the curse of anthropophagy once and for all. The implication, Cardano concludes, was that this barbarous rite had already been to a great extent abolished.

One objection remains to be refuted: America was not wholly bereft of edible fauna. Besides the tasty lizards and serpents much favoured by the Indians, there was a great abundance of poultry in the form of turkeys, and fish thrived. Cardano (who had studied medicine at Bologna) counters that this was poor food – indeed, a Lenten entertainment. Meagre and monotonous, it could not rival the good red meat from the quadrupeds of the Old World. If the Lenten fast were to last not for a few weeks, but all the year round, and every day's fare consisted of turtles and fish, people would undoubtedly lose not just their strength and vigour, but even their muscles and their very flesh. The infamy of cannibalism would then be inevitable.

Thus Cardano's explanation of the origins of anthropophagy postulates a chain of purely material causes. Divine Providence has nothing to do with it; nor do the cunning machinations of the Devil. There is no aspect of the problem which cannot be set down to the immanence of a Nature too poor to nourish an excess of population. South America (for this is the region constantly referred to) is not a boundless continent, but (as certain recent studies have indeed demonstrated with regard to the pre-Columbian period) an island with insufficient resources.[25]

As happens in a besieged town or a shipwreck, the absence of protein eventually produced aberrant social practices. This explanation, which may without anachronism be dubbed 'materialistic', anticipates in several respects the arguments of Diderot and Malthus. For Cardano's approach has further consequences: by describing an apparently unnatural appetite without any recourse to the symbolic register – which is deliberately confused and obscured at the outset – he comes to explain the religion of the first Americans in terms of the imperious need for food. Since necessity is the supreme law, human society is obliged to shift this drastic constraint, imposed by the environment, to the level of discourse and belief. Therefore, the essential function of religion is to persuade the victims and their relatives to bow to their executioners, and to convince the latter that they are acting in full obedience to divine law. Hence the commonly held belief among the Aztecs that the victims, after their violent death on the pyramid of the Sun, would live in eternal bliss among the gods.

Cardano gives a very precise definition of religion – though as yet it is only the 'mad' idolatry of the Americans – as a kind of overdetermination. It exists only in order to distract humanity from the dismal but necessary fact that, from time to time, the human race has to bring destruction upon itself.

10

Brébeuf and Robinson: The Missionary and the Colonist

꙳

Oh more than barbarous cruelty, oh more than cruel barbarity!

Claude d'Abbeville,
Histoire de la mission des Peres Capucins en l'Isle de Maragnon

Now we shall dip our pen in blood and paint a Picture of horror. It will show nothing save inhumanity, barbarity and rage.

Charles de Rochefort,
Histoire naturelle des Iles Antilles de l'Amérique

A taste for missionaries

The hypothesis of vengeance cannibalism, with or without accompanying honours, was the one most acceptable to missionaries of all allegiances, because it cast no doubt on the immeasurable goodness of God. Nor did it require them to despair of human nature, so diverse and yet the same in every clime and under every sky. Therefore, it was the explanation generally adopted by the Friars Minor and the Jesuit Fathers, in tropical Brazil and in the Caribbean islands, among the Iroquois and in Guyana. On this point, as on others, there was a seamless transmission from Jean de Léry to the Capuchin Claude d'Abbeville, a missionary in Maranhâo in 1612–13. D'Abbeville, whose description of the Tupinambas of Saint-Louis draws freely on that of his Huguenot predecessor, adds some comments of his own: 'It is not because they take such delight in eating this human flesh or because their sensual appetite tempts them to such foods. For I remember hearing from one of them, that after eating it they are sometimes constrained to vomit it up, since their stomachs are not well able to digest it ...'[1]

Even more – and even more literally – than Montaigne, d'Abbeville sees the Brazilian Indian as a Cannibal who spits. Vomiting expresses the primarily symbolic value attached to the ingestion of human flesh. D'Abbeville is in no doubt that this food is actually uneatable.

Therefore, a great deal of hatred must be felt before it can actually be swallowed; it takes a very tyrannical custom to overcome the natural repugnance it inspires: 'but they do what they do only in order to avenge the death of their predecessors and assuage the insatiable and more than diabolical rage which they have against their enemies'.[2]

D'Abbeville went further. Not content with telling his flock that this 'detestable and diabolical' practice was 'wholly contrary to the will of that great Toupan who expressly commands us to love our enemies', he conveyed to Japy Ouassou, 'principal of the Maragnans', that 'this custom is wicked and against nature'. It appears that the Tupinamba chieftain was more than half won over; he was already fully conversant with the theological outlook of the new arrivals. But d'Abbeville then puts into his mouth the following rather improbable confession: 'Thus I have several times desired to abolish it.'[3] In other words, he realized that the Capuchins would make very useful allies, having arrived from France at just the right time to help him civilize his decidedly brutish subjects.

Vengeance was not, of course, tolerable in the eyes of the Church of Christ. But that was not an invincible obstacle. Just as Satan would be vanquished on the last day by the celestial hosts, it was already obvious that under the benevolent aegis of their new instructors, the 'cruelty and barbarity of the Maragnans' was changing 'into gentleness and benignity'.[4] Nonetheless, this effort must continue to be supervised, and this newborn zeal patiently nurtured and energetically fostered, for the devil had not yet shot his bolt. Yves d'Evreux, who succeeded d'Abbeville at the Saint-Louis mission, was very much aware of this when he wrote that if the colonists were to leave, 'all the nations which have congregated there pell-mell to make alliances with the French, being enemies heretofore, would eat one another'.[5] This ominous prediction, which is also an express exhortation to pursue the task of colonization, does not in the least imply that such an apocalyptic outcome would be due to a bad disposition, or to the despotic constraints of the environment. If, by mischance, it were to come about, it would be imputable only to 'the tyranny of Satan' over those unfortunate peoples.[6]

Here, contrary to the outlook of Léry, who described old Indian women as witches, the diabolization is intended not to condemn the Other, but to save him. Of course, this charity was self-interested to a degree, since to wrest the Indians from 'the chain of unbelief' was simultaneously to turn them into humble and obedient subjects of King Louis XIII of France.

By pronouncing human flesh uneatable, d'Abbeville reaped a further benefit. He distanced himself and the Catholic mission at

Maranhâo from the 'cannibal obsession' which had weighed so continually on Léry and the little Huguenot community in Guanabara. But the repressed was soon up to its old tricks once again. It was insufficient to say that the savage 'gorges himself to the point of vomiting on the very flesh of his enemies'.[7] The loudly proclaimed repugnance for 'a food which humanity would spurn' (as the Abbé Raynal was to describe it later)[8] cannot keep the missionary's lips from uttering the irrepressible question: What can human flesh possibly taste like?

Jokes on this subject go back a long way. They go back to the beginnings of the missionary endeavour, and usually issued from its detractors.[9] Thus, Urbain Chauveton, a Protestant pastor from Geneva who in 1579 published the *Histoire nouvelle du Nouveau Monde*, a translation from the Italian of Girolamo Benzoni, makes ironical reference to the Spanish monks who had the singular misfortune to be eaten during Lent. With an irony worth of Voltaire's *Candide* he adds that 'Spaniards are not very good to eat, because the flesh is too tough'.[10] To palliate this disadvantage, he even proposes a tried and tested recipe: 'unless it is marinated and softened for two or three days before eating'. For the rest, Chauveton entirely agrees with the missionaries of the other persuasion. Like the propagators of the Catholic faith, he begins by pointing out that the Indians only eat their enemies – in this case 'an infinity of Spaniards' – in order to 'satisfy their vengeance', and not because they like the taste. Thus, the hypothesis most favourable to the Indian is here accompanied by a secret curiosity. What if human flesh were eatable after all?

What is most surprising is that this unanswered question is subsequently uttered by the missionaries themselves. It may be found in the writings of the Dominicans Raymond Breton and Jean-Baptiste du Tertre, who evangelized the Caribs in the seventeenth century. Breton, who was familiar with the area and had written a Carib–French dictionary, reports in his *Relation de l'Isle de Guadeloupe* that 'for some time' the natives had 'abstained from eating the flesh of Christians'. Not – as it might be thought – that this was a token of the progress of Christian doctrine among them. The beginning of wisdom came about by pure accident. After an attack on Dominica and the capture of 'a quantity of negroes' and 'five of our Fathers', whom they 'put on the *boucan* to eat them', the consumption of this unaccustomed flesh 'made them feel so sick, that they never dared touch it again'.[11]

Inspired by handwritten information from his co-religionist, with an intermingling of remarks from Montaigne and Léry, Jean-Baptiste

Figure 10 Top: 'Torture of Slaves in North America'. Bottom: 'Torture of Slaves in South America'. Joseph-François Lafitau, *Mœurs des Sauvages Ameriquains comparées aux mœurs des premiers temps* (1724). Copper-plate. Yale University: Beinecke Library.

du Tertre made an observation on the same lines: that the Caribs 'eat this meat because of rage and not because of appetite, to avenge themselves and not to feed themselves, nor for the pleasure they find in its taste'. For, he adds, 'most of them become ill after this execrable repast'.[12] Later, an anecdote confirms the harmful consequences of such feasting. This time it concerns a raid on San Juan de Puerto Rico, where the Cannibals 'made great disorder'. Among other things, 'they killed one of our friars, and cooked him on the *boucan*, of whom having eaten, several of them died, and they were subsequently afflicted with very great sickness'.[13] The experiment bore immediate fruit: 'Since that time,' du Tertre assures us, 'they have no longer any wish to eat Christians, but are content to kill them and leave them where they lie.'

Unfortunately, du Tertre tries to have his cake and eat it. The supposed uneatableness of human flesh does not seem to him incompatible with an emphasis on the wolfish rage of the women who greedily lick the *boucan*, here vividly described in imitation of Léry: 'They chew it over and over, clench it between their teeth, and are so afraid to lose some of it that they lick the bars on which a few drops of fat have fallen.'[14] In particular, du Tertre does not shrink from speculating on the difference in quality stemming from the diverse national origins of this most repugnant, and yet desirable, food: 'They have probably tasted the flesh of all the nations that frequent them. I have several times heard them say that of all Christians, the French were the best and the most delicate to eat, that Spaniards were so tough that they had trouble eating them at all.'[15]

Much later, a film by Nelson Pereira dos Santos was given the title *My Delicious Little Frenchman*. With a zeal which compels admiration, du Tertre tries to show the love (if that is the right word) which the Caribs naturally bear to France above all the other nations of Europe, a love so great that they are equally greedy for the words and for the flesh of her missionaries. Perhaps without realizing it, and to a curiously apologetic end, he then goes back to the ferocious polemical clichés formerly disseminated by the Calvinist Chauveton. Spaniards are as cruel as they are indigestible; but the French please both the palates and the ears of these barbarians, who thereby demonstrate their undeniable good sense, tact – and good taste.

Du Tertre's inconsequentiality is quite comprehensible. All in all, he, like the Calvinist Léry, still considers anthropophagy as a sign. The material substance of this sign is repugnant, but the message it carries is to the last degree cheering and salutary. The Cannibal's partiality to French missionaries and distaste for Spaniards is surely a direct and limpid expression of his political, ethnic and religious preference for the former. Surely, this bodily communion and fusion of the flesh must be a happy augury for the success of the colonial establishment and the spiritual harvest which it must bring.

Thus, it is no surprise to find how much importance the virtuous du Tertre attaches to the words of the indigenous inhabitants. He borrows from the Léry and Montaigne traditions to show the haughty loquacity of the prisoners before their executioners:

> ...which these poor unhappy and unfortunate victims ordinarily endure with a serene and constant visage, in no wise dismayed; they even defy them and proudly boast of having eaten the flesh of their fathers, telling them that they will eat only what they have eaten, and that they have relatives and friends well able to avenge their deaths.[16]

It is easy to recognize, in this farewell speech of defiance, the cannibal language which was at work in 'Of Cannibals'.

Like both Breton and du Tertre, the Protestant minister Charles de Rochefort, author of a *Histoire naturelle et morale des Iles Antilles de l'Amérique*, published anonymously in 1658, transfers the lofty tableau of Tupinamba cannibalism, depicted by Léry almost a century earlier, to the Lesser Antilles. His Caribs, like the 'Toüoupinambaoults' of his co-religionist, are possessed of inexhaustible eloquence. For example, they enjoin the French to stay peacefully at home instead of ranging the world in search of easy and illusory profits. This harangue, borrowed from the Marseilles adventurer Vincent Le Blanc, draws from the sagacious Rochefort (who may have suspected the plagiarism) the following aside: 'They said almost the same thing to Jean de Léry, as he reports in his History.'[17] With no less grandiloquence, they chide the Europeans for 'usurping their native land, as a manifest injustice': 'Your land must be a very bad one, since you have left it to take mine; or else you are full of malice, since you come here so joyously to persecute me.'

Rochefort is not completely taken in by this borrowed rhetoric. His conclusion resembles Montaigne's comments on the proud retort of the Indians rejecting the *requerimiento*: 'This plaint has none too Savage an air.'[18] At an earlier stage he commends the 'mild and kindly' nature of the Caribs, who die of sorrow when harshly treated, as they were by the perfidious English. His praise of these savages, who 'live without ambition, without regrets, without anxiety', whose virtuous simplicity would have drawn admiration from Socrates and Lycurgus, seems so excessive that it becomes hard to understand the sadistic violence which they proceed to deploy in their wars and their banquets of human flesh. At that point, hyperbole and omission are supplemented by allusions to classical mythology: the Sun dare not even glance at this repast worthy of Thyestes, and sets at midday.[19] It is best to draw a curtain across this horrid spectacle, in which man casts off his nature and assumes 'that of the most bloodthirsty and furious beasts'[20] – as the Greek painter Timanthus drew a veil over the face of Agamemnon in his picture of the sacrifice of Iphigenia, and as d'Aubigné did likewise across the anthropophagous mother of Sancerre and her butchered child.[21]

Here again, however, heroic discourse finally triumphs over the flesh. The Protestant Rochefort is writing a piece of propaganda in support of the colonization of Saint-Christophe, which might become a sort of utopian refuge. His apologetic and colonialist bent makes him stress the symbolic value of Carib anthropology. Following Montaigne, he gives a lengthy description of 'that bloody and gay defiance which comes from a Brazilian prisoner about to be devoured by his enemies'. The death-defying boldness of a similarly doomed Arawak is of like sort: 'His courage was shown not only on his lips, but also in the effects which followed his defiance.'[22] For, unlike the Tupinambas, the Arawaks were tortured by the victorious Caribs before being put to death. Their flesh was lacerated and tormented with burning brands, and the wounds were filled with pepper. They braved all these tortures with Olympian calm and further words of defiance.

Rochefort cannot conclude this portrayal of Carib anthropophagy without echoing du Tertre's assertion that human flesh was not very 'pleasurable' to the indigenous palate, and, in particular, that they much preferred a tender Frenchman to a more leathery Spaniard. Still in imitation of his predecessor, he states that the Caribs now abstain from torturing their victims and that 'they no longer eat Christians'.[23]

This view of Rochefort's represents a typical example of a fairly widespread attempt to tame both the Carib, who (it was hoped) could be turned into a good and honest subject, and a culinary practice which was as scandalous as it was repugnant. The Cannibals found the French to their taste, and, conversely, the French succeeded in imposing their religion, rule and customs on the readily convertible Indians. The assimilation appeared to be mutual, if a mild play on words be permitted, and if it was acceptable to equate the sacrifice of a few missionaries to savage appetites with the methodical enterprise of converting and subjugating entire populations.

The assimilation was taken still further by the Jesuits in Canada, who suffered exemplary agonies as the consenting parties to Iroquois anthropophagy. Throughout interminable scenes of torture, the victim would stimulate the cruelty of his tormentor for as long as he retained his wits. Let us take the famous example of the friars of

Brébeuf and Lalemant, who were tortured together during the Indian wars which culminated in the virtual extinction of the Huron nation. We have noted that during the moments preceding death logomachy played an important part in the ritual of honour cannibalism. Discourse was linked to the staging of a positive duel, in which the victim rivalled his executioner in ardour, magnanimity and eloquence. The word 'victim' is in fact inaccurate, as much so as it would be if applied to the martyr who cheerfully accepts his torment and sees a good death, attained in communion of thought and soul with his Saviour, as a triumph *in extremis*.[24]

What was extraordinary about the missionaries in Canada was that they consciously played on the parallel between the cannibal duel and the ordeal of the martyr. As he underwent his torment, the missionary not only sought to oppose his patience and firmness to the cruelty of the Indians, so as to show them by example what greatness of soul could be attained through the true faith; he also sought to win, one after the other, all the 'rounds' between himself and his torturers. It became a sort of judicial duel, and God was expected to intervene on behalf of the weaker but justified party, using the triumphant death-agony to display his own omnipotence and glory.

The torment of Jean de Brébeuf lasted three long hours, but that of his younger and stronger companion, Gabriel Lalemant, took seventeen. Both won the martyr's palm after a fearful series of ordeals. Lalemant was first stripped naked and covered in pine-bark, which was set on fire. At the same time, and in his presence, a necklace of red-hot axes was hung around the neck of Brébeuf. Their bodies were all wounds; the Iroquois laughed at them. The spectacle had aroused their appetites: 'They told one another that the flesh of the Frenchmen must be good, and they cut great strips of it from one or the other, and ate them.'[25] This roasting of the living was accompanied by fearful blasphemies, which the two martyrs endured stoically. Brébeuf was scalped. His side, like Christ's, was pierced, and immediately blood gushed from it in abundance and was drunk by the 'Barbarians'. Finally, his heart was torn out and promptly eaten. The concluding comment from Charlevoix, who enshrined this twofold agony in his *Histoire et description générale de la Nouvelle France*, reads like news of a victory: 'his life was one continual Heroism, and his death aroused the astonishment even of his Executioners'.[26]

The earthly destiny of Lalemant, who was stronger and whose torment lasted longer, reached a similarly exemplary conclusion. His temple was cloven with an axe, and the brain flowed forth, but he did not entirely lose consciousness. 'Then they tore out one of his eyes, and in its place they put a burning coal.'

Figure 11 'Ceremonies practised upon those who have died of cold in the snow, or have unhappily been drowned.' Joseph-François Lafitau, *Mœurs des Sauvages Ameriquains comparées aux mœurs des premiers temps* (1724). Copper-plate. Yale University: Beinecke Library.

The heroic end of Lalemant and Brébeuf, soon to furnish ideal material for Catholic hagiography, demonstrated the absolute success of their mission by means of the anthropophagic episode which was part of it. Normally, the Iroquois did not eat Christians, regarding them with the same distrust – or distaste – as the Caribs described by Breton and du Tertre. So when another Jesuit missionary, Jogues, was killed with an axe, his body was unceremoniously thrown into the river and his head hung on the palissade by way of a trophy.[27] Still more significant was the martyrdom of Bressani, another Jesuit in New France who was captured by the Indians along with his escort. The Huron who was with him was boiled and eaten, but Bressani was not considered worthy of such a fate. His nails were singed, his left thumb and two fingers of his right hand were cut off and his feet were dislocated. This rent and swollen flesh was just good enough to feed to the beasts. It was improper food for a man, but made a dish for hungry dogs: 'They reached such an excess of inhumanity, as to give dogs food upon his stomach, so that these ever-hungry animals should rend him, as they did in many places.'[28]

In the end, even the dogs scorned him, and Bressani, still alive, fell prey to worms which 'swarmed all over' his flesh. His body became so foul 'that no one could bear the stench of it any longer'. The Iroquois got rid of it by selling it to the Dutch, who were their allies against the French.

The relative failure of Bressani, who was to end his days in his native Italy, showing off his mutilated hands in the pulpit and edifying crowds of the faithful by his gestures and his eloquence,[29] brings out by contrast the full and complete success of Brébeuf and Lalemant. Instead of being rejected by the anthropophagous Indians, in a process which Lévi-Strauss might have described as 'anthropoemic' (from the Greek *emein*: 'vomit'),[30] and forced to return to Europe defeated, they received from their Iroquois tormentors the grace of a good death. That sanctification was obtained at the end of an exhausting contest, during which, stage by stage, their tormented bodies and their lipless, voiceless mouths maintained the honour of God to the furthest bounds of possibility. This paradoxical triumph, this – if it may be so described – perfection of felicity, was won through a symbolic fusion with the Other.

Cannibalism may well have been part of a vengeance ritual, but to the Jesuit historiographer it acquires perforce another meaning. It is one stage of a Passion, an imitation of the sufferings of Christ on the Cross. During that interminable agony, blasphemy alternated with torture, and spiritual torment aggravated the torment of the body. The irony of the torturers rings true indeed when they hurl at

Brébeuf the mocking words: 'You assured us a while ago that the more one suffers upon Earth, the happier one is in Heaven; it is in friendship for you that we do our best to increase your sufferings, and you ought to be grateful to us.'[31] The martyrdom of Brébeuf and Lalemant was the final proof of the power of love. While confirming their sanctity, it once again promulgated the universal redemption of humanity in the death and resurrection of the Son of God.

In their supreme self-giving, which repeated the first sacrifice upon Golgotha, Brébeuf and Lalemant reunited the sundered halves of humanity. For the unbelievers, even with blasphemies upon their lips, took communion in the blood of the just. When the wound opened in Brébeuf's side, 'all the Barbarians came thronging to drink of it'. This avidity, or rather 'hydropic thirst for human blood',[32] could not retain in Charlevoix's narrative the meaning it originally had – a physical passion for destruction and sadistic celebration. The protagonists believed they were avenging themselves, but against their own bodily impulses they were ensuring their own salvation. Like the board fixed on the Cross, bearing the inscription 'Jesus of Nazareth, king of the Jews', the ironic simulacrum of kingship turns into an eternal truth.

Here we reach a limit. The vengeance hypothesis, dear to the theologians who used it to preserve the unity of the human race and thereby save the Indian, here comes up against a figure of Eucharistic communion. The real anthropophagy of the Iroquois and the symbolic theophagy of the Catholic missionaries have met to overcome the sacrificial curse and to consecrate, in a oneness that is in no way a simulation, the unity of the Revelation.

However, it was not the paths of asceticism and martyrdom which were most frequently followed. In particular, the sublimity of the twinned martyrdoms of Brébeuf and Lalemant ought not to gloss over the failure of the Jesuit mission to Canada, a failure which is only symbolically and tardily compensated by Charlevoix's hagiography. While the Jesuit mission was being decimated year by year, other voices were raised to give a wholly different interpretation of cannibalism among the first Americans. As an illustration of this new, and soon to be dominant, attitude, we shall take *Cleveland*, by Abbé Prévost, a novel of doubt and errant conscience, in many ways a pioneering achievement.[33] Cleveland, a natural son of Oliver Cromwell, roams the world in search of an unattainable happiness. His wanderings bring him to North America, beyond the Appalachian Mountains, where he becomes the chieftain and lawgiver of the Abaqui Indians, a peaceable people whose lives he undertakes to bring into conformity with the law of Nature. But the neighbours of this fortunate nation are the ferocious Rointons, savages who 'wander unceasingly after beasts and men, whom they consider to be their most delicious quarry'.[34] All Cleveland's efforts to civilize them are in vain: one day they flee, abandoning their burning village and leaving the old and sick to perish in the flames.[35] Later on, Cleveland, his fiancée Fanny and their daughter fall into the hands of the Rointons along with their Abaqui escort. In the long description of the gruesome orgy which ensues, Prévost sticks broadly to the portrayal of vengeance cannibalism bequeathed by Montaigne and the sixteenth-century voyagers. The captured Abaquis defy their vanquishers to their last breath, boasting that they have previously done the same to them. However, in spite of their cruelty and the rather too obvious pleasure they take in torturing their victims and roasting them over a slow fire, the Rointons 'are not habitually anthropophagous, but only on occasions when most of the savages of America are anthropophagous likewise: that is to say, against enemy Prisoners whom they have taken in war'.[36] Despite this sage reflection, which the hero-narrator addresses to himself, he nonetheless fears the worst. And indeed, after a feast of human flesh lasting four days and nights, his daughter disappears in a throng of merry savages in the midst of which there is a flaming brazier. She is finally restored to him hundreds of pages and innumerable adventures later, at the gates of Paris. Later, but still long before the end of the novel, we learn that the custom of the Rointons is to 'spare the women in their barbarous and bloody executions', showing how true it is that 'the most inhuman Savages of America have this kind of respect for nature'.[37]

These considerations, scattered throughout the novel, represent Prévost's ethnographic reflections, following the voyagers whom he knew well and whose writings he was later to compile into his vast *Histoire des voyages*; but they do not deter him from blackening the portrait of Amerindian ritual cannibalism. The internal economy of the novel, which deliberately delays the denouement in order to sustain the dramatic suspense, contributes to this pessimistic view of the eaters of human flesh. Though Prévost retains the schema of honour cannibalism – exogenous and androphagous – he does not hesitate to make it much darker and more 'savage'. The cannibal banquet takes place by night, by the light of cooking fires in which flesh is hideously transformed and skin changes 'form and colour'.[38] The Rointons 'grind their teeth in a fearsome fashion'; they roar with sardonic laughter when their prisoners beg for mercy. Even their mouths are 'unusually large'. Their eyes 'gleam with cruelty and malice'.[39] They are 'stupid and pitiless' and scarcely deserve to retain the name of men.[40] Rather, they are 'Tigers in human shape'.[41]

All these characteristics bring the Rointons dangerously close to beasts. Prévost – betraying Montaigne and looking directly forward to Cornelius de Pauw and Sade – steers anthropophagy ineluctably away from civilized man and defines a type of polluted nature and degraded humanity which will soon be assumed to be inferior. The (sometimes unexpressed) desire for union now yields to a loudly proclaimed desire for exclusion. The failure of the novel's two American utopias, that of the Abaquis and that of the Nopandes, confirms this malediction against peoples who are no longer seen as primitive, but rather as degenerate.[42] Faced with the anthropophagi of America or anywhere else, the choice is now between 'reduction', as practised by the Jesuits of Paraguay, and destruction. In the former case, the savage is forced to bend to the rules of an ideal Nature which seem to have been expunged from his make-up by laziness, idleness and forgetfulness. In the latter – the solution which is to triumph with Robinson Crusoe – fear joins forces with cynicism, or at best with self-righteousness, to abolish the unendurable proximity of flesh and blood in the Other. The bloodthirsty *doppelgänger* which haunts the individual must at all costs be eliminated, like a recurring nightmare.

Robinson Crusoe

The fear of being eaten – swallowed up – haunts Robinson Crusoe throughout his sojourn on the desert island: fear of being swallowed by the sea after the shipwreck; fear of being devoured by wild animals when, as the sole survivor, he reaches land.[43] As a survivor, he will devote all his efforts to accumulating, lest he lack something. His terrors return with even greater violence when, after fifteen years of absolute solitude, he sees the track of a bare foot on the sand one day 'about noon':[44] Cannibals, without a doubt; man-eaters: he knows it, forebodes it. Robinson then has the same experience as Columbus two centuries earlier: he thinks so much about the Cannibals that in the end he encounters them.

But the embodiment of the fantasy is delayed, serving only to fortify and confirm his imagination. The revelation takes place little by little, each event being separated from the preceding one by a minimum of one or two years. It goes on so long that the appearance of the feared Other, the fearfully grinning spectre which springs, bloody and naked, from the exile's imagination, reads like an interminable psychoanalysis, the sessions spanning all the years of a life. First, the print of a single naked foot, much wider than Robinson's (he tries his own foot in it), strikes the poor castaway with uncontrollable terror, so that he immediately strengthens his fortifications and cowers within his stockade. After the footprint, this trace of a vanished presence, comes the blinding proof which Robinson has evidently been awaiting for months: a seashore 'spread with skulls, hands, feet, and other bones of human bodies'.[45] The ashes of the fire are surrounded by a sort of circular seat dug out of the earth, 'like a cockpit', scene of 'their inhuman feastings'. After this second stage in his cannibal initiation, Robinson considers the extermination of this entire race of cruel man-eaters. He is now at the stage reached by Columbus on his second voyage, when, landing on Guadeloupe, he discovered human remains, ready for eating, in an abandoned Carib village.[46] Assuredly, the Cannibals continue to elude capture. But they are no longer merely rumours passing from mouth to mouth, or fleeting tracks on a sandy beach. Their intrusive, obsessive presence has left a horrid physical impression.

The Cannibals are easily recognizable from the scene of their doings, the cockpit full of dismembered bodies. Without fully realizing it, Robinson is acting out a previous history, which is not entirely his own: an 'original sin' which he must expiate and which is connected with his disobedience to his father.[47] This original sin, which torments him and which he can only shake off by the exercise of even greater violence, also relates to the destruction of the American Indians, which is mentioned several times in the story. Friday, for example, though he has not knowledge of writing, is well acquainted with the exactions of the 'white bearded men', who had killed 'much mans', as he puts it.[48] Robinson realizes that he means the Spaniards, the conquistadors, 'whose cruelties in America had been spread over the whole countries and were remembered by all the nations from father to son'. But the honest Yorkshireman, with his Calvinist upbringing, would never dream of behaving in that way. On the contrary, he does his best to save Friday, body and soul, by restoring him to life and to the priceless gift of a reformed Christian conscience. But the cost is notably disproportionate: the youthful Carib is saved by means of a veritable carnage among his brethren.

Thus Robinson reinvents the Cannibals, step by step, just as Columbus originally invented them as bogeymen attired with bleeding heads and mutilated limbs. And the rediscovery has the same disastrous consequences. The terror of being eaten justifies, in anticipation, the destruction of this unhuman humanity. For Robinson, of course, puts his fears into practice, once in order to save Friday from his pursuers – killing two of them – and later to snatch Friday's father and a Spanish prisoner from these 'abominable creatures' – this time at a cost of seventeen or eighteen corpses, according to the scrupulous reckoning of Robinson himself.

Doubtless the massacre is not undertaken lightly. In both cases Robinson hesitates for a long time before intervening, as if he feared that to shed blood would make him more cannibalistic than the Cannibals themselves. In any case, is it right to strike people who have done you no wrong, 'whose barbarous customs were their own disaster'?[49] As Léry believed at an earlier date, the cannibalism of the Cannibals is clearly a sign that God has abandoned them to their accursed perceptions. Why add a human condemnation to this all-too-evident malediction? Is it not a sin of pride to usurp the decisions of the supreme Judge? In both cases, Robinson waits for a 'plain call from Providence' before taking action: Friday's inexplicable flight from his executioners, and the unexpected sight of a white man among the victims of the second group. At least this means that the barbarous act is performed under divine licence.

Apart from his tumultuous inner debates and his hesitations, Robinson is own brother to the Spanish papists whom he so detests, who spread Christianity at the sword's point. In a word, God fights on his side, as long ago he sustained the Crusaders of Castile in their remorseless struggle against the 'gentiles' of Mexico and Peru. The demographic reckoning is certainly comparable. Twenty Indians are killed and one is converted – perhaps two, if we are to count Friday's father. Robinson's genocide in miniature far surpasses the worst estimates suggested by present-day historians for the *conquista*. As he himself foresaw, in an extraordinary flash of lucidity, Robinson has become 'no less a murderer than they were in being man-eaters'.[50]

But let us return to Robinson's gradual discovery of the Cannibal evidence, which is accompanied by an inexorably rising tide of terror. After the single footprint, after the remains of the feast in the cockpit, comes the fire on the beach, which Robinson saw in December of the twenty-third year of his sojourn on the island.[51] In spite of his terror, he is still able to use his spy-glass to follow the smallest details of the scene as it unfolds, bearing out the worst imaginings of his own nightmares. Nine savages are sitting around a hearth, cooking a mysterious dish which they have brought for the purpose – whether alive or dead remains to be seen. After a victory dance – or a crude pantomime of one – they depart on the ebb-tide in the canoes which they had drawn up on to the sand. Robinson runs up, armed to the teeth, and is horrified to discover the usual evidence: 'the blood, the bones, and part of the flesh of human bodies, eaten and devoured by those wretches, with merriment and sport'.[52] The five canoes are already far out at sea, heading for the mainland.

Now Robinson knows that his fears were justified. The strange visitors are indeed Cannibals. They eat human flesh with undeniable
enjoyment. Besides that, they are naked; but, strange to say, in spite
of his spy-glass and voyeuristic attention to detail, Robinson could
not tell their sex.

The unanswered questions will be resolved in the next episode,
which takes place another eighteen months later. This is the decisive
episode of the rescue of Friday. The savages return for their annual
sacrifice, more numerous than ever and closer to Robinson, who feels
as helpless as ever, hidden in his 'cell'. Then comes the expected incident, the flight of Friday, which Robinson has foreseen in a dream.
Encouraged by this premonition, which he takes as a sign from
Divine Providence, he shakes off his lethargy, calls to the fugitive,
shoots one of his pursuers (Friday beheads the second with
Robinson's sword), and frightens off the others. The next day
Robinson and Friday, now his devoted servant, recognize the usual
proofs of savage voracity on the deserted beach. One is disturbed by
it; the other is not. But the inventory is striking enough: 'I saw three
skulls, five hands, and the bones of three to four legs and feet, and
abundance of other parts of the bodies.'[53]

To make any sense of this rag-and-bone assortment (worthy of one
of Prévert's poems), of these three dismembered and partially eaten
corpses, takes all Friday's dispassionate attention – or, rather, all his
greed, for it is obvious (as Robinson notes with alarm) that he 'was
still a Cannibal in his nature'. When he is ordered to assemble the
skulls, bones and stumps into a pile and reduce them to ashes, Friday,
Robinson is horrified to notice, looks with a hunger on the ghastly
remains. Only the threat of death can dissuade him from indulging
that appetite: the most scandalous evidence Robinson has met with
yet.

The fearful sight of these butchered bodies seems to hold a morbid
attraction for the exiled Puritan. The hatred of the flesh which he
feels, on both the erotic and the alimentary level, is equalled only by
his obsession with the latter. He is literally besieged by gruesome
remains, which appear over the years, in a sort of encircling movement, on all sides of the island, strewn over its fairest beaches. This
mingled fascination and disgust resurfaces when the Cannibals return
three years later, and then his destructive rage will know no bounds.
But he has a more immediate anxiety, which must be resolved at once:
it is Friday himself, tame as a cat, but clearly far from cured of his
appalling appetite. He must be coaxed out of it as soon as possible.
Robinson must assume responsibility for the education of a Cannibal.
His chief anxiety is to find out what makes a person anthro-

pophagous, and how he can be stopped from being so.

To the first question Friday gives a very clear answer: vengeance. The Caribs, as everyone has long known, eat only enemies taken in war. This, in 'savage' language, is expressed as follows: 'They no eat mans but when make the war fight.'[54] But Robinson clings to the alternative explanation: greed and rooted 'nature'. Thus, the deadlock between the two characters opposes the two main theories of the origins of cannibalism. However, the two viewpoints are unequally represented: since the novel is written in the first person, it is Robinson's view which prevails. This imposes a radically ethnocentric solution: anthropophagy is attributed to a perverse appetite.

Indeed, the narrator's stubborn adherence to this belief produces one of the most improbable, and most unintentionally comic, episodes in the story. Robinson, convinced that Friday has never eaten any meat other than human flesh, takes him goat-hunting so he can 'taste other flesh'.[55] He kills a kid, stews part of it, roasts the rest, and introduces the Cannibal to a food which he now apparently tastes for the first time. Friday's alimentary conversion is a complete success. Overcome with gratitude and greed, he promises his master that never again will he eat the flesh of any man.

Robinson can now complete his civilizing labours: having introduced him to meat, he teaches his servant to grind corn, sift flour and make bread. The novel presents Friday as a wild animal, a predator with a human face who cannot live except by killing and eating his adversaries; without that, he must be taught every detail of how to survive. But he is also like a docile, well-meaning infant, who is only too willing to learn. The young Carib appears to have forgotten every detail of his ancestral practices. He knows nothing of hunting or fishing, or preparing cassava. Robinson even teaches him how to make a *boucan* – an implement of incontestably indigenous origin.[56]

The unbridled anti-primitivism of the first part of the novel is, admittedly, counterbalanced by one of Robinson's 'Serious Reflections' in his old age. Musing on how he met Friday (now dead), he thinks that apart from their cannibalism, the savages are as human and gentle as most people, and also easily converted. Contrary to expectation, their appetite for human flesh is not all-embracing: it surfaces only when they have prisoners of war.[57] Despite these last-minute retouches to his sombre portrayal of the Caribs, Defoe's work is an effective contribution to the black legend of the Cannibals. It represents the normal English attitude towards them throughout the ages of discovery and colonization. Unlike the French, who, except in times of acute conflict (as in 1645–9), lived peacefully with them or made alliances with them, the subjects of His Britannic Majesty always saw them as enemies to be avoided, reduced to slavery or exterminated.[58] In return (as Rochefort remarked, following Breton and du Tertre), the Caribs called the English *Etoutou Noubi*, 'meaning ill-made enemies, because they are clothed', and showed them no quarter.[59] Besides the historical circumstances of their settlement in the West Indies, which began later than the French and remained for some time more precarious, the religious element in this English hostility should not be forgotten. Puritan Calvinism, as practised by Defoe and his like, involved a comprehensive rejection of the flesh. Having banished all traces of blood-sacrifice from the Eucharist, they were hardly likely to accept the resurgence of real flesh and real blood – the horror of the mutilated body, which ought to have been obliterated for ever by Christ's death on the cross.[60]

Robinson Crusoe has rightly been seen as a 'prophetic figure', a prefiguration of colonial self-righteousness a hundred years in advance of the reality.[61] Defoe's hero can indeed be seen as the type of new economic man,[62] an implacable individualist, all the more ruthless towards others because of his belief that Providence supports him, inspires his smallest deeds and continually justifies the excesses of his conquering and civilizing progress. *Robinson Crusoe* is again revolutionary in its paradoxical geography: a European dwelling on an American island, threatened with invasion and conquest by Carib Indians who visit it periodically from the nearby continent. To defend his property, his adopted country, this Island of Despair which, over time, he has turned into a kingdom rich in cattle, crops and even subjects, Robinson massacres the intruders or thrusts them back into the sea: never, at least in the first part of the novel, do they penetrate beyond the beachheads. This inverts the real historical situation, whereby the Indians, besieged in their islands, fought foot by foot against European colonists who decimated them periodically. We have already noted a similar schematic inversion in connection with the education of Friday, to whom Robinson teaches the basics of savage living in the wild. In reality, the invaders also came from a continent: not South America, but Europe, which was shedding its surplus population in all directions and sending fleets of heavily armed soldiers, zealous missionaries and starving adventurers across every sea.

This inverted schema, a typical ideological tool, is also a convenient smokescreen. The map of the world is turned back to front; island and continent change places. Inhabitants of the one accuse those from the other of barbarity; but, through an inversion of the most probable appearances, it is the former who are themselves all too obviously guilty of barbarous behaviour, carrying their deeds with them wherever they go. By justifying his repeated massacres of the Caribs, who have nothing to set against his arsenal of weapons save their naked skin and a few clubs quite unable to harm anyone except for the unfortunate brethren whom they sacrifice, Robinson becomes the prophet of a pitiless sovereignty, which will exact payment from its adversary for its own original sin.

One of the main lessons of the novel is perhaps this, which applies to Robinson even more than to the Cannibals: you will find nothing on the island save that which you have brought there yourself. Without the innumerable items salvaged from the wreck – seeds, provisions, sails, clothing – Robinson would never have survived even for a single year. As for the savages from the continent, who come to the island to perform their sacrifices, they have to bring their victims with them; the physical effort involved scarcely seems proportionate to the result. This remark applies even more forcibly on the moral level. Robinson comes to his island, at the mouth of the Orinoco, burdened with a paranoid outlook on the world. Despite all his efforts to create a miniature York in these tropical climes, the incessant burgeoning of evil remains apparent – in the Cannibal, if not in the caymans, sharks and other flesh-eaters which swarm in those latitudes.

As a consequence, the Cannibal, in the European mind, was to become progressively more insular. The island, apparently well able to restrain and circumscribe fantasies, was to work rather like a fixation abscess. It inscribed and absorbed evil, and so the latter was conjured, kept at a distance. We shall see how in Diderot, Sade and Jules Verne cannibalism is structurally linked with the isolation of an island. Unsurprisingly, by that time cannibalism was to assume its most degraded form, cannibalism by constraint. Amidst the boundless ocean – free from foreign competition as far as the eye could see, endlessly accessible to the ships and interests of the all-conquering West – the Cannibal Isles, narrowly encircled and closely watched, were to represent the last, scattered traces of an archaic terror, the fossil outlines of an initiating violence, where the modern conquerors would be altogether incapable of recognizing the very act which justified them.

11

The Enlightenment Cannibal: From Bougainville to Voltaire

The insular Cannibal: Bougainville, Diderot

The determinist hypothesis, of which the essential outlines had been sketched by Cardano in 1557, was to triumph two centuries later, towards the end of the Enlightenment. Diderot adopted the paradigm in *Supplément au voyage de Bougainville*, which he wrote in autumn 1772, and in the additions he made at about the same time to Abbé Raynal's *Histoire philosophique et politique des établissements et du commerce des Européens dans les deux Indes* ('Philosophical and Political History of the Settlements and Trade of the Europeans in the Two Indies'). He applies it both to Oceania and to early Britain.[1] It is first mentioned in an interchange between speakers *A* and *B* in the first part of *Supplément au voyage*. The dialogue form gives Cardano's explanatory model a new solidity. At last, anthropophagy is located in its proper place: the island, which is now simply a spatial expression of human isolation.

What, *B* asks, would happen if men were to 'go on multiplying on a little spit of land that is less than three miles across?' (In context, this refers to the Ile des Lanciers, discovered by Bougainville in March 1768.) *A* replies: 'probably they thin themselves out by eating each other. Perhaps you have there – in the very condition of island life – the origins of a very ancient and very natural form of cannibalism.'[2]

The trigger for this dazzling, but highly debatable intuition is a remark made by Louis-Antoine de Bougainville in his *Voyage autour du monde* ('Voyage Round the World'), dated 22 March 1768. The philosopher-navigator comes within sight of a little island covered with luxuriant vegetation, whence emerge fifteen naked warriors armed with long spears (hence the name 'Isle of Lancers'); and he wonders what link there is between this little group, isolated in the ocean, and 'the chain of other beings'.[3] How were they transported to that place and what happened as they began to multiply in such a confined space? In a report compiled in 1771 for *Correspondance littéraire*, in which he sketched the broad outlines for what was to become *Supplément au voyage*, Diderot pondered the enigma and declared himself unsatisfied with the unanswered question: 'M. de Bougainville knows nothing of it.' Happily, Diderot is able to furnish a solution, and he immediately formulates the hypothesis of cannibal insularity: 'To the last question I would answer, that either they exterminate or eat one another, or their multiplying is delayed by some superstitious law, or they perish under the sacrificial knife.'[4] War, anthropophagy and human sacrifice provide a triple solution to the enigmatic and vaguely disquieting silence of the Lancers.

The first interesting aspect of this very brief reflection by Diderot is that it uses the insular theory to focus very narrowly on the hypothesis of the natural origins of cannibalism. In the same way an island represents a special locus for *in vitro* experimentation in many other eighteenth-century fictions and philosophical writings: compare Foigny's *Hermaphrodites*, Morelly's *Basiliade*, Abbé Coyer's *Découverte de l'Isle Frivole* ('Discovery of the Frivolous Isle') and Restif de la Bretonne's southern archipelago. In the island locus, the power of reason acquires a transparency which makes it decisive. Unlike the continent, where objects and matter are completely heterogeneous, the island is utterly translucent. Within its bounds, which are themselves unequivocal – a fringe of foam, a ring of breakers on a coral reef – it is a simple object, secure from all outside contact. Every island encloses a singular phenomenon, a microscope slide ready prepared for the scientific gaze.[5] In the present case, the island offers the additional advantage of being intrinsically and structurally linked with the problem under discussion: it is a compendium of all possible states of siege, wind-driven ships, besieged cities, states of helpless isolation. The island implies and condenses the fact of cannibalism. It is, thus, the most eloquent illustration of Cardano's paradigm.

In the *Supplément au voyage*, just after his remark on the insular origins of cannibalism, Diderot lists the large number of practices, aberrant in the eyes of reason, which arise when a group is obliged to feed and survive in a restricted space. As well as anthropophagy, there is human sacrifice – reminding us of the ancient Mexicans – castration of males and infibulation of females, all of them customs which are supremely consecrated by religion and which tend to curb the increase in population. For Diderot, as for Cardano, cannibalism is really caused by the imperatives of survival, though its apparent causes are religion, idolatry and the honour cult – themselves never more than secondary overdeterminations which proliferate like parasites, a process Diderot calls 'fatal palingenesis'.

After the paradigm had successfully crossed the two centuries between Cardano and Diderot – doubtless via a good many intermediaries – it emerged in a simpler and more systematized form. It becomes, indeed, very much simplified, since it uses an Ocean island as its medium rather than the vast plinth of the American continent, as a result of which the experience of cannibal origins is 'miniaturized', and so becomes more attainable. And it is also systematized, in that superstition and its cruel and irrational practices are, in the last analysis, explained in terms of the quantitative relationship between people and place.

By glossing the *Histoire des deux Indes* and stuffing it with philosophical digressions, Diderot aimed to turn it into a sort of materialist and republican fireship which could incinerate the *ancien régime* and 'bring Brutuses to birth'.[6] That is why the exceedingly corrosive passage which the *Supplément au voyage* devotes to anthropophagy is reproduced almost word for word, though without the dialogue form, at the beginning of Book III.[7] Diderot adds remarks on abstinence, fasting and monastic rules in general. If it were possible to imagine 'a monastery of men and women very abundant in monks, with no chance of emigration', is it not obvious that cannibalism would one day be part of its rule?

One model drives out the other. Having accepted the materialist siege hypothesis (which he applies, somewhat maliciously, to early England – 'an attentive observer would find some traces of it in the Great Britain of today'), Diderot dismisses the classical explanation based on points of honour and vengeance, as applied to those everlasting Brazilians by Léry, Montaigne and Osorio. Similarly, the post-1770 editions eliminate one of the few witty remarks made by the industrious Raynal, the very wording of which owes much to the sixteenth-century texts: 'It appears that vengeance is the sole seasoning for a dish that humanity would spurn.'[8] Diderot disagrees: he puts a line through the untimely remark and replaces it with a cool reflection on the 'execrable *ius gentium*' of primitive peoples.

This reveals a certain doubt and fear: if one attempts to systematize the siege model, which is strictly determinist, is there not a danger of freeing cannibalism from all remaining taboos and making it appear, in the last analysis, rather attractive? Since religion has been revealed as an empty vessel, fear can no longer serve as a brake on the cannibal appetite. If the taste for human flesh becomes more widespread, if the tyrant comes to know of it and finds it agreeable to his palate, might he not use cannibalism as a tool to maintain his power?

If the two phenomena – tyranny and anthropophagy, both equally monstrous in Diderot's eyes and both secretly akin – were to come together, human society would doubtless be an abominable spectacle.

But it is too late to turn back. If such questions really do arise and never, for a single instant, seem absurd, it is because the paradigm defined by Cardano two centuries earlier has finally triumphed. The causes of cannibalism are both natural and material. This makes it all the harder for the body social to exorcise them. The first priority is to fight any kind of discretionary power, which (so to speak) concentrates the devouring menace over the head of every individual. Cannibalism has become a political allegory, an active metaphor for tyrannical regimes which trample both bodies and minds.

However, there is one obvious gap in Diderot's chain of reasoning. Between the insular microcosm and the extension of the metaphor to its maximum – almost universal – extent, natural determinism has somehow lost its way. How can one make the transition from the island to the rest of the world? How can a constraint, quite tangible when it is concentrated in a narrowly circumscribed location, persist when the location is enlarged to infinity? Diderot is obliged to entertain the concept of a persistent behaviour pattern: cannibalism can be exported to a further shore. Once the initial constraint had disappeared, the island peoples, after years of continental influence, had (he suggests) retained it as a pious custom. The reader will not be very surprised to find Diderot resuscitating Cardano's argument regarding the notion of custom and associating it, once again, with necessity:

> When these men had discovered a way to escape the narrow bounds within which they had been confined for centuries by physical causes, they brought their customs to the continent where they were handed down from age to age, and where even today they sometimes torture the philosophers who come seeking the reason.[9]

Malthus and the anthropophagous archipelago

The dispassionate theorist who was to perfect the explanation suggested by Cardano and extend it methodically, country by country, to the entire inhabited globe was none other than the Reverend Thomas Robert Malthus. In his celebrated *Essay on the Principle of Population*, first published in 1803 and considerably enlarged thereafter, he repeatedly includes the fact of cannibalism among the natural and necessary obstacles to population growth. Islands are the most obvious example, and Malthus quotes Raynal (alias Diderot), but only in order to refute him. Malthus was certainly shocked to find the French philosopher applying the paradigm to ancient England in the first instance; but in a way, it was even better suited to Great Britain, crowded as it was with the surplus population of the first Industrial Revolution. Malthus is determined to show that the compiler of the *Histoire des deux Indes* has been caught in his own metaphorical trap. Cannibalism may indeed be insular in origin, but there are islands and islands. By trying to confine it within the very narrow circle of a Pacific islet, Diderot and Raynal have botched the problem of how it expanded over three out of the four continents. The right line of argument postulates human 'islands': 'A savage tribe in America surrounded by enemies, or a civilized and populous nation hemmed in by others in the same state, is, in many respects, circumstanced like the islander.'[10]

It follows that the world – and in particular pre-colonial America, where a population subdivided into an enormous number of rival ethnic groups disputed possession of a land devoid of natural resources – could be seen as a conglomeration comprising an infinite number of population 'islands'. Any people living in the heart of a continent is under continual siege from all the others, and helps in turn to besiege them. The circle is complete, whether it is bounded by the sea, by mountains and forests or, most often, by mere contiguity with neighbouring circles. These barriers may not be visible, but they are real, and are even harder to cross than the confines of the seashore.

Malthus, extending the island paradigm to the entire inhabited world, provides the following neat summary: 'There is probably no island yet known the produce of which could not be further increased. This is all that can be said of the whole earth. Both are peopled up to their natural produce.'[11]

This definition of cannibalism in terms of insularity seems to have satisfied Malthus, and it is a model which can be transported to any point on the globe. A human society, wherever it dwells, is surrounded by limits to its natural expansion, and this often impels it towards a not always figurative autophagy. Suddenly, insular cannibalism becomes ubiquitous – the main advantage of which is to raise it to a remarkable level of abstraction. It can now be applied to any social or ethnic peculiarity: the Maoris of New Zealand, described by Cook on his third voyage; the Tupinambas, as described by Léry or Staden; Charlevoix's Iroquois; and so on. It matters little that the former are natives of Oceania, and the latter of Brazil or Canada. Cannibalism, in all its diversity, can always be reduced to the same model. Therefore, it is legitimate to confuse cultures and despise rituals – as Cardano did – and to set at naught the symbolic content which the actual perpetrators attached to their practices. The only thing which really counts is the mathematical relationship between a defined population and a location with a set of given dimensions.

This brutal reduction of the diversity of rites and cultures to an economic and ecological model opened the way to the most aggressive ethnocentrism. Strictly speaking, no doubt, the analysis could also be applied to 'civilized' peoples of the European type. Indeed, Malthus devotes a book of his *Essay* to the 'Checks to population in the different states of Modern Europe', from Norway to France and from Russia to Spain.[12] But it is very clear that these nations, with their elevated moral consciences, have in the course of their long history been able to solve the problem in a less crude way than by merely eating one another. Birth-control, the 'prudential check to marriage',[13] celibacy among certain social and professional classes – priests and teachers – can, by invoking the 'duty of moral constraint', make it possible to obey the imperious summons of Nature without overt violence. The exemplary success of these northern European societies makes any other practice, starting with the 'brutal' and 'odious' rites current among supposedly 'savage' peoples, seem unacceptable. All in all, the superiority of the European cultural model appears unassailable. This conclusion would not appeal to such as Diderot, whose 'apology for the Tahitian' is in many ways comparable to Montaigne's for the Brazilian.[14]

Candide among the Cannibals

Nonetheless, the Cannibal is still a fascinating paradox: less barbarous than the so-called civilized peoples, with all their polemical potentialities. In the article 'Anthropophagi' in his *Dictionnaire philosophique* (1764), Voltaire deftly and fleetingly plagiarizes Montaigne, adapting the final scene of essay I,31. The scene of the interview is no longer Rouen but Fontainebleau, and the elegant lightness of the *style Louis XV* has replaced the grim magnificence of Charles IX's reign. To make the savage's rejoinders more piquant, Voltaire turns him into a woman. We no longer hear the indignation of an unclothed king, but the astonishment of a 'lady of that country' – and the country has been shifted from Brazil to Louisiana, from the banks of the Rio de Janeiro to the banks of the Mississippi. The conversation immediately turns not to politics, but to gastronomy: 'I asked her if she had eaten men; she answered very frankly that she had done so.'[15]

Montaigne's manly interviewing technique gives way to a sophisticated badinage in which cannibalism becomes a transparent linguistic cover for eroticism. In the *Dictionnaire philosophique* the article on 'Anthropophagi' comes directly after the one on 'Amour' ('Love'), and it opens with the contrast between the pleasures of Venus and the greed for one's fellow humans: 'It is hard to pass from people kissing each other to people eating each other.'[16] Voltaire was surely the first to recognize the secret affinity supporting that unusual and shocking transition. From kissing to biting, the difference is only one of degree. And, after all, cannibalism is a particularly direct and effective method of becoming one with another person.[17]

This cannibalistic badinage, a re-writing of Montaigne adapted to eighteenth-century taste, is nonetheless intended seriously. The discussion soon sheds its gallantry in favour of philosophy, and the jesting tone yields to one of vehement exhortation. Voltaire transcends the amatory setting and recreates the vigorous impetuosity of Montaigne in 1580: 'I looked rather scandalised; she excused herself, saying it was better to eat one's dead enemy than to leave him to be devoured by wild beasts.' This is almost the tone of the famous tirade in the *Essays*: 'I think there is more barbarism in eating men alive, than to feed upon them dead'.[18] That pronouncement, in its turn, recalls Voltaire's cynical remark that 'We respect dead men more than the living.' Montaigne was criticizing judicial torture and the interminable agonies visited upon men condemned to death in his time. Voltaire uses the cannibal allegory to condemn warfare, the perfectly legal massacre of one's neighbour.

The main difference between Montaigne and Voltaire is that the latter does not take the allegory too seriously. The lady from the Mississippi is only a pretext, soon forgotten in order to concentrate on the message, which is all that really matters. This is confirmed by the way Voltaire, later in the same article, ferrets among the hardware of exoticism and comes up with the odd pronouncement that 'Nations which are called civilised are right not to put their victorious enemies on the spit.' The consequence would have been a raging epidemic, which would have had the direst effects on 'social virtues'.

Voltaire turns the same spit in the corresponding scene from *Candide*, in which the hero and his servant Cacambo are captured by the ferocious Oreillons, Xaraya Indians from Upper Peru, who take them for members of the Company of Jesus and make ready to roast and boil them, crying 'We'll have Jesuit for dinner! We'll have Jesuit for dinner!' To quench the culinary zeal of their tormentors, who, naked and armed with arrows, clubs and stone axes, are preparing the cauldron and the spit, Cacambo develops a line of argument in complete accord with the Cardano hypothesis. Noting cynically that 'the law of nature bids us kill our fellow men', he begins by approving the procedures followed by the savages, who, in the words of the innocent Candide, are representatives of 'pure nature'. He goes on to establish between his interlocutors and 'ourselves' a distinction which has nothing to do with morality, and everything to do with the varying intensity of natural constraint: 'We don't avail ourselves of the right to eat one another because we can find good food elsewhere. You have not the same resources as we have.'[19] The sole merit of westerners is that they were born in a more fertile terrain. Only the hazard of their birthplace gives them any claim to superiority. There is no room here for Divine Providence. Behind the irony of Cacambo, here acting as Voltaire's mouthpiece, there is an observation both lucid and despairing. The riches and resources of the earth are unequally distributed, and with no attention to privilege or election. The two hemispheres are as good (or bad) as each other, as the rest of the story makes clear.[20] In the southern hemisphere, as in the north, men treat one another like wolves.

Voltaire's *Histoire de Jenni* applies the same insight to North America, through the mouth of the atheist Birton. This free thinker agrees with the vengeful Blue Mountain Indians, who have killed and eaten Madame Clive-Hart, that 'the custom of putting one's fellow man in the pot or on the spit was the most ancient and the most natural ... it was an innate conviction that men were hunted before beasts, because it was much easier to kill a man than to kill a wolf'.[21]

To Voltaire, the universality of evil is a much more serious matter than cannibalism, which is a mere sideline, a particular illustration of a more general problem. Thus Cacambo is not exaggerating in the least when he says that 'it is undoubtedly better to eat your vanquished foes than to leave them to the crows and ravens'. 'Our stomachs', say the Blue Mountain warriors, 'are a more honourable grave.' The *Dictionnaire philosophique* repeats this almost word for word, while denouncing war as an absolute evil: 'We kill our neighbours in battles pitched and unpitched; and for the most paltry pay provide meals for the crows and the worms. That is the horror, that's the crime; what does it matter, when a man has been killed, if a soldier eats him, or a crow and a dog?'[22]

The crowning evil of this general allelophagy, inflating cannibalism into a universal symbol, is the fanaticism which overlies the natural constraint: 'It was superstition that caused the human victims to be immolated; it was necessity that caused them to be eaten.'[23] The scandal is not confined to the absurdities provoked by ungrateful Nature: it resides essentially in the increase of evils which is heaped upon an already deplorable state of affairs by so-called human 'reason'.

All in all, cannibalism is an indirect and allegorical way of attacking the infamy of religious intolerance and all its black-robed minions.[24] The relativism recalls Montaigne. But while the historical pessimism builds on the observations in 'Of Cannibals' and 'Of Coaches', the cannibal allegory has acquired a more sinister overtone. It is no longer underpinned by an idealized vision of the Indian as the man of Nature, heir to the heroic virtues of antiquity; it is underpinned by a caricature. In the intentionally conventional and schematic geography of *Candide*, the cauldrons and spits borrowed from the old *mappae mundi* submerge the horror in ridicule.

The horror – which makes us laugh when we ought to weep – is universal. The Oreillons, stupid and cruel as they may be, are full members of the human race. There is no further excuse for cannibalism; and yet no attempt is made to explain it. The environmental constraint takes us back to a first cause which is blind, unfathomable. Why (oh why!) must men be brought to eat one another and, worse still, invoke the most lofty and sacred principles by way of justification? In the final analysis the question is a metaphysical one, and, as such, it is destined to remain unanswered.

12

Cruel Nature: De Pauw and Sade

The Caribs of the Islands are the only ones who have kept their grim character and their chastened and thoughtful air: one would think that they were nostalgic for the time when they used to roast their captives and depopulate the Isle of Portorico.

Cornelius de Pauw, *Recherches philosophiques sur les Américains*

It is just as easy to eat a man as an ox.

Sade, *Aline et Valcour*

The degenerate America of Cornelius de Pauw

The island can be seen as the original location and symbol of cannibalism. But the necessity of cannibalism can be felt in another environment: a continent too poor to supply the needs of its population. Such, in essence, was Cardano's view of America. Voltaire, speaking through Cacambo, agrees that the deficiency is consubstantial with the New World itself: the latter is incapable of feeding its natural inhabitants. The next episode of *Candide* seems to contradict this, however: leaving the Oreillons, we suddenly find ourselves in the utopian land of Eldorado. The former are savages, living in great deprivation in a state of nature; the latter is a place of such extraordinary abundance that the most frugal meal becomes a banquet. In a poor village inn the visitors are served – as a first course – four soups, a boiled condor weighing two hundred pounds, two roast monkeys, 'a platter of three hundred humming-birds and another of six hundred colibris'.[1]

The negative hypothesis was adopted, and taken to extremes, by an author more rigorous than Voltaire and less enthusiastic than Diderot: the austere churchman Cornelius de Pauw, whose *Recherches philosophiques sur les Américains* was published in Berlin in 1768. The work provoked impassioned reactions and was to be the starting point of what Antonello Gerbi has called 'The Quarrel of the New World'. More immediately, it drew the author to the attention of Frederick II, who invited him to Court, but quickly tired of his stiffness and self-conceit.

The implacably learned de Pauw, deeply imbued with the spirit of encyclopaedism, hating the Jesuits and believing in the progress of the arts and sciences, shrinks from no detail, however painful or scabrous, that will support his thesis. That is why sexology takes pride of place in his portrayal of a degenerate continent. Indeed, as he explains in his 'Discours préliminaire': 'The knowledge of physical Man having been the first object of these Researches, it would be exceedingly strange if I were not to be pardoned for giving certain details that we pardon every day in those who describe insects, and devote whole volumes to the coupling of Slugs.'[2]

And he proceeds to tell the reader all that there is to know about the sexual practices of American natives, their ineptness in the act of love, the general ingratitude of Nature towards them, the smallness of their organs and the barrenness of their seed. This is a good indication of de Pauw's methods: he deliberately puts mankind on the same footing as the other creatures of Nature, while observing differences and degrees within the species. His argument, supported by a formidable assemblage of sources and comparisons, is that America is in an advanced state of degeneracy. This world, first glimpsed from the ships of Columbus, Vespucci and Cabral, scarcely merits the title 'New' – quite the reverse, in fact. It is as old as the Old World, but it is more obviously marked with the stigma of decline. Contrary to Montaigne's description of it as an 'infant world',[3] it is decrepit, in the last stages of a premature but unmistakable senility.

The question immediately arises: 'Was Nature so impotent that she never completed her handiwork?' Surely not: the admirable fabric must have been undone over many centuries and generations.[4] This is a proof *per absurdum*, which assumes the reality of Nature's fecund power; the counter-argument (adduced by the 'philosopher La Douceur' in a highly amusing pamphlet) is obvious enough: 'to prove that a thing has degenerated, one must begin by proving that it previously excelled in its natural quality'.[5] This is something which de Pauw, who had no access to any previous information on the subject, would have been quite incapable of doing.

While the *a priori* argument appears very shaky, it certainly abounds in *a posteriori* illustrations: the endless deserts and the barren earth; the proliferation of harmful animals which alone can thrive in those desolate regions; the absence of edible quadrupeds, and, consequently, the extraordinary ignorance of pastoral farming; the 'excessive laziness' of the natives[6] and the rudimentary state of their agriculture; their small size and feeble physique; the inability of their

minds to rise to any higher conception, etc. What a merciless indict-
ment! It spares no area of Nature, no sphere of human activity. Never
had denigration been taken to such lengths.

The portrayal was bound to raise hackles. De Pauw was in fact
aiming principally at the apologetic writings of the missionaries, chief
among them the 'Edifying Letters' written by Jesuits who praised the
nature of the New World in order to increase the value of the spiritual conquests which they had achieved in those distant regions. The
intransigent de Pauw gives not the slightest credence to that literature, which, as he put it, took the reader to 'the heart of all absurdities
and prodigies'. He adds a perfidious swipe at the Jesuit worthies: 'It is
astonishing that so many falsehoods must be set down to the account
of those who, as they claim, have preached the truth at the uttermost
ends of the earth.'[7]

But the members of the Company of Jesus were not the only ones
to be annoyed by so unremittingly sombre a picture. The naturalist
Buffon, though agreeing about the inferiority of the new continent,
refused to equate the creatures of nature and those of human society.
The oneness of the human race, compromised by the exaggeration of
the *Recherches philosophiques*, must be safeguarded. Natural determinism set limits which it was imprudent to ignore. De Pauw's
systematized vision had the paradoxical effect of goading Buffon into
a contrary reaction.[8] The American who emerged from the ensuing
dispute had regained his physical strength, if not the inclination to
use it. He remained indolent, contemplative, even lazy; but – in
Buffon's eyes at least – he was no longer degenerate.

De Pauw, though he invites caricature, is deserving of close study.
He combines two seemingly incompatible, but actually closely inter-
linked attitudes. On the one side, he expresses, in the crudest imaginable terms, the contempt of a progressive man for 'primitives'
incapable of overcoming their perverted nature, being, indeed, more
inclined to submit pleasurably to it; on the other, a loathing for wars
of conquest disguised under bogus humanitarian pretexts.[9] His
'Preliminary Discourse' gives the measure of this ambiguity. With the
eloquence of an encyclopaedist, de Pauw excoriates the atrocities of
the *conquista*. The apparently euphoric opening sentence, 'There is no
event more memorable among men than the Discovery of America',
is immediately contradicted by the sequel, which sets the tone for the
book: 'the greatest misfortune ever suffered by mankind'. That misfortune affected more than the 'few million Savages' who were exterminated at the outset: it also brought torment upon the 'dread
vanquishers', who were 'smitten with an epidemic disease which,
attacking both the mainsprings of life and the sources of generation,

soon became the most dreadful scourge of the habitable world'.[10]

De Pauw's assessment of the cost of the conquest – of which both sides must pay a part – springs from an extremely traditional way of thinking. From the sixteenth century onwards, most of the apologists for Spain, including Gomara, Oviedo and Thevet, had balanced the accounts in a rather peculiar way: on the one side were the treasures brought back from the New Indies; on the other, the millions of souls won for God. The result was a deficit, which, contrary to all historical reasoning, favoured America, not Europe. De Pauw, whose aims are wholly secular and 'scientific', performs the same kind of calculation. When he balances the genocide of the Indians against the spread of syphilis in Europe, he takes little account of the extermination of whole peoples who, in the course of a few decades, were swept from the face of the earth. He greatly overdramatizes the tragedy of venereal disease, whose demographic consequences were not even remotely comparable to those of the deportation of the Indians of Central America, of their ruthless exploitation in the mines and the Caribbean pearl-fisheries and of their reduction to a state of general drudgery. His outlook is overtly and exclusively European. When he speaks of 'man' he means only those whose 'humanity' is fully developed, meaning his compatriots of modern Europe, men of the Renaissance and the Enlightenment. It is in this restrictive sense that he writes: 'As a quintessence of misfortune, Man, already sinking beneath the burden of his existence, found the seeds of death in the arms of pleasure, and at the heart of ecstasy; he believed himself irretrievably lost; he thought that wrathful nature had sworn his ruin.'[11]

The high-flown oratory, intended to chill the reader's blood, rings rather hollow, and the eloquence seems out of place, to say the least, in view of the fact that the Europeans had already ruined other races or planned to exterminate them, not because of some hypothetical plan formed by 'wrathful nature' – a strange metaphysical ghost to haunt the mind of this unrepentant rationalist – but for the joint benefit of a warrior caste, a merchant class and a punctilious colonial administration.

De Pauw, carried away by his own eloquence, suddenly delivers himself of an apocalyptic prediction:

> The Annals of the universe do not, and perhaps never will, present any similar era. If such disasters could happen more than once, the Earth would be a dangerous place, where our Species, succumbing to its ills, or weary of fighting its own destiny, would suffer total extinction, and would abandon this Planet to happier or less persecuted beings.[12]

De Pauw does not offer the prospect of a better life in another world: he foresees the death of humanity in a desacralized universe, or its collective emigration to a kinder planet. It was fortunate that the new dogma of the plurality of worlds, which since Fontenelle had been generally accepted, was available to take over from discredited religious thinking.

Nonetheless, this emotional analysis of the discovery of the New World culminates in an outright condemnation of colonial endeavour. If, since the dawn of the modern age, all Europeans had remained at home instead of rashly going to sea, they would have saved humanity from partial destruction and spared themselves serious discomfort. The lessons of history do not seem to have served any useful purpose, however: 'Nonetheless, scheming Politicians never cease, by their seditious writings, to encourage Princes to invade the Austral Lands.' The spectre of victorious expansion has returned, with its train of havoc, 'its torrents of blood', and, worse still, its probable backlash – epidemics. The happiness of Europe depends on disavowing the voyages of Kerguelen, Bougainville and their ilk.

De Pauw fails to see the contradiction between his dream of progress and the withdrawal of an (as he sees it) all-conquering Europe. 'Now if equity fails, prudence will tell him to leave the Austral Lands in peace, and better cultivate his own.'[13] Here we recognize a geopoliticized version of Candide's famous 'We must cultivate our own garden.' Is this world-weary moral compatible with the spread of the Enlightenment and a general increase in human welfare? Can it really be extended to the whole planet? Nothing is less certain.

This author recognizes geographical limits and recoils from the abuse of European 'superiority'; but he is no philanthropist. Worse was to come later: writers from Gobineau to Raymond Cartier were to couple the dogma of inequality with conscious egoism and engender a refusal to share wealth equitably among peoples. Perhaps in de Pauw we have the germ of a sort of right-wing anti-colonialism. In that sense, he could be seen as a precursor, though a stumbling one who makes up for the shortcomings of his analytical tools by an eloquence of unusual intensity.

Meanwhile, the fundamental inequality of the two worlds seems to de Pauw to supply a brilliantly simple explanation of the clash of 1492: 'What Physician of Antiquity would ever have suspected that the same Planet had two such different Hemispheres, one of which had been vanquished, subjugated and as it were swallowed up by the other as soon as it became known, after a lapse of centuries lost in the night and abyss of time?'[14] This upheaval 'was wholly instantaneous, because, through an almost incredible destiny, there was no equality between the attack and the defence'. It is this initial insight – startling, almost revolutionary – which produces the image of an America which for all its diversity, is degenerate, even to the last and least of its creatures.[15]

The metaphor of swallowing up immediately hints that cannibalism had a hand in this sudden catastrophe. The Old World devoured the New – all the more easily because the latter was already devouring itself. Among the perceptible tokens of degeneracy in that other half of the globe – circumcision and infibulation, poisoned arrows and all the variegated manifestations of the 'brutish mind of the American'[16] – de Pauw has no trouble in identifying universal anthropophagy. There were Cannibals everywhere: 'they were to be found from North to South, the length and breadth of the new Continent'.[17] This observation was to some extent to be confirmed by modern anthropology. But it is hard to agree with de Pauw that it 'proves' that the first inhabitants of America were less refined, and therefore on a lower level of humanity.

De Pauw has no trouble finding reasons for this deplorable state of affairs: a whole string of them, in fact. Doubtless, one must allow for some exaggeration on the part of the Spanish chroniclers, who were anxious to endow their defeated adversaries with all possible vices, the better to justify their own crimes. The ancient Romans did the same to Carthage, accusing Hannibal of feeding his soldiers on human flesh.[18] The fable of 'instinctive Anthropophagi', who had more canine teeth than other men, must also be rejected.[19] In spite of its naive exaggeration, the materialist explanation is the most probable. Violent hatred and the thirst for vengeance, suggested by Pigafetta (among others),[20] can explain only isolated cases; they certainly cannot account for the inveterate practice of populous nations. That would be like inferring from the murders of Concini and de Wit – the former's liver and lungs were eaten, and the latter's heart – that the French and Dutch were habitually anthropophagous.[21] De Pauw sees those executions as no more than 'the rage of a few obscure and raving villains', but happily without influence on the rest of society. He prefers not to acknowledge that seventeenth-century Europe, which saw the triumph of civilized attitudes, undoubtedly preserved traces of archaic ritual.

Thus, the real causes of American cannibalism are materialistic. It sprang from 'the harsh necessity of savage life' and then became a habit. 'Custom, which makes all abuses tolerable, must have continued to act after the necessity ceased to exist.'[22] De Pauw's variant on the determinist hypothesis is more nuanced, but also more systematic, than his predecessors'. His subtle analysis covers all the facts.

There is no apparent exception which is not eventually fitted into the initial framework.

Famine causes only the odd, isolated case of anthropophagy. To produce a whole cannibal society, there must be laws and a received religion, and the 'fearful and arbitrary right of conquest' must be acknowledged. On the other hand, these tyrannical customs cannot be maintained unless they are occasionally replaced, and apparently justified, by environmental constraints. The theoretical construct is backed by a rigorous criticism of the sources. De Pauw does not believe in spontaneous but durable habits of allelophagy, as described by pseudo-Vespucci and his imitators. Cannibalism, while omnipresent in America, has not had the devastating consequences which are sometimes imagined. Carib voracity seems to have been reduced to manageable dimensions; in twelve years they apparently ate six thousand islanders from Puerto Rico, but this was because they regarded them as their arch-enemies and treated them according to the laws of war. De Pauw also pours scorn on another legend, that children intended for eating were castrated 'so as to tenderise them'. Emasculation probably was practised in the West Indies before the coming of the first Europeans, but it was inspired, as in the Old World, 'by the sombre and unquiet spirit of jealousy' rather than by 'the alleged refinement of the Anthropophagi'.[23] On the island of Puna, as at Constantinople, eunuchs were used to guard the despot's harem, not to grace his table.

Similarly, it seems odd when we find a people who are highly civilized and yet practise anthropophagy. The Mexicans are no exception to this. Their human sacrifices satisfy a hunger more spiritual than carnal. The barbaric custom of offering a victim's bleeding limbs 'to the most ardent devotees' is a kind of 'legal expiation', 'dictated by the most extreme fanaticism', and not a means of survival.[24] As for the Aztecs, de Pauw seems to think that they sacrificed no more than one victim per year: so which of the two peoples was barbaric, the Aztecs or the Spanish Catholics, those intolerant and bloodthirsty conquerors who deliberately exaggerated the cruelty of their victims? At this point de Pauw, carried away by his criticism of his sources and his hatred for Jesuits and all missionary orders in general, seems to be falling into what we now call 'denial', but what he himself calls 'an almost insane historical pyrrhonism'.[25] Well aware himself of the danger, he denies that he has comprehensively rejected 'all that can be read in the most truthful, or least suspect Accounts of the Atacacapas of Louisiana, the old Caribs of the Islands, the modern Caribs of Maranhâo, the Tapuiges of Brazil, the Cristinals, the Pampas, the Peguanchez and the Moxes'. To show his distance from historical revisionism, he returns to the origins of anthropophagy and the gradual processes by which the first men were induced to eat one another: 'What could be more natural than a Savage, driven mad by hunger, should eat his prisoner, his enemy? The idea that Savage has, that his prisoner belongs to him, seems well founded: that he may eat him, if he likes such meat, is a logical consequence which he draws from his principles.'

We should not conclude from this that there are nations which feed exclusively on human flesh, 'an absurd supposition if ever there was one'.[26] Similarly, de Pauw undertakes to refute the legends of man-breeding stud farms and markets selling human flesh, which could, according to credulous historians (promptly echoed by the authors of the *Encyclopédie*) be seen among the ferocious Jagas of Africa.[27] Sade, a careless reader of the *Recherches philosophiques*, was to seize on this characteristic to nourish his tale *Aline et Valcour*. In the pivotal episode of the 'History of Sainville and Léonore' we read about the disgusting butchers' stalls of the Jagas and the anthropophagous kingdom of Grand-Macoro, their neighbour, a 'powerful and magnificent' monarch who 'serves human flesh on his own table and also those of his courtesans' – both fables which de Pauw had done his best to debunk in favour of comparative anthropology and simple common sense.[28]

De Pauw's approach to cannibalism is now sufficiently clear. His first impulse is to rationalize: the first cause was purely material, but it was soon overlaid with superstition and habit. Second, he reduces its scope and destructiveness, which was exaggerated in the crazed and calculating imagination of conquistadors and priests. In any case, American cannibalism has now ceased to be more than an unpleasant memory: 'Europeans have totally exterminated most of the American Peoples who treated their captives most inhumanely; and they have accustomed some others to be less ferocious, less excessive in their resentment.' Hence, 'today there are fewer Anthropophagi in the New World than many people imagine'.[29] Finally, cannibalism, far from being universal, is found only among the most indigent peoples. Its existence points up the contrast between men who have been left to their own brutish ways and those who have been led by the Enlightenment towards the highest degree of civilization. It is theoretically possible to pass from the first group to the second (or vice versa – progress or regression), but it should be borne in mind that de Pauw has carefully blocked the channels of communication between the two worlds and the two humanities. This removes the threat of contamination. Instead of being part of the underlying human condition, the temptations of cannibalism are and remain a matter for the Americans alone.

One revealing anecdote shows the horror that continues to lurk in a discourse that otherwise seems under perfect control. Francis Bacon, in his *Sylva sylvarum*, had advanced a most ingenious hypothesis: that syphilis, the 'Naples evil', had originally been caused by anthropophagy on the part of the French besiegers of the city, to whom certain shameless merchants had sold barrels of human flesh under the pretence that it was tuna. To corroborate this event, which had allegedly taken place during the Italian wars in the time of Charles VIII of France, Bacon compares the West Indian Cannibals who eat human flesh and are subject to venereal disease. Their most dangerous poison is in fact a mixture of human blood and fat, or flesh.[30] In the *Recherches philosophiques*, de Pauw devotes the final part of the section 'Of Anthropophagi' to refuting 'this paradox or hypothesis' to which Bacon, the Lord Chancellor of England, had unwisely lent the weight of his authority.[31]

Yet de Pauw, while contradicting the facts adduced by the learned Chancellor, does not contradict his thesis. It is generally accepted that there is a profound analogy between alimentary and sexual taboos. Moreover, by creating a genealogical link between 'the horrible custom of eating men' and venereal disease, Bacon had unconsciously emphasized the oneness of the fear which both inspired. Because 'alimentary incest' seems to produce the same effects as unbridled fornication, the contact with another person's flesh should be avoided in both its guises, the culinary and the sexual. It is noticeable that Bacon's arguments are not condemned – and in the same breath, refuted – until the very end, as if to betray, *in extremis*, what de Pauw's discourse had left unsaid. America is indeed the location of the Other, the unspeakable, the taboo. It is better to leave it to its original self-government.

Having thus placed the lurking terror at a distance, de Pauw is free to dilate, without anxiety, on the variety of tastes in human flesh. Some like it raw, others cooked. The Iroquois prefer the neck; the Caribs, the flesh of the thigh and calf. The latter, just like the mastiffs which were used by the Spanish to hunt down the Indians, baulked at eating women.[32] The same observation is made by Prévost in *Cleveland*,[33] and in the missionary letters. In connection with the holy missionary martyrs, the question was whether their flesh was or was not tastier with added salt. Voltaire had established that savages enjoyed Jesuits for dinner. Was this 'sincere desire'[34] to be attributed to the particular tastiness of Jesuits, or was it, as de Pauw believes, due to 'graver and more serious reasons'?

Following this line of thought, de Pauw outlines his own typology of American cannibalism. Intuitively anticipating the fundamental

distinction which modern anthropologists make between endo-cannibalism and exo-cannibalism, he distinguishes three kinds of anthropophagi: those who kill their captives and eat them; those who
'touched only the appendages of the human body', eating the umbili-
cal cords and cauls of newborn babies or mixing blood into the sacred
bread; and those who ate relatives who had died of wounds or sickness.[35] De Pauw cannot refrain from deploring the aberrations of the
human mind, in an expressive aside which prefigures the more stirring passages of Diderot and his continual digressions in the *Histoire
des deux Indes*: 'Since men are capable of imagining all things and of
abandoning themselves blindly to the extravagance of their ideas,
their actions are all too often dictated by crazy impulses and momentary caprice, to the despair of those who seek to account for them, or
to unveil their causes.'[36]

Shaking off his momentary discouragement, de Pauw doggedly
continues with his task: all the research, verification and classification
has finally revealed the intellectual challenge originally posed by the
existence – disputed at the time – of anthropophagi. It has not been
well attested, categorized and mapped. This makes the enigma less
scandalous. De Pauw has accomplished the task he set himself at the
beginning of the chapter: 'we must keep to the facts, set them out as
they are, or as we believe them to be, without hatred, or prejudice, or
respect, except for truth'.[37]

Sade's African fantasy

Sade places his novels under that same sign of truth: if they give a
good deal of space to anthropophagy (and to so many other base and
shameful activities), it is because he claims to be probing the truth of
the human heart.[38] From the freedom with which Sade adapts ethnographic data to the needs of his fantasies, he almost seems to be deliberately setting out to contradict de Pauw. In the fantastic Africa of
Aline et Valcour he describes the 'public butcheries' in which monkey
and human flesh are eaten indiscriminately.[39] As we have seen, de
Pauw had already dismissed, and convincingly disproved, that particular legend.

Despite such minor betrayals, Sade's analysis of cannibalism is
drawn from de Pauw. Both loudly proclaim their allegiance to the
'philosophical' spirit. In de Pauw can be found the triumph of materialist explanation, with the denunciation of superstition as a corollary;
Sade broadly follows this. Moreover, the horror inspired by cannibalism had to be removed before Sade could develop the cruel refine-

ments which mark his work, from *The Hundred and Twenty Days* to *The Story of Juliette*. In a note in *Aline et Valcour*, Sade expressly acknowledges his debt to the author of *Recherches philosophiques*, whose name he abbreviates as 'Paw'. But he regrets that the latter did not find a better explanation of the 'first cause' of anthropophagy: 'when one has read and re-read this passage, one finds one is no wiser than before'.[40]

Sade loves cataloguing even more than de Pauw does: witness the learned typology of simple, double, criminal and murderous passions set forth by the bloody drama of *The Hundred and Twenty Days*. The same passion for nomenclature, the same obsession with the number four, feature in the note on the origins of anthropophagy in *Aline et Valcour*. Outdoing his predecessor in taxonomic exactness, Sade distinguishes four possible causes. First, superstition or religion, 'which are almost always synonymous'. Second, disordered appetite, 'having the same cause as hysterical vapours in women'. Third, and more traditional, vengeance. The fourth cause is twofold: 'refined debauchery or need'. Thus, natural constraint and (more or less ritualized) vengeance, the two main explanatory models for cannibalism before Sade, are supplemented by the refinement of debauchery and an anarchic drive, which he defines as a sort of alimentary hysteria. The characters in his novels are precise and complete illustrations of this kind of behaviour. As well as the many perversions enumerated in *The Hundred and Twenty Days*, and others scattered through the rest of his work, one need only think of the more fully rounded characters of the Comte de Gernande and the ogre, Minski. The first, in *The New Justine*, kills his wife, sucks her blood and serves up what is left of her at a dinner party.[41] Minski is the Apennine giant in *The Story of Juliette*, whom the heroine meets on the volcano of Pietra-Mala, as if he had just risen from the infernal regions. We soon learn that he lives entirely on human flesh, and, for the purpose, keeps a breeding population of both sexes in the innumerable rooms of his castle, drawing on them for the alternate pleasures of the couch and the table.[42]

It remains to be seen which of these four – or rather five – causes came first, giving the force of law to a custom which Sade, speaking through the debauchee Sarmiento, sees not as a form of moral corruption but as a practice in conformity with Nature: 'It is just as easy to eat a man as an ox.'[43] Sade leaves the question open and ironically invites learned academies to discuss it. It would be a worthy subject of debate, needing only a Rousseau to develop it.

Let us look in more detail at *Aline et Valcour*, an 'esoteric' work published in 1795, but developed and retouched by Sade during the

upheavals of the Revolution. One of the oddities of this 'philosophical novel' is that it builds cannibalism into an economic and political
system. As an institution, it is attached to a geographical configuration which is a variation on a recognizable archetype. For Diderot it
was an island; for de Pauw an inferior continent; for Sade, the spatial
configuration of anthropophagy is an enclosed kingdom at the heart
of a vast continent, the most barbarous and mysterious of all continents: Africa, which since Pliny and antiquity had been considered
'fertile in monsters'. This adage had been frequently cited since the
Renaissance: 'from Africa there is always something new'. Such is the
bloody and debauched anti-utopia of Butua, with its monstrous customs and crueller laws. In obedience to geographical probability,
Sade situates it near to the ferocious Jagas, between Benguela (the
port of Angola, founded by the Portuguese) to the west and Kaffir
country to the south.[44] In the general schema of the book, and especially in the 'History of Sainville and Léonore', a long picaresque
excursus recounted episodically through a series of letters, Butua is
the pendant of an idealized island called Tamoe, one of the Society
Islands recently explored by Cook, and distinguished by the common
happiness and equality of its citizens. In this island city, which is a
compendium of all the clichés of the utopian literature popular at that
time, all meat-based foods are prohibited. Butua, by contrast,
expresses its despotism in the goriest sexual and alimentary terms.[45]

Butua, like the legendary Jagas before it, is a sort of condensation
of the fear and excess which the Enlightenment philosophers projected on to the Other in their immense labour of rationalization.
Sade's description may merely be building on his contemporaries'
most gloomy and terrifying attempts at ethnographical reconstruction. But it is not all that much wilder than the description given
under the heading 'Jagas, Giagas, or Giagues' in d'Alembert's and
Diderot's *Encyclopédie*. Sade's fictional Butua is in fact largely
derived from that 'ferocious, rude and anthropophagous nation',
which exhibits 'the strange phenomenon of the most atrocious inhumanity, authorised and even ordained by religion and the laws'.

The ruler of this realm, unvisited by caravans and unknown to
European travellers, is the prince Ben Mácoro, a despot, a sodomite
and a cannibal. Every month, all the provinces of his empire render
him a tribute of women. The twelve thousand captive women in his
harem are divided into four classes – just as there are four causes of
cannibalism, four months in the long winter of Silling and four cate-
gories of passions inventoried and practised in *The Hundred and
Twenty Days*. The strongest of these women belong to Mácoro's personal guard: they are redoubtable archers, and totally naked. The

second class comprises the palace servants and gardeners. The third, made up of young virgins aged between sixteen and twenty, supplies the human sacrifices required by a bloodthirsty idol. Those in the fourth class, aged between childhood and puberty, provide the despot with his minor amusements.[46]

Generally speaking, the women of this country live in the vilest humiliation. 'Fulfilling the same functions as our beasts of burden in Europe',[47] they are treated with less consideration even than those. Their husbands whip them on to the fields, where they work naked, harnessed to the plough and burdened with children hanging at their breasts. As a result, the population is diminishing, and is already 'nearly annihilated'. The kingdom is, in the most literal sense, devouring itself. Butua endures a living death inflicted by the same kind of murderous self-consumption as is sometimes practised by the villainous inhabitants of the castle of Silling in *The Hundred and Twenty Days* upon their victims.[48]

The anti-utopia is inexorably swallowing itself. Not only do the inhabitants eat enemies taken in war – preferably young warriors – they inflict the same fate on all subjects who disobey their tyrannical and arbitrary laws,[49] on mere beggars and on 'all those incapable of earning a living'.[50] And corpses are occasionally eaten, provided that their flesh is in good condition.[51] If not, they are simply left under a tree. Sade evidently has a sovereign contempt for the fine distinctions noted by de Pauw, Buffon and the like. To present 'the cruellest and most dissolute people on earth' he readily merges the most abominable transgressions and freely intermingles endo-cannibalism and exo-cannibalism, omophagy and necrophagy, representing everyday life in Butua as a chronicle of uninterrupted debauchery.

He explains that originally these horrid customs were motivated by natural constraint. Butua's isolation in the heart of southern Africa required severe measures to control the population, as happened on the Isle of Lancers beloved of Bougainville and Diderot, or in Malthus's American archipelago. But this rigorous policy soon turned into 'a horror of propagating their own kind'. The original necessity quickly gave rise to the arbitrariness of custom, following a mechanism frequently described by Enlightenment philosophers.

'A population which had become too large was forced to authorise those ancient customs,' remarks the Portuguese traveller Sarmiento, 'a people which had become too numerous, so confined that it could not find more space or form colonies, must inevitably destroy itself.' This 'cannibalized European', as Sade calls him,[52] is an accomplice of the cannibalistic despot, serves him and closely imitates his most reprehensible appetites, but he also serves the interests of his former

compatriots. If Ben Mácoro and his subjects abandon their over-zeal-
ous Malthusianism – Malthusianism by debauchery? – they will,
Sarmiento asserts, be able to benefit from a substantial excess of population. The realm 'would grow rich from its surplus subjects, if it
would only communicate with us'.[53] This is a scarcely veiled way of
saying that the black slave trade would give the Butuan autarchy,
now 'very near its ruin',[54] a much-needed economic boost. The slave
trade would restore the vigour which is simply being wasted by self-
consumption.

Nonetheless, Butua is doomed: if it continues with its murderous
orgies it will perish within the century. Already the population numbers no more than thirty thousand souls, in an area as large as
Portugal. The insularity of this anti-utopia is made still worse by
what Sade calls 'isolism'.[55] The men of Butua behave as despots in
their own families, indiscriminately debauching their wives, daughters, sons and slaves: they are true Sadean libertines, interested only in
their own pleasures. In their innumerable sexual encounters with the
most diverse objects they remain obstinately alone, rejecting all
notions of reciprocity. The crazed autarchy of Sade's negro utopia
thus returns us to the island: sexual 'isolism'; the isolation of the
prince's harem, which receives, month by month, a flood of women
from the principal provinces, to be swiftly consumed in a succession
of orgies, hard labour and sacrifice; the solipsism of a people ignorant
of everything beyond their own frontiers, who have forgotten the
past and 'never foresee the future'.[56] The Sadean anti-utopia declines
the principle of insularity in every possible case.

As with the Isle of Lancers in Diderot's *Supplément au voyage de
Bougainville*, it is the very nature of the place which originally condemned its isolated population to anthropophagy. But here the regu-
lating principle runs mad, completely out of control. The process
accelerates to a dizzying speed: the appetite of the social body con-
sumes the entire organism. Indeed it seems that 'this unhappy people,
eager for its own end, eagerly imagines everything likely to hasten
it'.[57] So the island becomes narrower. Its frontiers come closer
together as its population diminishes. The geographical container is
swallowed up as its social content swallows itself. Soon the cannibalistic anti-utopia will be a no-place, a white space on the map of Africa
– which is as rich in deserts as in monsters.

Sarmiento has still more to say about Butua. The pride of its pre-
tentions is in inverse proportion to its present poverty. This people
without a future calls itself 'the oldest on earth'. 'Once,' he declares,
'it ruled the whole continent, and especially the sea; but now it knows
nothing of it.' 'Its position amidst other lands, its perpetual disputes

with the peoples of East and West, which prevent it from extending thither, will probably long continue to prevent it from knowing its nearest coasts.'[58] The island travels further and further from the sea, until it loses sight of it altogether.

Butua's self-devouring is the clearest rendition of a phenomenon which can be observed in other Sadean fictions. The location normally represented on a smaller scale is here enlarged to a continent, albeit an enclosed one. The same location is found, for example, in the castle of Silling, cut off from the rest of the world by night and snow, and in which, in the course of one cruel winter of interminable agonies, two-thirds of the original occupants perish. According to the meticulous calculations of the narrator of *The Hundred and Twenty Days*, of the original forty-six 'subjects' 'thirty were immolated and sixteen returned to Paris'.[59] Minski's isolated castle, set in a mountain lake, surrounded by forests and by three concentric walls, is a yet more fearful abyss. To reach it one must travel in a 'black bark like a Venetian gondola', with a giant steersman – very like crossing the Styx with Charon.[60] One enters through dungeons full of skeletons, which echo with the screams of the tormented. It is indeed a Hell which is visited by the fearless Juliette and her companions in debauchery. There, hundreds of captives of both sexes await them, their ages ranging from infancy to adulthood, all doomed to be tortured, humiliated and finally eaten, ending up in the giant's kitchen, or in the maw of the wild beasts he keeps in his menagerie.

Autarchy is not really the right word for this implosion of energy; it was inadequate even when applied to Rabelais's Abbey of Thélème, which, enriched by opulent tribute from every corner of the world, produced nothing in return save pleasure and musical harmony.[61] In fact, the Sadean castle of torment, in its various representations (debauched convent, African utopia), is separated from the outside world in so far as it is the point of no return. It receives a continual convergent influx of victims swept up from the surrounding countryside, or even from 'all the large cities of the world' where the frightful Minski keeps his agents.[62] It is a bottomless pit, with seemingly direct access to Hell, in which the whole of humanity might be lost, in all its fragility and grace. It is like a volcano (to Sade, volcanoes symbolize the criminal disorder of nature); but this volcano is inside out: it does not spew out, but swallows up, endlessly. In the same way, the crater of Vesuvius 'swallows' the beauteous Olympe Borghese: Juliette and Lady Clairwil, having stripped her of her clothes and money, throw her down it out of idle curiosity.[63] For 'several minutes' the two criminals can hear the echoes of their friend's body bouncing from wall to wall, rent by the sharp corners of the pumice-stone and gradually being 'disorganized' as she returns into the abyss. The mouth of the volcano, which in its most disordered eruptions devours itself, and in the present case devours an insatiable libertine, is an appropriate metaphor for the autophagous regime which rules the Sadean universe. Or, to use an anachronistic image (which Sade might not find unacceptable), the Sadean world, with its suggested correspondences between individual and cosmos, has the self-destructive voracity of a 'black hole', a stellar mass which sucks up swarms of molecules from disintegrating matter as it inexorably swallows itself.

As in all Sadean fortresses – dark and devouring mouths – the anti-utopia of Butua is a no-place, but in a very specific sense. It will not cease to exist in the sense that it will disappear from human memory. The place of its disappearance is stamped with an enduring terror. Horror impregnates the very sand on which the Jagas have sacrificed and eaten their captives. Honest Sainville, who has witnessed the scene, refuses even to pull up roots from that sand to feed himself.[64]

The Sadean volcano, though at first sight it looks like a prolongation of Bougainville's and Diderot's islands – which both produced and circumscribed the fact of cannibalism – is in fact quite different. Its living, moving lips represent no rigid closure. It is on the slopes of Vesuvius that Juliette and her accomplice recline to pleasure themselves after the vertiginous fall of their victim. Sade's intention is not to prevent contagion; on the contrary, he advocates transgression, the passing of boundaries: even at the risk of one's own life, one should yield to all the caprices and disorders of nature. The dizzying allure of the abyss is the obverse of that readiness.

This takes Sade still further from de Pauw. His preferred continent, cruel Africa, bears only a limited resemblance to the degenerate America of the learned and philosophical *Recherches philosophiques*. Sade does not see a repellent, but a salutary disjunction between the cannibal country and the reassuring norm of civilized human beings – meaning the late eighteenth-century Europeans. For Sade, the cannibal is the naked truth, the substrate of the European finally laid bare. He would echo the words of the giant Minski, returning from the voyage to Africa which introduced him to anthropophagy:

> In a word, it was there I observed man in his constitutionally vicious, instinctively cruel, and studiously ferocious form, and as such he pleased me, as such he seemed to me in closer harmony with Nature, and I preferred these characteristics to the simple crudeness of the American, to the knavery of the European, to the cynical depravity of the oriental.[65]

Obviously, this dark primitivism contains an element of contemporary prejudice and deliberate intention to shock. But beyond its ethnocentric caricature of the four continents it reveals the most terrifying thing of all, the 'inhumanity which is concealed deep in all of us',[66] which reaches its highest pitch in Sade's ogreish variant of cannibalism.

13

Cannibalism and Colonialism: Jules Verne

~:~

Cannibalism told to the children

We have seen that it was Cardano's determinist theory of the origins of cannibalism which finally carried the day; and it persisted into the modern era, Diderot's primitivist nostalgia notwithstanding. The latter, as an admirer of Montaigne, may have been justly worried by the fearful consequences of cannibalism caused by necessity; but he could no longer accept the 'honour' hypothesis, which was by then decidedly out of date, ruined by the decline of the aristrocratic values with which it had originally been associated. Voltaire, too, broadly accepted the determinist theory. He preserved the taste of Montaigne's elegance and piquant paradox, but the cynical conclusion to the Oreillons episode in *Candide* puts a definite end to two centuries of belief in Brazilian cannibal magnanimity. Finally, de Pauw and Sade systematized the materialist explanation, forever blocking the access to higher levels of transcendence and aesthetic or moral values.

Montaigne faded gradually out of the picture[1] – a corollary of the triumph of the natural-determinist model of cannibalism. Plainly, it is the most intolerant hypothesis which is also the most 'modern'. It is also the most totalitarian, in that it purports to explain not only the table manners of native tribes, but also their entire system of cultural practices and beliefs. To gauge the distance which had been covered since the time of Montaigne and Cardano one need only re-read the appropriate chapter from an illustrated work for younger readers 'in which cannibalism is treated theoretically'.[2] At the beginning of Part III of Jules Verne's *Les Enfants du Capitaine Grant* (1868), which takes the reader to New Zealand (then inhabited chiefly by cannibalistic Maoris), Paganel the geographer pronounces a learned discourse on the causes of cannibalism. The narrator then proceeds to endorse Paganel's hypothesis: 'the savages began by eating human flesh to satisfy their insatiable appetites; then the priests regulated and blessed their monstrous customs. The meal became a ceremony. That's all.'[3]

First came obedience to natural necessity: 'there are few quadrupeds, or even birds, in this inhospitable country'; then, overdetermination by abominable religious practices. (Much later, the same sequence was to appear in Brecht's *Threepenny Opera: 'Zuerst kommt das Fressen, und dann kommt die Moral'*.)

Such is the lesson, then, as presented for the youthful reader. And there is more to come. The theoretical preface, which reduces Maori culture to the filling of Maori bellies, is swiftly followed by a practical demonstration. The adventurers are captured by a tribe which has revolted against its English overlords, and are given a front seat at the gory spectacle of a Maori chieftain's funeral: an object lesson to reinforce the teacher's masterly presentation. The next scene, which shows slaves being slaughtered and literally torn to pieces by a howling mob of savages, is far from echoing the remote and dispassionate tone of sixteenth-century ethnographic description. Where Thevet or Léry would have confined themselves to meticulous observation, and Montaigne to elegant ellipsis, Verne produces a clumsy pastiche of epic style.[4] Hyperboles in dubious taste ('the ghastly mob swarmed under a rain of blood'), tired metaphors ('fierce tigers on their prey', 'lion-tamers', 'wild beasts') and the showers of overstrained epithets intended to chill the juvenile blood: all are well-worn literary techniques exposing the fact that the scene is pure fantasy. The libidinal content is so obvious that it is quite impossible to give any credence to this depiction of a bestial orgy, despite the attempt at realism implied by the 'scientific' prelude described above. There is one conclusive phrase which finally betrays the shameful desire projected by the westerner on to the rent and rending body of the native: 'Glenarvan and his companions, gasping with horror, tried to conceal this abominable sight from the eyes of the two poor ladies.'[5]

This is no surprise to the reader: the phantasmagoria is seen – as a denizen of dreams or nightmares is seen in a picture by Fuseli – through European eyes, as an obscene spectacle which must at all costs be veiled from the female gaze. Only European man, meaning an adult male at the peak of mental and bodily vigour, can and must look – albeit with a brief, but salutary gasp of horror. The sight will confirm him in his belief that he has exclusive rights to membership of the human race.

This same smug condescension is perceptible in an earlier book, *Five Weeks in a Balloon*, the first of Verne's 'Extraordinary Journeys', published in 1863. It is set on the vast stage of southern and equatorial Africa, from Zanzibar to Senegal. As they float above a continent which is still inaccessible, and in part 'forbidden', the curiosity of three intrepid English travellers is fed on boundless and unshadowed space, spread out like a map beneath them. But that is not all: they are also able to measure both the distance and the dizzying hierarchy of difference which separate the men in the balloon – masters of reason and science, observing by means of the latest scientific instruments – from the brutish and superstitious earthbound natives crawling at their feet, who invariably mistake them for gods, and either worship them or do their best to devour them, in order to appropriate their magical powers.

The most revealing scene of all takes place above the country of the appropriately named Nyam-Nyams, scattered tribes of brutal natives whose double name mimics the noise of mastication.[6] The balloon flies over two tribes at war with each other, who, not content with ferocious fighting during which they wallow in the blood and guts of the wounded, also bite their adversaries and cut off their quivering limbs for immediate consumption. The new Icaruses are torn between excitement and revulsion: one of them, the hunter Dick Kennedy, cannot refrain from putting a bullet through the head of one of the chiefs, a kind of black Hercules, who, wielding axe and assegai, is cleaving a bloody path through the enemy ranks, dismembering and eating his victims even before they are properly despatched.[7]

The nausea and disgust, which are amply expressed in the exclamations and interjections of the three observers, betray a profound contempt for the 'crazed mob' which is running in useless pursuit of the balloon. This violent rejection, symbolized by the safe and easy murder of the most powerful Negro, cannot quite mask a lurking fear: the perception (hastily glossed over) that there is a hidden affinity between this unspeakable savagery and the uniformed warfare of modern nations. 'If great generals could thus look down on the theatre of their exploits,' exclaims the good Dr Fergusson, 'they would perhaps end by losing their taste for bloodshed and conquest.'

While condemning his companion's murderous impulse, the doctor may, by implication, be betraying a secret ambition: does the obvious superiority conferred on them by their aerostatics and their firearms justify them in bringing down the vengeance of heaven upon the anthropophagous heads? Are they supposed to 'play the part of Providence'? This momentary doubt must be taken to imply that the speaker is convinced of the higher purpose of their mission.[8]

At this early stage of Vernian cannibalistics, no explanation is proposed. The reaction is pure horror: these uncouth creatures, scarcely even apologies for men, still untouched by the redeeming wing of civilization, are nothing more than carnivorous animals. This ignorant cannibalism positively calls for the pacifying mission of the West, its remedy and opposite. The imagined spectacle of anthropophagous rage is rather like a film in negative of the leading European nations, as they set out to tear Africa apart limb from limb.

Here, we already have a sufficient demonstration of the sorry 'modernity' of Cardano's paradigm. By pushing the rationalization of medical and economic determinism as far as it would go, resolutely ignoring the symbolic dimension of cannibal rituals, he suppressed every potential for alterity. But at the same time his kind of 'scientific' discourse and apparent (but only apparent) neutrality left room for older imaginings, which had been suppressed since the beginning, and for which the 'savage' body could provide a valuable, if unwilling, support.

This positivist thinking, which reached its zenith in the nineteenth century, nourished the ideology of the great age of colonization. (It would be well worth studying the cannibal myth from 1830 to 1960 with that fact in mind.) Nonetheless, while the determinist model enjoyed considerable success, it seems likely that the paradigm inherited from Léry, Montaigne and Thevet also continued to be productive, though for a long time it remained underground. Lafitau, Lahontan and Robertson, all of whom revived the hypothesis of vengeance cannibalism, stood out against the irresistible rise of utilitarian anthropophagy which derived from Cardano and Malthus.[9] But it was not until anthropology had established itself as an independent discipline that Montaigne's 'Of Cannibals', and a whole series of texts from before and after it, gained a new lease of life and finally lost the 'verbal paradox' label which respected and complacent critics had attached to them.

From island to raft

The island reappeared in one final avatar: the raft. Indeed, Géricault's *The Raft of the Medusa* is the logical culmination of the Cardanian model. The circumstances of this dramatic shipwreck, which took place in July 1816, are well known. Thanks to the incompetence of her captain, Duroy de Chaumareys, the frigate *Medusa*, carrying the new governor of Senegal (Monsieur Schmalz) accompanied by an infantry battalion, was wrecked – in fair weather and at high tide – on the Arguin reef off Mauritania. The ship was abandoned in total confusion. Since there was an insufficiency of lifeboats – priority being given to the governor, his family, his staff and the ship's officers – a raft was hastily constructed for the unfortunate infantry. It was loaded to capacity with 152 men, crowded together and up to their knees in water. The boats were supposed to tow it, but soon left it to its fate. There were desperate struggles and outbursts of collective insanity. Every night dozens of passengers disappeared: some were swept away by the waves, others jumped in of their own accord. Soon the raft was heaped with corpses, which served the survivors as both mattresses and food. The wounded, including one woman, were pitilessly thrown into the sea. When the raft was found after drifting for thirteen days in a shark-infested sea, it carried only fifteen gaunt and half-naked occupants. Their food supply consisted of strips of human flesh hanging up to dry on ropes and mast.[10]

The drama is best commemorated today by Géricault's horrific 'machine', exhibited at the Salon of 1819. This dramatic manifesto of macabre romanticism does not include the cannibalistic episode, which is only hinted at by the stripped bodies lying about the raft. The painter was more audaciously realistic in his preliminary drawings of severed heads, arms and legs, based on anatomical specimens from the Beaujon hospital, and in the sketches which portray, stage by stage, the interminable death-agony of the shipwrecked soldiers. One of them, 'a breath of Goya', shows chalk-white bodies illuminated, as if by lightning, under a black sky: among the attitudes of prayer, depression or revolt, one man crouches, hungrily chewing on the arm of another.[11] The finished work sublimates the horror into a gesture of hope. The victims, stirring themselves out of the torpor of starvation, rise to catch a glimpse of a sail appearing on the horizon, still not knowing if it is coming towards them or going away, sealing their fate or bringing deliverance.

Rather than making a lengthy examination of this masterpiece, with its heightened rhetoric swaying between hope and despair, I shall turn back to Jules Verne and his novel *Le Chancellor*, a free adaptation of the narrative by Savigny and Corréard, two of those who 'miraculously' escaped from the *Medusa*.[12] Verne often imagines islands as glorified rafts: witness the chunk of rock which is detached from Labrador by an earthquake in *Le Pays des fourrures*, on which the fur traders continue their trapping for months, as if nothing untoward was happening.[13] Another example, closer to the shipwreck scenes in *Le Chancellor*, is the vast 'Jangada' (in the novel of the same name), which bears its load of trees, ploughed fields and homesteads majestically down the Amazon, like one mobile landscape gliding through another, a square garden drifting through the primeval forest.[14] *A Floating City* and *Propeller Island* can also be ranked with these geographical fictions, these 'unmoored peninsulas', to borrow a phrase from Rimbaud.[15] The raft is, as it were, a socialized version of the island, which becomes mobile and floats as it is remade in the image of its human inhabitants. It is an island without foundations, or any resources other than those provided by human industry.

This means that social violence is more apparent than elsewhere. Cannibalism is no longer seen from a distance, through the stakes of a palissade or from a travelling balloon. This time, the observer is on the spot, and is in imminent danger of infection.

The narrator of *Le Chancellor* is Jean-Richard Kazallon, a passenger on the doomed ship of the book's title, which is carrying cotton from Charleston to Liverpool, but is destined never to reach its destination. After a few days the cargo catches fire. The blazing ship is wrecked on a reef in mid-ocean, is kedged off with a shattered hull, becomes almost totally submerged, and is soon reduced to a few square feet of makeshift raft drifting before the trade wind. The stores are exhausted and hunger sets in. The twenty or so survivors are progressively reduced to eleven, and they yield to a cannibalistic obsession. But this obsession is experienced differently by the two clans sharing the restricted space on the raft. The division is social and cultural: forward is the crew, mostly made up of uneducated brutes who seem to have no religion; aft, under an awning to protect them from the burning sun, are the passengers, tactful individuals and skilled conversationalists, among them the narrator, two Frenchmen (a M. Letourneur and his son) and Miss Herbey, an orphaned English girl. The necessary go-between for the two groups is the captain, Robert Kurtis. Those most likely to be eaten face those who will probably eat them, while the status of the captain remains in doubt – although it is scarcely possible to believe that this energetic and generous man could be a cannibal.[16]

Faced with the possibility of cannibalism, the first group feasts on the idea itself, their imaginations alternating between eating and being eaten, albeit recoiling with equal horror from the thought of attacking either bodies or corpses. The second group will endure cannibalism, but in secret, under cover of darkness, or protected by the very unspeakability of the act. For the narrator, evidently an apostle of innuendo, uses exclamation marks to conceal the detail of those culinary operations which he has not seen – which he willed not to see. The result is that no one escapes cannibalism, in either thought or deed.

No one, however, actually becomes a victim of cannibalism. All that is eaten is the corpse of the over-fed cook, who hangs himself in despair after his last, carefully hoarded morsel of bacon has been stolen. They also use the foot of Lieutenant Walter, who has died of disease, as fish-bait. Even the boatswain, one of the most ferocious in his hunger, says to the narrator: 'Monsieur, it is better to eat a dead man than a living one!'[17] His interlocutor is not so sure, although the argument has a long and honourable ancestry. It seems to have been invented by Montaigne;[18] Voltaire and Sade repeated it with emphasis two centuries later. We have seen the alarming consequences which Sade drew from it. The boatswain may know his French classics, but the narrator is not won over by what he regards as sophistry. In fact, where cannibalism exists – and if we except the vivisection practised by (for example) the Iroquois, or among the violence of the Wars of Religion – it is nearly always the dead body which is eaten, whether it has been killed for the purpose or not. Thus, the difference between a living man and a dead one is of considerably less importance than the alimentary taboo itself.

The novelist must find a way of heading off this descent into rampant allelophagy. Of course, there is a happy ending which relieves the unbearable constraint; but even before this, Verne, as a good Catholic, has suggested an alternative solution. Instead of a class struggle translated into cannibalistic terms, he suggests a Eucharistic communion. The social microcosm of the raft is about to be torn (chewed?) apart. The poor have physical strength on their side, and make ready to devour the rich, who are weaker and whose education or religious convictions make it impossible for them even to contemplate breaking the taboo. The only way to reconcile the shattered community with itself is for one man to sacrifice himself voluntarily for the good of all. This heroic gesture is made by M. Letourneur.

Lots must be drawn, and the moment draws remorselessly nearer: 'For several days it had been an obsession which no one dared to speak out loud.'[19] One by one the names are drawn out of a hat. At the supreme moment, M. Letourneur senior, who is in charge of the process, volunteers to take the place of his crippled son. He is 'half smiling', redolent of the odour of sanctity.[20] The sea story has taken a decided step towards mawkish piety. It is not hard to imagine the astonishment and disappointment of readers of Edgar Allan Poe's *The Adventures of Arthur Gordon Pym*, from which Verne sought inspiration and to which he tried to provide a sequel in *Le Sphinx des glaces*, when they find Poe's inexorable tragedy culminating in would-be edifying contrivance. The puritanical and vaguely fantastic odyssey of Poe's original seems to have collapsed into a Sunday-school story, which is not really redeemed by the surrealistic nature of the epilogue. The contrast is still sharper with Savigny and Corréard's account of the shipwreck of the *Medusa*. Throughout the starvation episode Verne follows the *Medusa* survivors' narrative quite closely, but he makes some decisive modifications. They suggested the division of the raft into fore and aft, with officers and important passengers – the cool, calm and collected, the polished socialites – on the one side and ordinary men, mutinous brutes with a greed for human flesh, on the other. Verne glosses over the reality: on the *Medusa* raft it was the former, better armed and more cohesive group which ate the latter, not vice versa.[21]

To return to Verne's narrative: pretty Miss Herbey, struck by an inspiration which can only be described as providential, persuades the others to reprieve the victim for one more night. But the sun rises on an empty ocean: the respite is over. Here begins the final act of sublime renunciation and heightened emotion. The martyr, dressed in rags, arms bare to the shoulders, holds out his arms to be chopped off his living body, like Christ holding out his arms to suffering humanity.[22] The carpenter's axe is already raised, but just then the salt water turns fresh, as the ship enters the vast outfall of the Amazon. An hour later they sight land, pre-empting imminent sacrifice.

This cannibalistic crucifixion combines the Last Supper and the agony on the Cross into a single scene. It will also be seen that father and son have changed places. Now it is the father who gives his life for his only son, the only person he cares about and who has been singularly ill-favoured by nature and fortune. At the beginning of their ordeal, Letourneur senior had sacrificed part of his own ration to prolong the life of his offspring. Finally, he offers him the only thing he has left: his own lean and suffering flesh. This evokes a Christological image which had recently been brought back into favour by Musset and other romantic poets: that of the pelican in her piety, wounding her own breast to revive her young with her body and blood. Letourneur's act of sublime devotion is a very faithful imitation of the poet Clément Marot's line: 'The Pelican, who for her beloved slays herself'.[23]

Though the parody of the Passion is not pursued to the bitter end, the benefits are the same. The community is reconciled by simulating the ritual murder of one of their number. 'And now, after we have been through so much together, after miraculously escaping so many dangers, is it not natural that we, the passengers of the *Chancellor*, should be united in indissoluble friendship?'[24] The answer is obviously yes: the miracle has really happened. The survivors have become one flesh, members of one body.

There is, however, one limitation. Social prejudice remains, reinforced by the red alert endured by the passengers. The proclamation of unanimity does not extend to the crew, a feeling which is not spelt out, but is implicit in a sentence exempting the captain from any fault which has been committed: 'Robert Kurtis is and will always remain a friend of all his companions in misfortune.' This implies that his men, whose carnal appetites were only too plain, are not to be associated with this collective redemption through mystical friendship.

The saccharine piety of the ending does not purge all the terrors of the voyage. The hunger and physical closeness experienced on the raft have brought out the underlying bestiality which exists in every human being, always ready to return to the surface and sweep away the fragile barriers of reason and good behaviour. And the proximity of a familiar but alien proletariat has aroused a social terror incomparably more frightening than anthropophagous tribes gesticulating in remotest Africa, or dancing their dances of death on the volcanic rock of a New Zealand so far off as to be more or less legendary.

Montaigne's Cannibal made a prediction which has now come to pass. Western society has become the isolated battlefield of a merciless struggle. Its members are devouring one another, hurling reciprocal accusations of cannibalism. The crews of the *Grampus* or *Chancellor* are never seen without a handspike, knife or axe. In both cases the lurking fear, which infallibly sees the Other as a cruel and ravenous butcher, is justified. The negro cook of the *Grampus* goes on the rampage and slaughters twenty-two people one after the other; the crew of the *Chancellor* mutiny, and are quickly repressed. On both ships there is an anthropophagous epilogue: both incidents confirm the positive existence of a silent fear which ineluctably sees in the Other a cruel and famished butcher. In bourgeois eyes, a sailor or workman is a ferocious animal; but it is true enough to say that the bourgeoisie lives on the blood and sweat of the other two.

'If those Cannibals still try to make heroes of us . . .', threatens the *Internationale*. The words are familiar enough; in context they are anti-militaristic, but they could be taken as a definition of capitalist society as a whole. The exaltation of warlike heroism is a blind, a convenient way to disguise the butchery of the majority who are served up as cannon fodder. Honour and patriotism are mere futile pretexts. As for religion, which preaches love for one's fellow men and pretends that rich and poor can be brought together into one mystical body, its opium has lost its savour, and its sedative virtues are no longer very convincing.

In the positivist, liberal nineteenth century, when voracious progress was cynically attempting to arrogate the promises of the spirit, the Eucharistic symbol lost its sovereign efficacy. It no longer offered a plausible alternative to the ravages of class hatred. Letourneur, preferring to lose his arms rather than his life when it comes to the crunch (' "Cut them off – tomorrow you may have the rest" ')[25] shows how little belief there really was in this sublime, but scarcely practicable, exchange. The new Christ is a trader in his own flesh, selling off his members one by one. Society is dislocated and will remain so.

The utopian fusion of communism, for all its classless society free of distinction, property and privilege, still excludes a substantial number of people: in particular, the bourgeoisie, or, more broadly, the 'haves', the bogeymen who can effortlessly reincarnate themselves in a series of astonishingly diverse and unexpected adversaries. This became clear later, under Stalin, with the methodical annihilation of the kulaks, peasants who were no more than comfortably off, but were guilty of hanging on to their own means of production. Just as in *Le Chancellor* the Eucharist is reduced to a pale imitation, similarly the mystical communion of the new age remained imperfect. Not only because it was incapable of rising above the satisfaction of material needs – though it confined its ambitions to doing just that – but more especially because it stopped half way: its recipe for general salvation assumed the exclusion or annihilation of the Other, who had suddenly taken on a thousand faces and one role, that of scapegoat.

In those conditions the horror of reality always threatened to creep back from under the metaphor. Once it was no longer sublimated, cannibalism reappeared under the most dreadful guises. Stalin's classless society culminated in the state-sponsored perversion of the Gulag, where, in their humiliation and despair, the inmates sometimes cut off pieces of their bodies and ate their own living flesh.[26] At the same time, Hitler's new Germany was constraining its victims, shut in the hell of its ghettos and concentration camps, to devour one another. Indeed, whatever social system is actually envisaged – Soviet or Nazi ogre, or capitalist Leviathan – it is a fact that the ancient metaphor of the lean and the fat, the eaters and the eaten, still haunts the frame of political discourse. Montaigne saw the cannibalism of the Cannibals as an extreme revenge. The trouble with cannibalism in modern Europe is that it often represents nothing but itself: an archaic regression which, for want of a better term, is described as bestial;[27] an unreasoning, inexcusable brutality which defies all new religions.

Epilogue
The Return of the Cannibal: Swift, Flaubert and the Medusa

People die; rafts rot.

Julian Barnes, *A History of the World in 10½ Chapters*

'I have just been reading some medical literature on hunger and thirst – and among other things I have read the arguments of Dr Savigny, the doctor on the raft of the *Medusa*. Nothing could be more dramatic, dreadful, or frightening. What providential meaning could there be in all these tortures?'[1] This question – which evidently remained unanswered – was addressed by Flaubert to Madame Jules Sandeau in a letter dated 28 November 1861. The author was just finishing *Salammbô*, which was to be published the following year. He was on the last chapter but one, in which the mercenaries who have rebelled against Carthage die of starvation in a hollow of the desert hills. Usually, when Flaubert writes in his letters about his 'Punic novel', he either complains about the interminable hard labour or becomes frankly flippant: 'I'm perpetrating a few jokes which will make respectable stomachs heave', as he told the Goncourt brothers at a slightly later date.[2] In an earlier letter he had adopted a zestful tone, half Rabelaisian and half Sadean (Sade being the author most often quoted in his letters to male correspondents): he forecasts that he will be accused of 'exalting anthropophagy', nourishing the grievance in advance.[3] He glories in the violence of his own imagination, brandishing it like a slogan: 'Here I am in cannibal style.'[4] When he gets to the sacrifice of children to Moloch, one of the most famous scenes of the novel, he alludes with ogreish relish to the 'grilled kiddies', an expression he repeats more than once.[5] Inviting the Goncourt brothers to a reading of the first chapters of *Salammbô*, he describes the event as if it were an oriental dinner at which they will be 'served with human flesh, bourgeois brains and tigresses' clitorises fried in rhinoceros fat'.[6] He is still congratulating himself on the way he has 'upset the bourgeois', 'revolted the nerves and hearts of sensitive persons' and 'convinced people that I am a pederast and a cannibal'.[7]

As Claude Rawson has shown, *Salammbô* must have been written in a mood of triumphant sadism[8] – a sadism which can be traced back to Flaubert's youthful journeyings, when he strode with Maxime du Camp over the fields and beaches of the west coast of France and visited the slaughterhouse at Quimper, visualizing 'a cannibal Babel with slaughterhouses for men' and listening for 'something resembling a human death-agony' in the bellowing of slaughtered calves. A letter to Madame Sandeau, which discusses the *Medusa*, conceals a profound anguish under a noisy display of orgiastic gaiety, which he nurtured, week by week and month by month, from 1859 to 1862. The imagined colours of blood and flesh, the avalanches of bodies broken, devoured and consumed, are all suddenly wrecked on a reef of reality. The rampant imagination of the visionary novelist, reassuring in its very excess, is suddenly struck dumb, 'taken aback'. The eye of Medusa is upon him.

Admittedly, there is nothing particularly cheerful about the 'Observations on the effects of hunger and thirst experienced after the shipwreck of His Majesty's frigate *Medusa* in 1816', recorded by the ship's surgeon Jean-Baptiste Henry Savigny, who was one of the fifteen survivors.[9] The starvation on the raft; the incessant heat which drove the victims mad, so that they dreamed of rippling streams and flowery meadows, and leapt, laughing and shouting, into the waves; the remorseless anthropophagy practised by the survivors on the corpses of their companions, perhaps their friends; their cruelty to the wounded, whom they tossed into the sea as useless mouths: all this was enough to make anyone disgusted with the human race and inclined to cast doubt on Divine Providence. Flaubert goes beyond Sade to rejoin Voltaire and the total pessimism of Candide's gloomy companion, Martin.

There are several ways to escape from this lurking terror and disgust. The first is black humour. In 1799 Jonathan Swift suggested that starvation in Ireland could be palliated by substituting one-year-old children for butcher's meat: every child would provide sufficient for four meals. This would lighten the burden on mothers, and give them a little income so they could fatten up their other offspring. The rich would have a dainty dish for special occasions; the skin would make admirable gloves for ladies and summer boots for fine gentlemen. Public wealth would increase. As an additional advantage, the number of papists would decrease in relation to the number of

Protestants. Despite appearances, Swift is not sticking to the raw data
(literature always tends to recoil from raw data).[10] As Claude Rawson
has noted, the *Modest Proposal* fails to mention those cases of cannibalism which had been fairly common in Ireland during the previous
century, as its readers must have known.[11] Thus, in spite of its deliberate exaggerations, it falls short of the very reality it aims to
denounce. What Swift does do is allegorize, bringing in the mythical
'inhabitants of Topinamboo' (the allusion is scarcely unexpected in
such a context).[12] By a brilliant inversion, he makes fictional cannibalism into an allegory of the real thing: an imagined anthropophagous
economy, based on commerce in children's flesh, becomes a
metaphor for a society in which the organized misery of English
overlordship, together with religious hatred and a contemptuous attitude towards the entire population, is effectively forcing men to
devour one another. This seems to be what really lies behind the
author's black humour. More subtly still, there is an element of repulsion, setting the whole human race one degree beyond despair.[13]

Another method is to set the fear at a distance, so deeply veiled in
fancy and exoticism that the monstrous becomes aesthetic. The travel
and adventure literature of the nineteenth century evinces a fascination with unfortunate victims dying by inches on rafts, and with
starving shipwrecked sailors. These dizzying but distant scenes, with
their pathetic wrecks drifting over shark-infested seas, under burning
suns or skies of lead, combine an inextricable tangle of attraction and
repulsion, the lure of the abyss and shuddering recoil from the
unknown. Maritime cannibalism becomes a poetic experience, a
plumbing of depths. They have something of the same flamboyancy
as Baudelaire's *Invitation au voyage*.

Flaubert, an exact contemporary and acquaintance of Baudelaire,
chooses as his setting Carthage in the fourth century BC. There, far
away from the dull, bourgeois, modern world, he relocates the
extravagant orgies which fill his enthusiastically Sadean imagination.
The result is the operatic glitter of *Salammbô*. Anthropophagy fits in
comfortably with the torrid eroticism, the din of battles, the sacrifice
of children to Moloch. In the penultimate chapter, 'The defile of the
Axe', the theme of siege cannibalism is raised to epic heights. Forty
thousand mercenaries have been lured into a rocky defile by
Hamilcar Barca, and, hopelessly trapped, prepare to die. They devour
one another, and the lions and jackals complete the process.[14]

However, the surface of the finished novel betrays none of the
libidinal violence, so nakedly revealed in the letters, that filled
Flaubert's mind as his creative processes alternated between euphoria
and agony. Artistic asceticism vanquishes the author's morbid fasci-

nation with anthropophagy. Four years of back-breaking labour have contained the cannibal terror, but not suppressed it altogether.

Indeed, what is most striking about *Salammbô* is the supreme detachment of the horror. However minute the description, there is no tendency to wallow in it. Verne's reticence had been, to say the least, in doubtful taste: 'Were it not for the frightful tumult of the orgy, the shouting ... the captives would have heard the victims' bones cracking between cannibal teeth.'[15] Instead of this hypocritical modesty, which seems laughable today and which demonstrates the obscenity of hearing and seeing, rather than what ear and eye actually perceive, Flaubert gives us exact sensations: 'Their chests cracked like broken boxes' is his description of the mercenaries being crushed beneath the feet of Hamilcar's elephants.[16] The voluble commentator retires from the space between scene and reader and leaves the former to tell its own mute and riveting story. Against the background of that awful silence, the slightest indications take on a striking importance.

The self-destruction of a mass of men – twice twenty thousand – is put under a microscope. The description of hunger is clinically complete: blue-mottled skin, beginning to turn leaden and hang loose like an oversized garment; blackened nails, rabid madness, convulsions, hallucinations which drive some to sing and others to develop obsessive nervous twitches. Flaubert obtained medical information from his brother Achille and another doctor, Merry Delabost; and, as we have seen, he had read the tales of the *Medusa* survivors, Alexandre Corréard and Jean-Baptiste Savigny. His description is so minute and so well documented that it could almost relate to an open-air hospital or lunatic asylum on the desert fringe. In fact, it gives a wholly different impression. The distancing in time and space doubtless contributes to this transfiguration of horror into a picture so rich and strange. Moreover, the 'intensity of seeing' which the artist and novelist Fromentin perceived in *Salammbô*,[17] together with the musical rhythms of the prose, filter the brash cruelty of the event through the magical transparency of a dream world.

Montaigne himself had found a certain 'beauty' in cannibal warfare – as much as 'this human infirmity may admit'.[18] Thevet and Léry before him had taken a dilettante pleasure in the spectacle of Tabajars and Margajats tearing one another to pieces: 'Never was there such a goodly pastime'; 'we amused ourselves judging of the blows'.[19] The man-eater had a tendency to become an aesthetic object. Cannibals were admired for their boldness and generous self-outpouring both on the field of war and in the sacrificial enclosure designed by the *malocas* of the enemy village.

The same tendency in the observer towards generous emotional involvement is apparent in Lévi-Strauss's attitude to the Nambikwaras in the mid-twentieth century: a kind of echo of the generous cast of mind the observer thinks he can discern in the observed. This emotional communion, latent in *Tristes Tropiques* as in all other ethnographical studies, leads to 'a teleology and an eschatology: the dream of a full and immediate presence closing history, the transparency and indivision of a Parousia, the suppression of contradiction and difference'.[20] But between Montaigne, Léry, even Flaubert, and Lévi-Strauss there is a small difference, a revealing detail which changes the face of the world: and it is cannibalism. In *Tristes Tropiques*, anthropophagy appears only as a learned allegory counterbalancing the 'anthropoemy' of our developed societies, which vomit up, rather than swallowing down, any individual with disquieting powers – criminals, drop-outs, aliens.[21] The reversed perspective transfers the argument from the concrete to the abstract. The real is emptied of content so as to feed the symbolic.

But it is irreducible reality that permeates the *Essays*, as it permeates *Salammbô*. In both, the feeling of overwhelming admiration is indissolubly linked to its opposites, disgust and fear. The aesthetic attitude assumed by Montaigne, as well as Flaubert, is reconciled in both with an unfathomable lucidity. Each realizes that a human society, a scale model of humanity as a whole, is literally devouring itself. When the Tupinamba Indians described by Thevet, Léry and Montaigne eat their enemies, they are really eating themselves. In 'Of Cannibals' the prisoner makes this clear to his executioners: 'These muscles (saith he) this flesh, and these veins, are your own, fond men as you are, know you not, that the substance of your forefathers' limbs is yet tied unto ours? Take them well, for in them shall you find the relish of your own flesh.'[22]

There can be no question that Montaigne admires the 'native virtue' of the Cannibal. It reminds him of the lost warrior ideal so dear to the feudal nobility. But this admiration is counterbalanced by the mirror image of the situation in France, where quarrels over points of honour encourage the catastrophic fashion of duelling, and the rivalries of the ruling class have unleashed civil war and plunged the state into ruin.[23] Thus, while Montaigne's Brazilian chapter creates the figure of the Noble Savage, it also reveals the savagery of the French noble. In his 'Defence of Seneca and Plutarch', Montaigne observes that 'in these our miserable days' there are numerous 'effects of patience, of obstinacy and stiff-neckedness'. He expresses amazement at the suicidal resolve of Protestants, rejoicing and chanting psalms as they walk eagerly into martyrdom, and exclaims: 'How many have been seen, who have patiently endured to be burnt and roasted for unknown and wilful opinions, which they had borrowed of others?'[24] In his eyes, any exhibition of excessive and superhuman 'virtue' is crazy rather than reasonable, more akin to insanity – however holy – than to common sense.[25] Significantly, he demonstrates this reservation by placing his description of martyrs who defy their impotent tormentors under 'biting snippers' and even 'in the middest of a flame' in the chapter entitled 'Of Drunkenness'.[26] This is some indication of the gulf between Montaigne and his contemporary, d'Aubigné, poet of the 'triumphant martyrs'.[27]

Montaigne hated cruelty – both those who inflicted it and those who willingly experienced it – and he was not impressed by these spectacular deaths, men roasted alive as a stimulus to sanctity. To him, there is little difference between the drunkard who is unaware of his own actions and the martyr patiently undergoing the actions of others – just as he sees little difference between the heroism of the Maccabees or early Christians and the 'invincible courage' of the Cannibals, who were themselves not inconsiderable drinkers. The catastrophe is in the final reckoning: an elite devouring itself, consuming the entire social body in its own ruin. The gesture may look very fine, Montaigne thinks, but it is fatal nonetheless: 'So are there triumphant losses in envy of victories.'[28]

The agony of the Carthaginian mercenaries has the same intimate mixture of beauty and disaster. But Flaubert no longer offers the counterpoint of a France afflicted with civil war, with a governing class bleeding itself white. Or, if there is such an echo, it is a more distant one: when *Salammbô* was published France had had ten years of bourgeois imperialism and still had eight years to wait for the Commune – which Flaubert was to greet with execration. Social anxiety was therefore not the order of the day. The symbol, detached from immediate circumstances, becomes universal. In the chapter 'The defile of the Axe' Flaubert tells us that the defile is 'a kind of hippodrome' surrounded by mountains.[29] For weeks on end it becomes a theatre of duels worse than those of Roman gladiators, torments crueller than those endured by any martyr in the arena. Over the half-eaten corpses, which are covered by the first drifts of sand, towers, like a silent question, the stony eye of Medusa. She had fascinated an entire century, and it is towards her that the starving mercenaries turn their dying gaze. This famine, inspired by one shipwreck, itself inspired another. From the ocean to the desert, from the *Medusa* to *Salammbô*, the question shifts and strengthens. Between *Salammbô* and Joseph Conrad's *The Nigger of the 'Narcissus'* it returns, as it were, to the place of origin. The morbid imaginings of the dying barbarians, the 'noisy streets, the taverns, theatres, baths and barbers' shops where stories were told'[30] prefigure the equally vague and despairing reveries of Conrad's sailors, as they remember 'the noise of gaslit streets, the steamy heat of taprooms, or the scorching sunshine of calm days at sea'.[31]

The crazed, starving shipwrecked sailors, the forgotten mercenaries who long equally for life and death, turn a present nightmare into a dream of escape, a return towards unattainable pleasures, a vain search for an innocence forever lost. It is the writer's task to capture that mirage. The unspeakable horror of cannibalism, no longer legitimated as a social ritual or conjured by a higher necessity, is captured in a work of art. Of all scandals, that is perhaps not the least.

Appendix I
The Cannibal Speaks: From Montaigne to Jean-Jacques Rousseau

Montaigne's Cannibals are orators, so loquacious and so quick in their answers that they are not always easy to follow. This is shown in the conversation which took place between the author of the *Essays* and the Brazilians in Rouen in autumn 1562. To the questions which were put to the newly arrived Cannibals, 'they answered three things, the last of which I have forgotten, and am very sorry for it'.[1] Montaigne thinks that nothing can make up for this sad loss, which he blames on the 'foolishness' of the lagging interpreter and his own unreliable memory.

This, however, made no allowance for the inventiveness of his readers: for example, that of Jean-Jacques Rousseau, who two centuries later undertook to fill the gap. 'Of Cannibals' foreshadows an equally famous and vehement 'declamation', the *Discours sur l'origine et les fondements de l'inégalité parmi les hommes* ('Discourse on the Origin and Foundations of Inequality among Men'). 'Declamation', in the strictest sense of the word, is what we find in this piece of vaulting eloquence, which includes the famous and inspired sentence, 'Let us therefore begin by setting aside all the facts.'[2] Like 'Of Cannibals', and like La Boétie's *Servitude volontaire* (with which it has often been compared),[3] Rousseau's *Discours* turns its back on historical truths, and engages, with complete intellectual freedom, in a pure hypothesis which is taken to its logical conclusion: men are by nature equal; inequality is the result of a series of misfortunes in which the invention of personal property played a significant role. The *Discours* ends with an oratorical amplification of Montaigne, or more precisely, of Montaigne's Brazilian: 'since it is manifestly against the Law of Nature, however defined, that an infant should command an old man, an imbecile guide a wise man and that a handful of people should live in abundance of superfluities while the hungry multitude lacks necessities.' Thus the peroration of the *Discours* turns the twofold scandal denounced at the end of essay I, 31 (the child, meaning the young Charles IX, ruling over adults; the poor fainting with hunger at the rich man's gate) into a triple cadence.

Rousseau makes excellent use of Montaigne's fortunate lapse of memory. By correcting it and inventing the missing reply, he adds the scandal of the imbecile guiding the wise man, an anomaly that to him is just as much to be feared, and hardly less eloquent of contemporary social injustice.[4] In fact, this thought would have been fundamentally alien to the author of the *Essays*. Montaigne did not see the profession of letters as a potential rival to the profession of arms, the only 'vocation' worthy of the gentleman he aspired to be.[5] To the orphan Rousseau, on the other hand, it was in every way a profession: the wisdom of the intellectual was to him a higher virtue than the aristocratic qualities of swaggering courage and conspicuous extravagance that Montaigne discerned in the proud Brazilian anthropophagi, whose appetite for vengeance scarcely displayed the virtue of prudence.

Rousseau allows the Cannibal to retain his exalted violence of speech, but he retains nothing else. All fleshly presence has vanished. This amnesia in Rousseau concerning the appetite for flesh, which Montaigne linked directly to the eloquence of the savage, is not really surprising. In *Emile*, Rousseau had roundly condemned the eating of meat. Indeed, the 'meat-eater' was an 'unnatural murderer' who devoured his 'fellow creatures', 'creatures of flesh and blood' who 'lived and felt as he did'.[6]

So, at the end of a long series of transmissions and transformations, the Enlightenment version of cannibal eloquence comes from the lips of a dedicated vegetarian!

Appendix II
The Cannibal in Canada: Chateaubriand Reads Montaigne
~:~

The fortune of Montaigne's essay on Cannibals in the romantic period was rather extraordinary. Attention was not confined to the heroic idealization of the savage, the Spartan uprightness of the warrior defying death: it also extended to the local colour. There was particular interest in the fragments of folklore scattered through this Brazilian chapter. Goethe made it the basis of two German poems: the 'Love-Song of an American Savage' (*Liebeslied eines Amerikanischen Wilden*), which is a versification of the 'Song of the Serpent', and the 'Death-Song of a Prisoner' (*Todeslied eines Gefangenen*), in which the executioners are told that they will find in the captive the taste of their own flesh.[1]

Montaigne's political message has sunk definitively into the background. The voice of the Cannibal no longer shouts, insults or defies: it sings of love and death, yielding the native taste of immemorial folk poetry. The 'imagination' in which Montaigne found 'anacreontic' graces is now compared to the Song of Songs, the Psalms and the Persian Bulbul, ageless manifestations of national spirit.

This new dignity accorded to the literary and aesthetic object makes allowances for a certain inaccuracy of memory. For example, in a passage from Chateaubriand's *Mémoires d'outre-tombe* ('Memoirs from beyond the grave') the narrator describes a visit to North America during which he met a pretty Indian girl called Mila who sang him 'a very agreeable song'. He identified it as the 'Song of the Serpent': 'Serpent, stay; stay, serpent . . .' But when he attempts to recite the end of 'Of Cannibals' from memory, the imaginary traveller gets his geographical location wrong: the Tupinamba become Iroquois, who naturally wear no kind of breeches or hosen![2]

Notes

ᴗ:ᴗ

Introduction: To Meet a Cannibal

1 On Sunday, 1 November they heard mass in the pillaged cathedral. See René Herval, *Histoire de Rouen* (Rouen: Maugard, 1949), vol. II, p. 81.

2 All quotations from Montaigne's *Essays* are taken (with modernized spelling) from the reprint of the 1603 translation by John Florio (Menston, Yorks.: Scholar Press, 1969). In this edition the seminal essay 'Of Cannibals' is book I, ch. 30 (not 31, as in the French editions). See *Essays*, I, 30 [31], p. 106.

3 On the 'Brazilian pageant' of 1 October 1550 see Jean-Marie Massa, 'Le Monde Iuso-brésilien dans la Joyeuse Entrée de Rouen', in *Les Fêtes de la Renaissance* (Paris: Editions du CNRS, 1975), vol. III, pp. 105–16, and my 'Rouen et les "Nouveaux Horizons"', in Alain Parent (ed.), *La Renaissance et le Nouveau Monde* (Quebec: Musée du Québec, 1984), pp. 243–9.

4 Gustave Flaubert, letter to Louis Bouilhet, written at Croisset on 26 December 1853, in Jean Bruneau (ed.), *Correspondance* (Paris: Gallimard 'Pléiade', 1980), vol. II, p. 487. On the Kaffirs' reputation for savagery, which goes back at least to the eighteenth century, see Danièle Prégardien, 'L'Iconographie des *Cérémonies et coutumes* de B. Picart', in D. Droixhe and Pol.-P. Gossiaux, *L'Homme des Lumières et la découverte de l'autre* (Brussels: Editions de l'Université de Bruxelles, 1985), pp. 183–90.

5 Flaubert, to Louis Bouilhet, in Bruneau (ed.), *Correspondance*, p. 487.

6 Ibid., p. 488. As we have seen, this was not actually the 'coronation' of Charles IX, but merely a solemn entry into a reconquered Rouen. Pierre Villey draws attention to this passage in his edition of the *Essais* (Paris: PUF, 1965/1978), but gives it a rather cavalier résumé: 'Flaubert, who had been to see some Kaffirs at Croisset . . .'

7 On this impenetrability of the Brazilians' words in a text which gives an imperfect account of them, see Michel de Certeau, *Heterologies: Discourse on the Other*, trans. B. Massumi (Minneapolis: University of Minnesota Press, 1985), ch. 5, 'Montaigne's "Of Cannibals": The Savage "I"', pp. 67–79.

8 Montaigne, *Essays*, I, 30 [31], p. 100.

9 This pamphlet, first published in London in 1774, was reprinted in Paris at the end of 1792. On this treacherous adaptation, see Miguel Abensours's and Marcel Gauchet's preface to Etienne de La Boétie's *Discours de la Servitude volontaire* (Paris: Payot, 1976), pp. xi–xii.

10 Annie Le Brun, *Soudain un bloc d'abîme. Sade. Introduction aux œuvres complètes* (Paris: Jean-Jacques Pauvert, 1986).

11 Notes by Régis Michel in the *Géricault* catalogue (Paris: Réunion des Musées nationaux, 1991), p. 236.

12 Alexandre Corréard, in collaboration with Henri Savigny, *Relation du naufrage de la frégate 'La Méduse', faisant partie de l'expédition du Sénégal*

en 1816. Quatrième Edition entièrement refondue, with eight engravings by M. Géricault and other artists (Paris: chez Corréard, 1821), ch. VII, note 1, pp. 156–7.

13 On these events see below, ch. 13.

14 Arthur Rimbaud, 'Mauvais sang', in *Une saison en enfer*, in S. Bernard and A. Guyaux (eds), *Œuvres* (Paris: Classiques Garnier, 1983), p. 215.

15 William Arens, *The Man-Eating Myth. Anthropology and Anthropophagy* (New York: Oxford University Press, 1979). On Arens's 'craze for denial' and his undoubted similarity to the negationist historians of the Holocaust, see the useful comments by Pierre Vidal-Naquet, 'Du Cannibalisme, de son existence et des explications qui en ont été données', in *Les Assassins de la mémoire. Un 'Eichmann de papier' et autres essais sur le révisionnisme* (Paris: La Découverte, 1987), pp. 14–19.

16 This is especially true of Anthony Pagden, *The Fall of Natural Man: The American Indian and the Origins of Comparative Ethnology* (Cambridge: Cambridge University Press, 1986), pp. 80–7. See especially p. 83 and p. 226, note 154. My criticisms are aimed only at this particular detail in an otherwise notable work.

17 Cornélius de Pauw, *Recherches philosophiques sur les Américains, ou Mémoires intéressantes pour servir à l'Histoire de l'Espèce humaine*, 2nd edn (Berlin, 1771), vol. 1, part 2, section III, p. 255, note *.

18 Arens's little work has attracted several learned refutations, including those by Thomas S. Abler, 'Iroquois Cannibalism: Fact not Fiction', *Ethnohistory* 27/4 (Fall 1980), pp. 309–16; Donald W. Forsyth, 'The Beginnings of Brazilian Anthropology. Jesuits and Tupinamba Cannibalism', *Journal of Anthropological Research* 39/2 (Summer 1983), pp. 147–78; and idem, 'Three Cheers for Hans Staden: the Case for Brazilian Cannibalism', *Ethnohistory* 32/1 (1985), pp. 17–36.

19 For a good example of an archaeological investigation along these lines, see Christy G. Turner II and Jacqueline A. Turner, 'The First Claim for Cannibalism in the Southwest: Walter Hough's 1901 Discovery at Canyon Butte Ruin 3, Northeastern Arizona', *American Antiquity* 57/4 (1992), pp. 661–82. But see also the cautious article 'Anthrophage, anthropophagie' by C. Perlès in *Dictionnaire de la Préhistoire* (Paris: PUF, 1988). Recent excavations by Jean Courtin in the cave of Fontbrégoua near Salernes in the Var region of France have uncovered the remains of ten or so humans who were probably victims of cannibalism some 4000 years BC.

20 As is shown by the recent survey edited by Pierre-Antoine Bernheim and Guy Stavridès, *Cannibales!* (Paris: Plon, 1992).

21 René Girard, *Violence and the Sacred*, trans. P. Gregory (Baltimore: Johns Hopkins University Press, 1977), p. 276; Isabelle Combès, *La Tragédie cannibale chez les anciens Tupi-Guarani* (Paris: PUF, 1992).

22 Title of ch. 11 of Girard, *Violence*, p. 274.

23 This expression was known in Montaigne's time from Christine de Pisan's *Livre du corps de policie*, a fifteenth-century treatise on government and the virtues of the Prince.

24 Montaigne, *Essays*, II, 12, p. 305.

25 Sigmund Freud, *The Future of an Illusion* (London: Hogarth Press, 1962), p. 39.

26 For an attempt at a dialectical synthesis between these two currents of thought see Georges Guille-Escuret, 'Cannibales isolés et monarques sans histoire', *L'Homme* 122–4 (April–December 1992), pp. 327–45.

Chapter 1: Birth of the Cannibal

1 This etymology, which is now universally accepted, is given in the OED and in Collins English Dictionary (3rd edn, 1991).

2 Cecil Janes (ed.), *The Voyages of Christopher Columbus* (London: Argonaut Press, 1930), p. 177. For a commentary on this part of the journal see especially Juan Gil, *Mitos y utopías del Descubrimiento*, I. *Colón y su tiempo* (Madrid: Alianza, 1989), pp. 30–2.

3 Pliny the Elder, *Natural History*, VI, 30, and especially VII, 2; Solinus, *Polyhistor*, ch. 31; St Augustine, *City of God*, XVI, 8; Isidore of Seville, *Etymologiarum libri XX*; Migne, *Patrologia latina, vol. 82, col. 421* (lib. XI, ch. III): '*Cynocephali* appellantur eo quod canina capita habeant, quosque ipse latratus magis bestias quam homines confitetur: hi in India nascuntur.' On the tradition of monstrous races and the diverse interpretations of them through the Middle Ages and up to the Renaissance, see Jean Céard, *La Nature et les Prodiges. L'insolite en France au XVIe siècle* (Geneva: Droz, 1977), part I, pp. 21–75. The motif of the dog-headed man occurs in the legendary geography of India and ancient China as well as in the cosmography of Greek and Latin antiquity, as shown by David Gordon White in *Myths of the Dog-Man* (Chicago and London: University of Chicago Press, 1991). In every case it is used to stigmatize the barbarism of peoples who were little known and therefore feared, casting doubt on their membership of the human race. On Columbus's contribution to this widespread belief see pp. 63–4.

4 Hartmann Schedel, *Die Schedelsche Weltchronik*, fol. xii (facsimile of the 1493 German edition in the collection *Die bibliophilen Taschenbücher*, Dortmund, 1978). For a commentary of the woodcuts see Céard, *La Nature et les Prodiges*, pp. 74–5.

5 Janes (ed.), *Voyages of Christopher Columbus*, p. 180.

6 Ibid., p. 117: the Indians 'said that the *caniba* had only one eye and the faces of dogs'.

7 In Isidore and in the Nuremberg Chronicle, the Cynocephali come immediately before the Cyclopes: see above, note 3.

8 Janes (ed.), *Voyages of Christopher Columbus*, p. 215.

9 Ibid., p. 183. Alexandre Cioranescu, in his French edition of Columbus's works (*Les Œuvres de Christophe Colomb*, Paris: Gallimard, 1961, p. 408, note 256) observes in this connection that 'We know that the correct form of the native word is *cariba*, whence "Caraib", but the form *caniba* remains unexplained. It would be interesting to see whether the latter form, which prevailed and gave us the word "cannibal", can in fact be explained by Columbus's desire to dabble in a little etymology and see the word as an echo of the "Khan" whom he was seeking.' Raymond Arveiller, in his *Contribution à l'étude des termes de voyage en français (1505–1722)* (Paris: Editions d'Artrey, 1963), p. 146, doubts whether 'the comparison with the Latin *canem* or the Italian *cane*' had much influence on the final form of the word.

10 Janes (ed.), *Voyages of Christopher Columbus*, p. 197

11 Ibid., p. 203, dated Monday, 17 December 1492. Cf. Cioranescu, *Œuvres de Christophe Colomb*, p. 114.

12 Peter Martyr of Anghiera, *De Orbe Novo* (Paris: E. Leroux, 1907), 'Première décade', ch. II, pp. 23–4. On the author, rightly termed a 'literary discoverer

of the New World', see the classic work by J. H. Mariéjol, *Un Lettré italien à la cour d'Espagne: Pierre Martyr d'Anghiera, sa vie et ses œuvres* (Paris, 1887), and the very useful description by Numa Broc in *La Géographie de la Renaissance (1420–1620)* (Paris: CTHS-BN, 1980), p. 25.

13 For a good account of Amerigo Vespucci's four voyages to America between 1497 and 1504, see Albert Ronsin, *Découverte et baptême de l'Amérique* (Montreal: Editions Georges Le Pape, 1979), book I, ch. V, pp. 81–96.

14 Lorenz Fries, *Uslegung der Mercarthen oder Cartha Marina, darin man sehen mag, wo einer in der Welt sey, und wo ein yetlich Landt, Wasser, und Stadt gelegen ist. Das alles in dem Büchlin zufinden* (Strasbourg: Johann Grüninger, 7 September 1525. In his dedication to the printer, 'Johann Grieninger Bürger und Buchtrucker zu Strassburg', Lorenz Fries, alias Laurentius Friess, describes himself as a 'natural philosopher' (*natürlicher Philosophus*). I consulted the second edition of 1527 in the John Carter Brown Library, Providence, fol. xv verso: 'Von Canibalien das. 60. ca.' Cf. fol. xx recto: 'Von dem land Prasilia das. 82. Cap.' A third edition was published in 1530, again by Johann Grüninger at Strasbourg, with the title *Underweisung und usslegunge der Cartha Marina*.

15 Although the dates are not always correct, see the exhibition catalogue *Mythen der Neuen Welt. Zur Entdeckungsgeschichte Lateinamerikas*, ed. Karl-Heinz Kohl (Berlin: Frölich and Kaufmann, 1982), p. 25, fig. 15. The commentary by Hugh Honour, on pp. 22–47, is entitled 'Wissenschaft und Exotismus. Die europäischen Künstler und die aussereuropäische Welt.' Cf. Philip P. Boucher, *Cannibal Encounters. Europeans and Island Caribs, 1492–1763* (Baltimore and London: Johns Hopkins University Press, 1992), p. 19. Boucher compares this woodcut with the tall stories retailed by John Mandeville, who mentions both the peaceable Cynocephali and the islands of the anthropophagi, where children are fattened for the table.

16 In a letter from Amerigo Vespucci to Lorenzo di Pietro Medici describing his third voyage along the coasts of Brazil (1501–2), printed in Paris in 1503 and in Venice in 1504, under the title *Mundus Novus*. In the compendium translated by Marthurin du Redouer in 1515, *Sensuyt le Nouveau Monde et navigations faictes par Emeric de Vespuce Florentin* (Paris: BN, Rés. 4° P. 8; G. Atkinson, *La Littérature géographique française de la Renaissance*, Paris: Picard, 1927, no. 10), this culinary simile occurs in part V, ch. CXVI, fol. 74 recto.

17 Also reproduced in Karl-Heinz Kohl (ed.), *Mythen der Neuen Welt*, p. 24, fig. 14: 'Das volck und insel die gefunden ist durch den cristlenlichen künig zu Portigal oder von seinen underthanen.'

18 Loys Guyon de La Nauche, *Les Diverses Leçons de Loys Guyon, Sieur de La Nauche, Conseiller du Roy, et Esleu au bas Lymosins, suivans celles de Pierre Messie, et du Sieur de Vauprivaz. Divisées en cinq livres. Contenans plusieurs Histoires, Discours et faits memorables, recueillis des Autheurs Grecs, Latins, François, Italiens, Espaignols, Allemans, et Arabes* (Lyon: Claude Morillon, 1604; 2nd edn, 1610), book IV, ch. 3, pp. 161–3. On this chapter, see Jacqueline Bolens-Duvernay, 'Les Géants Patagons ou l'espace retrouvé. Les débuts de la cartographie américaniste', *L'Homme* 106–7 (April–September 1988), pp. 156–73, esp. pp. 161–3. But the author wrongly believes that these remarks derive from Pero Mexia, following the English translation of 1613, *The Treasurie of auncient and moderne times. Containing the learned Collections, judicious Readings, and memorable observations … translated*

out of that worthy Spanish gentleman Pedro Mexio. And M. Francesco Sansovino, that famous Italian. As also, of those honourable Frenchmen, Anthonie Du Verdier, lord of Vauprivaz: Loys Guyon, sieur de la Nauche, counsellor unto the king: Claudius Gruget, Parisian, etc., 2 vols (London: W. Jaggard, 1613–19). Thus, Duvernay neglects the considerable debt owed by this 'Treasury' to French authors such as Léry and Montaigne. She also unduly postdates this (as she sees it) very valuable evidence of the survival of the Cynocephalus beyond the classical era.

19 Jean de Léry, *Histoire d'un voyage faict en la terre du Brésil, autrement dite Amerique* (La Rochelle (Geneva): Antoine Chuppin, 1578; expanded editions appeared in 1580, 1585, 1599–1600 and 1611). On this work and its author, see my *Le Huguenot et le Sauvage. L'Amérique et la controverse coloniale, en France, au temps des guerres de Religion* (Paris: Aux Amateurs de Livres, 1990), chs II and III.

20 See the alphabetical list of authors cited in Guyon de La Nauche, *Diverses Leçons.*

21 Léry, *Histoire d'un voyage*, 2nd edn (1580; facsimile by Jean-Claude Morisot, Geneva: Droz, 1975), ch. VIII, p. 98. Cf. English translation by Janet Whatley, *History of a Voyage to the Land of Brazil* (Berkeley: University of California Press, 1990), p. 58.

22 Guyon de La Nauche, *Diverses Leçons*, p. 585.

23 On this see Claude Rawson, *Order from Confusion Sprung. Studies in Eighteenth-Century Literature from Swift to Cowper* (New Jersey and London: Humanities Press, 1992), ch. 2, pp. 68–70: 'Gulliver, Marlow and the Flat-Nosed People: Colonial Oppression and Race in Satire and Fiction'.

24 Claude Lévi-Strauss, *Tristes Tropiques* (Harmondsworth: Penguin, 1976) p.81.

25 Montaigne, *Essays*, trans. John Florio (Menston, Yorks: Scholar Press, 1969), I, 30 [31], pp. 106–7.

26 Guyon de La Nauche, *Diverses Leçons*, book IV, ch. 3, p. 595.

27 Aelian, *Nat. an.*, IV, 16, after the Indian fables of Ctesias of Cnidos. Quoted by Gil, *Mitos y utopías*, vol. I, p. 30.

Chapter 2: The Cannibal *à la mode*

1 Peter Martyr d'Anghiera, *De Orbe Novo* (Paris: E. Leroux, 1907), 'Première décade', p. 12. On the earliest images of the Cannibal in modern European literature, see Peter Hulme, *Colonial Encounters* (London: Methuen, 1986); Philip P. Boucher, *Cannibal Encounters* (Baltimore and London: Johns Hopkins University Press, 1992), ch. 1.

2 See below, ch. 8, 'The Spitting Cannibal'.

3 Martyr, *De Orbe Novo*, I, 1, p. 12. Translated from the French edition of 1533 (Atkinson, no. 45), which is entitled *Extraict ou Recueil des Isles nouvellement trouvees en la grand mer Oceane ou temps du roy Despaigne Fernand et Elisabeth sa femme, faict premierement en latin par Pierre Martyr de Milan, et depuis translaté en languaige françoys* (Paris: chez Simon de Colines, published on '12 January 1532' [1533 new style], fol. 4 recto. The translater was Antoine Fabre. For a succinct analysis of this edition of the first three 'Decades', see Gilbert Chinard, *L'Exotisme américain dans la littérature française au XVIe siècle* (Paris: Hachette, 1911; Geneva, 1978), pp. 16–17.

4 *Sensuyt le Nouveaue Monde et navigations* (Paris: BN, Rés. 4° P 8; Atkinson, no. 10) fol. 55 recto. The expression occurs in part IV, in relation to voyages to Colombia. It is in fact a straight translation from Martyr, *De Orbe Novo*, I, 1, p. 12. For an identical view of cannibalism by Cardano, see below, ch. 9.

5 François de Belleforest, *Histoire universelle du Monde* (Paris: Gervais Mallot, 1570), book IV, fols. 315 verso–316 recto. The source given for this passage is 'Americ Vespucce Florentin', or, more accurately, the *Mundus Novus* adapted from Vespucci (1503–4), which enjoyed considerable success all over Europe. See notes 14–18 below.

6 Martyr, *De Orbe Novo*, I, 2, p. 23: 'Other fragments of human corpses were fixed on spits for roasting.' Cf. Sebastian Münster, *Cosmographia universalis* (Basel: Heinrich Petri, 1565; 1st Latin edn, 1544), p. 1259: 'and after splitting them down the middle, they take their steaming intestines and eat them; they do the same with the extremities; but they chop up the other limbs, salt them and keep them as we keep sausages and hams.'

7 For all this iconography see Frauke Gewecke, *Wie die neue Welt in die alte kam* (Stuttgart: Klett-Cotta, 1986), plates 6–8. Cf. Münster, *Cosmographia universalis* pp. 1215 (heads on poles emerging from the chimney and window of a house), 1218 (men roasting on a spit), 1259 (naked butcher brandishing an axe and cutting up human bodies).

8 Jean de Léry, *Histoire d'un voyage faict en la terre du Brésil* (Geneva: Antoine Chuppin, 1580 edn), ch. XV, p. 219: 'Error on the Maps showing savages roasting human flesh on spits as we do our meat.'

9 François Rabelais, *Pantagruel*, in *Gargantua and Pantagruel*, trans. Thomas Urquart (Chicago and London: William Benton, 1952), ch. 14, p. 92.

10 Don Honorius Philoponus, *Nova typis transacta Navigatio. Novi Orbis Indiae Occidentalis admodum reverendissimorum PP. ac FF. Reverendissimi ac Illustrissimi Domini, Dn Buelli Cataloni Abbatis montis Serrati, et in universam Americam, sive Novum Orbem Sacrae Sedis Apostolicae Romanae à Latere Legati, Vicarii, ac Patriarchae: Sociorum a Monachorum ex Ordine S.P.N. Benedicti ad supra dicti Novi Mundi barbaras gentes Christi S. Evangelium praedicandi gratia delegatorum Sacerdotum. Dimissi per S.D.D. Papam Alexandrum VI. Anno Christi 1492* (Munich, 1621). For a brief description of this volume and reproductions of four of its nineteen line engravings, see the exhibition catalogue *Die Neuen Welten in alten Büchern. Entdeckung und Eroberung in frühen deutschen Schrift- und Bildzeugnissen. Ausstellung in der Staatsbibliothek Bamberg* (Bamberg, 1988), pp. 84, 85, 255–7. The two most highly coloured plates are between pages 16 and 17, 32 and 33 of the original edition.

11 Tzvetan Todorov, *The Conquest of America. The Question of the Other* (New York: Harper and Row, 1984), pp. 14–33: 'Columbus as Interpreter'. On this semiotic and moral approach to the *conquista*, see the qualified review by Giuliano Gliozzi, 'Tre studi sulla scoperta culturale del Nuovo Mundo', *Rivista storica italiana* XCVII/1 (1985), pp. 160–76.

12 Martyr, *De Orbe Novo*, I, 2, p. 24.

13 Ibid., p. 23. I translate from the French version of 1533, *Extraict ou Recueil des Isles* (Atkinson no. 45; see note 3 above), fol. 7 recto.

14 For a detailed account of the circulation of travellers' tales in the early Renaissance, see Numa Broc, *La Géographie de la Renaissance* (Paris: THS-BN, 1980), p. 27. On Vespucci's French reputation, see the recent article by William Kemp, 'Les éditions du *Nouveau monde et navigations de Vespuce*

(1517–v.1532): diffusion du premier récit de voyage "américain" imprimé en français', *Bulletin du Bibliophile* (1993).

15 Rudolf Hirsch, 'Printed Reports on the Early Discoveries and their Reception', in Fredi Chiappelli (ed.), *First Images of America* (Berkeley, Los Angeles and London: University of California Press, 1976), vol. II, pp. 540ff. Cf. W. G. L. Randles, *De la terre plate au globe terrestre* (Paris: Armand Colin, 1980), *passim*.

16 Albert Ronsin, *Découverte et baptême de l'Amérique* (Montreal: Editions George le Pape, 1979), book I, pp. 87–8.

17 That this was an unlicensed addition was shown by Alberto Magnaghi, *Amerigo Vespucci. Studio critico* (Rome: Arti Grafiche Affini Roma, 1924), vol. I, ch. II.

18 On this point see W. G. L. Randles, ' "Peuples sauvages" et "états despotiques": la pertinence, au XVIe siècle, de la grille aristotélicienne pour classer les nouvelles sociétés révélées par les Découvertes au Brésil, en Afrique et en Asie', *Mare Liberum* 3 (1991), pp. 299–307.

19 All references are from Randles, ' "Peuples sauvages" ', p. 301, notes 21–4. On the idea of 'hard' primitivism, see G. Boas and A. O. Lovejoy, *Primitivism and Related Ideas in Antiquity* (Baltimore, 1935), p. 275.

20 *Sensuyt le Nouveau Monde et navigations* (Paris: BN, Rés. 4° P. 8; Atkinson, no. 10), fol. 73 verso.

21 Chinard, *L'Exotisme américain*, p. 11, seems to exaggerate the contrast between Columbus, man of the fifteenth century, and Vespucci, whom he sees as the model of the humanist explorer. In fact, it was in many ways Columbus's vision that had the brighter future, in spite of its etymological divagations and prophetic obsession. It is symptomatic that Chinard fails to notice the anthropophagous hysteria so complaisantly evoked by Vespucci.

22 *Sensuyt le Nouveau Monde*, fol. 74 recto.

23 Belleforest, *Histoire universelle du monde* (1570), fols 315 verso–316 recto.

24 On this see the article by Juha Pekka Helminen, '¿Eran canibales los Caribes? Fray Bartolomé de Las Casas y el canibalismo', *Revista de Historia de América (México)* 105 (January–June 1988), pp. 147–58.

25 On these abuses see further Vicenta Cortés, 'Los Indios Caribes en el siglo XVI', *Proceedings of the Thirty-Second International Congress of Americanists* (Copenhagen, [1956] 1958), pp. 726–31.

Chapter 3: The Cannibal Comes to France

1 Geoffroy Atkinson, *Littérature géographique de la France*, nos 10–13 and 20–1. I owe the re-dating (1517 instead of 1515) to the article by William Kemp, 'Les éditions du *Nouveau Monde et navigations de Vespuce* (1517–v.1532): diffusion du premier récit de voyage "américain" imprimé en français', *Bulletin du Bibliophile* (1993). The privilege granted to the bookseller Galliot du Pré for this edition does indeed bear the date 16 January 1516 (old style).

2 Given in the colophon as 'le 12 janvier 1532'.

3 Contrary to the assertions of Marcel Françon, 'Cannibales, Rabelais et Montaigne', *Bulletin de la Société des Amis de Montaigne* 6/13–14 (January–June 1983), p. 106. The conclusion of this note, that 'This word [Cannibals] referred to Levantine anthropophagi', is, of course, unacceptable.

4 See Marcel Françon's introduction to his edition of the *Chroniques admirables du puissant roy Gargantua,* preface by Henri Dontenville (Rochecorbon: Editions Charles Gay, 1956), pp. lviii–lix.
5 As claimed by Marcel Françon, 'Sur l'exotisme chez Rabelais et chez Montaigne', *Francia, Periodico di Cultura Francese* (October–December 1975), p. 79, referring to W. W. Comfort, 'The Literary Role of the Saracens in the French Epic', *PMLA* (1940), pp. 628–59. The same note by Françon puts the utopia of *Gargantua* in the Orient, 'whereas the Utopia of Thomas More could convincingly be identified with Peru' (p. 76). There is no justification for this distinction, since More's imaginary island has recently been identified, even more arbitrarily, with the India of d'Albuquerque. According to this hypothesis, Hythlodeus is the pseudonym of Duarte Barbosa, whom the author himself met at Antwerp. For further explanations, see Luis de Matos, 'L'Expansion portugaise dans la littérature latine de la Renaissance' (doctoral dissertation, Paris, Sorbonne, 1959), summarized by Michel Mollat du Jourdin in his article 'Humanisme et Grandes Découvertes (XVe–XVIe siècles)', *Francia. Forschungen zur Westeuropäischen Geschichte* 3 (1975), p. 232.
6 As suggested by Raymond Arveiller, *Contribution à l'étude des termes de voyage en français* (Paris: Editions d'Artrey, 1963), under 'Cannibale', pp. 142–6, note 23.
7 François Rabelais, *Pantagruel,* in *Gargantua and Pantagruel,* trans. Thomas Urquart (Chicago and London: William Benton, 1952), p. 126.
8 Ibid., *Gargantua,* p. 65.
9 Jehan Mallart (or Jean Maillard), *Premier livre de la description de tous les ports de mer de lunivers. Avecques summaire mention des conditions differentes des peuples et adresse pour le rung des ventz propres a naviguer, c.*1546–7 (Paris: BN, MS fr. 1382) fol. 46 recto.
10 Ibid., fol. 47 verso.
11 Ibid., fol. 49 verso.
12 Jean Alfonse, known as Jean Fonteneau or Alfonse de Saintonge, *La Cosmographie avec l'espère et régime du Soleil et du Nord,* edited and annotated by Georges Musset (Paris: E. Leroux, 1904), p. 337; cited by Arveiller, *Contribution à l'étude,* p. 146.
13 Ibid., p. 339.
14 Antonio Pigafetta, *Le Voyage et navigation faict par les Espaignols es Isles de Mollucques, des isles quils ont trouvé audict voyage, des Roys dicelles, de leur gouvernement et maniere de vivre, avec plusieurs aultres choses* (Paris: Simon de Colines, n.d. [1526]), fol. 6 recto. Cf. Arveiller, *Contribution à l'étude,* pp. 142–3. On Magellan's encounter with these Brazilian 'Cannibales', see Philip P. Boucher, *Cannibal Encounters* (Baltimore and London: Johns Hopkins University Press, 1992), p. 21.
15 N. (Jean Arnaud) Bruneau, gentleman of Rivedoux, *Histoire veritable de certains voiages perilleux et hasardeux sur la mer, ausquels reluit la justice de Dieu sur les uns et la misericorde sur les autres* (Niort, 1599; Paris, BN, Rés. G. 2889): 'Another voyage to Peru, in which we see the violence of a wind called Hurricane, with the perils endured by those that encounter it', p. 83. On Captain Bruneau, see the article by Alain-Gilbert Gueguen, 'Duplessis-Mornay et l'*Histoire véritable*', *Bulletin de la Société de l'Histoire du Protestantisme Français* 136 (April–June 1990), pp. 209–18.
16 Bruneau, *Histoire veritable,* p. 97.

17 Cecil Janes (ed.), *The Voyages of Christopher Columbus* (London: Argonaut Press, 1930), 22 December 1492, p. 211. Cf. pp. 236–7: Tuesday, 15 January 1493, when the lure of the gold was offset by fear of the Caribs.

18 Vladimir Propp, *Morphologie du conte* (Paris: Seuil, 1970), ch. 2: 'Méthode et matière'.

19 Christopher Columbus, *La Découverte de l'Amerique*, ed. Soledad Estorach and Michel Lequenne (Paris: La Découverte, 1979), p. 92. Cf. Alexandre Cioranescu (ed.), *Les Œuvres de Christophe Columb* (Paris: Gallimard, 1961), pp. 197–9.

20 Daniel Ménager, 'La politique du don dans les derniers chapitres du Gargantua', *Journal of Medieval and Renaissance Studies* 8/2 (Fall 1978), pp. 179–91. Cf. the recent studies by Philippe Desan, *L'Imaginaire économique de la Renaissance* (Mont-de-Marsan: Editions Inter-Universitaires, 1993), ch. 11.

21 Rabelais, *Pantagruel*, ch. 32; *Gargantua*, ch. 38; both in *Gargantua and Pantagruel*, trans. Urquart. On these two parallel episodes, see my article 'Dans la bouche des géants', *Cahiers Textuels* 34/44: François Rabelais/Aurélien d'Aragon (Paris: Université de Paris, 7, 1989), pp. 43–52.

22 François Rabelais, *Brief Declaration*, in *The Complete Works*, trans. D. Frame (Berkeley and Los Angeles: University of California Press, 1991), p. 593. Judging by the order in *Briefve declaration*, which puts the word 'Canibales' in sixth place, the definition actually applies to the occurrence in the intro-ductory epistle to Odet de Coligny. After that, the meaning of the word is never again made clear, and there is no hint whether or not that meaning remains unchanged in chapters 32 and 66.

23 Lazare Sainéan, *La Langue de Rabelais* (Paris: E. de Boccard, 1922–3), vol. 2, p. 518. At the close of the century the cosmographer Thevet, in a manuscript entitled *Grand Insulaire*, 'Guide to the Islands' (Paris: BN, MS Fr. 15452), mentions several 'Pearl' islands or groups of islands near the American main-land. E.g. fol. 215 recto: 'The Isle of Cubaga or Pearl Island' (Cubagua, off the coast of Venezuela); fol. 281b: 'Pearl Island or Tararequi' (the Pearl Archipelago in the Gulf of Panama). There is little point, then, in lining up expert critical opinions on this point to use as Aunt Sallies, as Marcel Françon has done in a note entitled 'Rabelais et les Canibales' (*Bérénice* 1, November 1980, p. 55); cf. Françon, 'Cannibales, Rabelais et Montaigne', pp. 106–8. Sainéan and Guy Demerson are both right, and they agree on the essentials, namely that the islands of the 'Perlas' are indeed to the west, on the threshold of the newly discovered lands. [Translator's note: Guy Demerson edited Rabelais, *Œuvres complètes* (Paris: Le Seuil, 1973).]

24 Rabelais, *Gargantua and Pantagruel*, trans. Urquart, p. 233.

25 Ibid., pp. 273–4.

26 Pierre de Ronsard, *Continuation du Discours des Miseres de ce temps* (1562), in Paul Laumonier (ed.), *Œuvres complètes*, vol. XI, p. 49, lines 235–6. In this context the word 'Cannibals' evidently means, by metonymy, 'the land of Cannibals'. In conjunction with 'Peru' and 'Canada', thought of as being in the West Indies, and Calicut, in the East Indies, it might agree geographically with the position in André Thevet's *Les Singularitez de la France antarctique*, namely the north-eastern part of South America, as opposed to the Spaniards' Peru, which is in the west and south. The passage probably contains an allu-sion to the unsuccessful attempts at conversion of the savages made by mem-

bers (particularly Huguenots) of Villegagnon's short-lived 'France Antarctique' colony in 1555–60.

27 Shortly after the first War of Religion the lawyer Fabriel Bounin, less savage and more genuinely conciliatory than Ronsard, urged the factions in the kingdom to live together in peace and understanding. He suggested to King Charles IX that the civil war should be exported to the furthest corners of the world, the barbaric confines that were its natural home. This oratorical exhortation, which momentarily echoes Ronsard, draws on the catalogue of newly discovered, far-distant peoples in Sebastian Münster's *Cosmographia universalis*: 'Sire, the planning and fighting of such wars and bellicose impressions should be left to the Indians of Calicut, the Cannibals, the islanders of Madeira and the Canaries, and the Barbarians of the furthest Garamanths, as things unworthy of the name of Frenchman.' See Gabriel Bounin, *Harangue au Roy, à la Roine, et aux hommes françois, sur l'entretenement et reconciliation de la Paix, en entree dudict Seigneur en ses villes. Par Gabriel Bounyn advocat en la cour de Parlement à Paris, et Lieutenant de Chateauroux en Berry. A Madame de Savoye, Duchesse de Berry* (Paris: Robert Estienne, 1565; Paris, Bibliothèque Mazarine, Rés. 41915–1), fol. 10 recto. The exact marginal note is 'Munstere li. 5'.

28 François Garasse, SJ, *Les Recherches des Recherches et autres Œuvres de Me Estienne Pasquier, pour la defense de nos Roys, contre les outrages, calomnies et autres impertinences dudit Autheur* (Paris: Sebastien Chappelet, 1622), p. 827.

29 Ibid., p. 686.

30 Rabelais, *Le Quart Livre* in Frame (ed.), *Complete Works*, p. 309.

31 Despite the ingenious hypothesis of V.-L. Saulnier in 'Pantagruel au large de Ganabin ou la peur de Panurge', *Bibliothèque d'Humanisme et Renaissance* XVI (1954), pp. 58–81, reprinted in *Rabelais. II. Rabelais dans son enquête* (Paris: CEDES-CDU, 1982), pp. 142–8, under the title 'Ganabin, ou le spectre de la police'. Saulnier sees this 'Thieves' Island' as an allegory of the Châtelet and the Conciergerie, prisons and police headquarters, which were, of course, hostile to the Pantagruelists.

32 Rabelais, (*Cinquième Livre*, ch. 30 in Frame (ed.), *Complete Works*, p. 681).

Chapter 4: Brazil, Land of Cannibals

1 The importance of Verrazano's second voyage in terms of long-term consequences, despite its apparent failure, is emphasized in Michel Mollat du Jourdin's indispensable study of this Florentine navigator: *Giovanni et Girolamo Verrazano, navigateurs de François 1er. Dossiers de voyages établis et commentés par Michel Mollat de Jourdin et Jacques Habert* (Paris: Imprimerie Nationale, 1982), ch. III, pp. 91–115.

2 Guillaume de Saluste du Bartas, *La Seconde Semaine* (1584) ed. Y. Bellenger et al. (Paris, STFM, distr. by Klincksieck), book VII, 'Les Colonies', lines 459–60.

3 For a brief account of these Brazilian festivities in 1550 see the paper by Jean-Marie Massa, 'Le monde luso-brésilien dans la joyeuse entrée de Rouen', in *Les Fêtes de la Renaissance*, vol. III, pp. 105–16. Cf. Mollat du Jourdin, *Giovanni et Girolamo Verrazano*, pp. 151–3.

4 Rouen, Bibliothèque municipale, MS Y 28. See Stéphane de Merval (ed.),

L'Entrée de Henri II Roi de France à Rouen au mois d'octobre 1550. Orné de dix planches gravées à l'eau forte par Louis de Merval, Société des Bibliophiles Normands (Rouen: Imprimerie de Henry Boissel, 1868), fol. xvii verso.

5 Jehan Mallart (Jean Maillard), *Premier livre de la description de tous les ports de mer de lunivers* (Paris: BN, MS fr. 1382), fol. 48 recto, lines 1967ff.:

> North-westerly and south-easterly doth flow
> The Maron, and far backward doth he go
> Toward th'Antarctic and its distant sounds;
> The lands of Spain and Portugal he bounds.

6 André Thevet, *Histoire de deux voyages aux Indes Australes et Occidentales*, c.1587–8 (Paris, BN, MS fr. 15454), fol. 133 recto. See also my book *Le Huguenot et le Sauvage. L'Amérique et la controverse coloniale, en France, au temps des guerres de Religion* (Paris: Aux Amateurs de Livres, 1990), pp. 222–3, notes 75 and 76.

7 Elisabeth Chirol, writing in the catalogue of an exhibition entitled *La Renaissance et le Nouveau Monde*, ed. Alain Parent (Quebec: Musée du Québec, 1984), p. 231, suggests that this carved emblem slightly predates Henri II's visit to Rouen. The double oak panel is also reproduced in Mollat du Jourdin, *Giovanni et Girolamo Verrazano*, p. 150, fols 43 and 44, and in the catalogue of the exhibition *La Renaissance à Rouen* (Rouen: Musée des Beaux-Arts, 1980), pp. 25–6, nos. 22–3.

8 *C'est la deduction du sumptueux ordre plaisantz spectacles et magnifiques theatres dresses, et exhibes par les citoiens de Rouen ville Metropolitaine du pays de Normandie, A la sacree Maiesté du Treschristian Roy de France, Henry second leur souverain Seigneur, Et à Tresillustre dame, ma Dame Katharine de Medicis, la Royne son espouse, lors de leur triumphant joyeulx et nouvel advenement en icelle ville. Qui fut es jours de Mercredy et jeudy premier et second jours d'Octobre, Mil cinq cens cinquante* ('The deduction of the sumptuous order, pleasant spectacles and magnificent theatricals prepared and exhibited by the citizens of Rouen, capital of the province of Normandy, for his sacred Majesty, the very Christian King of France, Henri II their sovereign Lord, and the very illustrious Lady Catherine de' Medici the Queen his wife, on the occasion of their triumphant, joyous and recent arrival in that city which took place on Wednesday and Thursday, 1–2 October, 1550.) (Rouen: chez Robert le Hoy, Robert et Jehan dictz du Gord, 1551) (BN: Lb31.25), fol. K 4 recto: '… to prove which, several persons of this realm of France, in sufficient numbers, having long dwelt in *the country of Brazil, and cannibals*, will in good faith attest that the appearance of the preceding figure is a perfect simulacrum of the truth.'

9 Ibid., fols K 2 verso–K 3 recto. Wood engraving, 17.8 × 26.3 cm, reproduced in the exhibition catalogue *L'Amérique vue par l'Europe* (Paris: Musées Nationaux, 1976), p. 69 (the caption appears mistakenly on pages 15–16).

10 André Thevet, *Les Singularitez de la France Antarctique, autrement nommee Amerique: et de plusieurs Terres et Isles decouvertes de nostre temps* (Paris: chez les Héritiers de Maurice de la Porte, 1557), ch. 61; Jean de Léry, Histoire d'un voyage faict en la terre du Brésil (Geneva: Antoine Chuppin, 1578), ch. V.

11 Guillaume Le Testu, *Cosmographie universelle selon les navigateurs, tant*

anciens que modernes, MS atlas, paper (1556), Vincennes, SHAT, DLZ 14, fol. lxv recto. The passage is transcribed in my *L'Atelier du cosmographe ou l'Image du monde à la Renaissance* (Paris: Albin Michel, 1991), pp. 190–1.

12 The region was inhabited by Tupinamba Indians, as was the hinterland of Rio bay where Villegagnon had settled more than fifty years earlier. Thevet's localization of the Caribs/Cannibals in the 'Marignan' region is thus purely fanciful. The most detailed descriptions of the 'France Equinoxiale' venture are the accounts by the Capuchin fathers Claude d'Abbeville and Yves d'Evreux. See the critical bibliography by Jean-Paul Duviols, *Voyageurs français en Amérique (colonies espagnoles et portugaises)* (Paris: Bordas, 1978), pp. 68–78. See also Maurice Pianzola, *Des Français à la conquête du Brésil (XVIIe siècle). Les Perroquets jaunes* (Paris: L'Harmattan and Geneva: Editions Zoë, 1991). See also below, ch. 10, pp. 125–30.

13 Thevet, *Les Singularitez*, ch. 61, fol. 119 verso: 'the mainland where the Cannibals are, which country divides the lands of the King of Spain from those of Portugal'.

14 Ibid.

15 On these 'dragomen', who were mostly of Norman origin, see my 'Le Français ensauvagé: métissage et échec colonial en Amérique (XVIe–XVIIe siècles)', in Jean-Claude Carpanin Marimoutou and Jean-Michel Racault (eds), *Métissages*, vol. 1, *Littérature-Histoire* (Saint-Denis: Université de la Réunion and Paris: L'Harmattan, 1992), pp. 209–19.

16 For the detail of this montage see my *André Thevet, cosmographe des derniers Valois* (Geneva: Droz, 1991), pp. 100–14.

17 André Thevet, *La Cosmographie universelle* (Paris: Pierre L'Huillier and Guillaume Chaudière, 1575), vol. II, book XXII, ch. II, fol. 956 recto: 'And because I speak of Cannibals, do not think that I take the name as broadly as the Spaniards who have written on them without knowing the truth, who very falsely have called the whole country, known as the Antarctic, and as far as New Spain, Cannibals, meaning Anthropophagi: whereas I name only those who are properly called Carybes, or Caraibes, who live along this Promontory [Sâo Agostinho] and neighbouring Islands, not approaching within a hundred leagues of Castille D'Or; and so far are they from reaching, as some have thought, as far as the Isle called L'Espaignolle, on the Arctic side and towards the Antarctic, that they do not extend beyond the Bay called All Saints.' This passage is transcribed and annotated by Suzanne Lussagnet in *Les Français en Amérique pendant la deuxième moitié du XVIe siècle. Le Brésil et les Brésiliens par André Thevet* (Paris: PUF, 1953), p. 271, note 1.

18 Thevet, *Les Singularitez*, ch. 60, fol. 118 verso: 'as far as Cape Saint-Augustin, which we attempted to round, and so were becalmed for the space of two months or thereabouts, so great is it and so far projecting into the sea'.

19 See below, ch. 7.

20 Toussaint de Bessard, *L'Aigle-compas de Toussaincts de Bessart, d'Auge en Normandie, avec son usage, accompaigné des demonstrations pour l'intelligence d'iceluy* (Paris: de l'imprimerie de Hierosme de Marnef et Guillaume Cavellat, 1572; BN: V.8424–4), epistle, fol. 2 recto: 'to show in their hours of repose what difference there is between politic [civilized] men and the Androphagi'. Toussaint de Bessard claims to have sojourned for ten years 'in the land of America below the tropic of Capricorn, in the place called Cap de Frie and river of January'.

21 Thevet, *Cosmographie universelle*, vol. II, fol. 956 recto, following on from the passage quoted in note 17. Not transcribed by Lussagnet in *Le Brésil et les Brésiliens*.

Chapter 5: The First Ethnographer of the Tupinamba Indians

* 'Worse than an inhuman Scythian, you saw the Cannibal who swallows up and devours human flesh.'

1 I shall not attempt to give a complete bibliography of *Essays*, I, 30 [31], and shall mention only the works which I have consulted while writing the present book: Gilbert Chinard, *L'Exotisme américain dans la littérature française au XVIe siècle* (Paris: Hachette, 1911; Geneva, 1978), ch. IX, 'Un défenseur des Indiens: Montaigne', pp. 193ff.; Jean Plattard, *Montaigne: 'Des Cannibales'*, Les Cours de la Sorbonne (Paris: CDU, 1940); Charles-André Julien, *Les Voyages de découverte et les premiers établissements* (Paris: PUF, 1948), ch. VII, pp. 420–31; Hugo Friedrich, *Montaigne* (Paris: Gallimard, 1968), pp. 218–19; Alphonse Dupront, 'Espace et Humanisme', *Bibliothèque d'Humanisme et Renaissance* (1946), pp. 61–6 and 90; René Etiemble, *L'Orient philosophique au XVIIIe siècle*, Les Cours de la Sorbonne (Paris: CDU, 1956–7), pp. 34–52; Raymond Lebègue, 'Montaigne et le paradoxe des Cannibales', in *Studi di letteratura, storia e filosofia in onore di Bruno Revel* (Florence: Olschki, 1965), pp. 359–64; Pierre Michel, 'Cannibales et Cosmographes', *BSAM* (July–September 1967), pp. 23–7, and 'Les cosmographes disciples du ouy-dire', *BSAM* (January–March 1968), pp. 34–5; Bernard Weinberg, 'Montaigne's Readings for "Des Cannibales" ', in *Renaissance and Other Studies in Honor of William Leon Wiley* (Chapel Hill: University of North Carolina Press, 1968), pp. 261–79; Giuliano Gliozzi, *Adamo e il nuovo mondo. La nascita dell'antropologia come ideologia coloniale, IInda parte* (Forence: La Nuova Italia, 1977), ch. 1, note 3, 'Montaigne: dall'Atlantide al Nuovo Mondo', pp. 199–219; Michel de Certeau, *Heterologies: Discourse on the Other*, trans. B. Massumi (Minneapolis: University of Minnesota Press, 1985), ch. 5, 'Montaigne's "Of Cannibals": The Savage "I" ', pp. 67–79; Gérard Defaux, 'Un cannibale en haut-de-chausses: Montaigne, la différence et la logique de l'identité', *Modern Language Notes* 97 (1982), pp. 919–57, reprinted in Defaux, *Marot, Rabelais, Montaigne: l'écriture comme présence* (Paris and Geneva: Champion-Slatkine, 1987), pp. 145–77; Michael J. Giordano, 'Re-Reading "Des Cannibales": "Veritable Tesmoignage" and the Chain of Supplements', *Neophilologus* 69 (1985), pp. 25–33.

2 Montaigne, Essays, trans. John Florio (Menston, Yorks: Scholar Press, 1969), I, 30 [31], p. 100.

3 For this rhetoric of astonishment see Joseph R. de Lutri, 'L'humour de la déception dans le chapitre "Des Cannibales" ', *BSAM* 5/14–15 (1975), pp. 103–7, and section in ch. 8 below, 'Montaigne, or the paradox of "Cannibals" ', pp. 94–7.

4 On this 'sociological revolution' and its applicability to eighteenth-century literature, see below, ch. 8, note 31.

5 Lebègue, 'Montaigne et le paradoxe', p. 359, points out this possible influence, following Geoffroy Atkinson, *Les Nouveaux Horizons de la Renaissance française* (Paris: Droz, 1935). See Guillaume Postel, *De la Republique des Turcs* (Poitiers: Enguilbert de Marnef, 1560), I, pp. 62–3. On

the scope of the 'sociological revolution' in Postel, see my 'Guillaume Postel et l'"obsession" turque', in *Guillaume Postel 1581–1981* (Paris: Guy Trédaniel, 1985), pp. 265–98, reprinted in *Ecrire le monde à la Renaissance. Quinze études sur Rabelais, Postel, Bodin et la littérature géographique* (Caen: Editions Paradigme, 1993), pp. 189–224.

6 Jean de Léry, *History of a Voyage to the Land of Brazil*, 2nd edn (1580), trans. Janet Whatley (Berkeley: University of California Press, 1990), 'Preface', p. liv: 'I am content to gratify him so far as to name him not only simple "Cosmographer", but also, what is more, so general and universal a one, that – as if there were not enough remarkable things on this entire globe, not in this world (of which, however, he writes both what is and what is not) – to fill out and augment his idle tales, he goes so far as to seek his nonsense in the realm of the moon.'

7 Ibid., p. lxi.

8 Chinard, *L'Exotisme américain*, p. 196. It is to Chinard that we owe the discovery of Montaigne's immediate source for the whole beginning of the essay, and this decisive study can be said to have inaugurated the real critical history of ch. I, 30 [31]. Marcel Bataillon, 'Montaigne et les conquérants de l'or', *Studi Francesi* III/9 (September–December 1959), pp. 353–6, hints very suggestively that the extent of Montaigne's debt to Chauveton goes well beyond this lifting of three pages. For other passages in the *Essays*, particularly the entire chapter 'On Coaches' (III, 6), Chauveton was, if not the intermediary, at least the 'filter' between Montaigne and his Spanish sources. It was thus through the sometimes rather distorting spectacles of a Calvinist pastor that Montaigne was able to read Gomara and Oviedo, and so confute the Spaniards with the evidence of their own historians.

9 Guy Mermier, 'L'essai "Des Cannibales" de Montaigne', *BSAM* 5/7–8 (1973), pp. 27–38. See especially p. 28. The best structural analysis of this chapter is incontestably Edwin M. Duval's 'Lessons of the New World: Design and Meaning in Montaigne's "Des Cannibales" (I, 31) and "Des Coches" (III, 6)', *Yale French Studies* 64 (1983), pp. 95–112, especially pp. 95–104. The author distinguishes five successive viewpoints in the essay and shows how the definitions of 'barbarian' and 'savage' slide imperceptibly from the positive to the negative. At the beginning the Cannibal is a man of nature and esteemed as such; later, he is admired for his artistic talents (his songs are worthy of Anacreon).

10 For example, Gliozzi, *Adamo e il nuovo mondo*, pp. 205–6, strives to show that the ellipses and omissions in Montaigne's borrowings from Chauveton produce a very significant shift in the dispute over whether America was a continent or an island. While Chauveton was arguing from the strictly political viewpoint of national territorial claims (the Atlantis argument, which he rejects, would seem to suggest that the New World belongs to Spain, since it was once joined on to it, but drifted away), Montaigne adopts a more theoretical viewpoint, which involves interim acceptance of polygenesis.

11 On Thevet's importance to the anthropology of the Brazilian peoples see, especially, Alfred Métraux, *Religions et magies indiennes d'Amérique du Sud* (Paris: Gallimard, 1967), ch. 11, and Suzanne Lussagnet, *Les Français en Amérique pendant la deuxième moitié du XVIe siècle. Le Brésil et les Brésiliens par André Thevet* (Paris: PUF, 1953). The recent study by Isabelle Combès has confirmed this judgement: see *La Tragédie cannibale chez les anciens Tupi-Guarani* (Paris: PUF, 1992), p. 31.

12 André Thevet, *Cosmographie universelle* (1575; Lussagnet (ed.), *Les Français en Amerique*, p. 207), vol. II, book XXI, ch. XV, fol. 947 recto: 'and even the vermin which is born on man, such as big red lice, which they often have on their heads, they hold them in such contempt, that if they are bitten by them they avenge themselves with their teeth'.

13 Ibid., fol. 944 recto (Lussagnet, p. 192): 'The greatest vengeance, which these Savages perform against their enemies, and which is more than bestial, is to eat them.'

14 The manuscripts are in the Bibliothèque Nationale, numbered MS Fr. 15454 (*L'Histoire*) and MS Fr. 1452–3 (*Grand Insulaire*). For a description of the MSS and the dates of the two works, see the bibliographical note to my *André Thevet, cosmographe des derniers Valois* (Geneva: Droz, 1991).

15 André Thevet, *Les Singularitez de la France Antarctique* (Paris: chez les Héritiers de Maurice de la Porte, 1557), ch. 40, fol. 77 recto. The same woodcut appears in *Cosmographie universelle* (1575), vol. II, fol. 946 recto.

16 Théodore de Bry, *Americae Secunda Pars* (Frankfurt, 1592). This volume contains the complementary accounts by Hans Staden, an arquebusier from Hesse who was taken prisoner by the Tupinikins, and Jean de Léry, who was their friend.

17 Sebastian Münster, *Cosmographia universalis* (Basel: Heinrich Petri, 1565; 1544), pp. 1215, 1218, 1259. See above, ch. 2, note 7.

18 Thevet, *Les Singularitez*, ch. 39, fols 73–5: 'The manner of their combats, by both land and sea.' The borrowing from Vespucci is in ch. 24 (see my edition of *Les Singularités*, Paris: La Découverte, 1983, p. 49).

19 Ibid., fol. 74 recto.

20 Ibid.

21 Ibid., ch. 40, fol. 76: 'How these Barbarians put their enemies to death, which they have captured in war, and eat them'; cf. my edition, p. 86. For the meaning of this 'calendar' see Combès, *Tragédie cannibale*, p. 55.

22 Ibid., ch. 40, fol. 77 recto; Léry, *Histoire d'un voyage*, pp. 217–18.

23 On this, see the comments by Yvonnne Verdier in *Façons de dire, façons de faire. La laveuse, la couturière, la cuisinière* (Paris: Gallimard, 1979), pp. 24ff.

24 Thevet, *Cosmographie universelle*, vol. II, book XXI, ch. XV, fol. 946 recto–verso (Lussagnet, p. 203). For other details on the distribution of parts of the body among the guests, see Isabelle Combès's detailed tabulation in *Tragédie cannibale*, pp. 62–3.

25 Thevet, *Les Singularitez*, ch. 40, fol. 77 verso.

26 Ibid., ch. 41, fols 78–9.

27 Ibid., fol. 79. Cf. the slightly expanded version in Thevet, *Cosmographie universelle*, vol. II, book XXI, 15, fol. 947 verso (Lussagnet, pp. 208–9). A very similar anecdote is told by Léry, *Histoire d'un voyage*, ch. XV, p. 225: 'Margaja baptised in Portugal, a prisoner, whom we sought to save.'

28 Thevet, *Cosmographie universelle*, vol. II, book XXI, ch. 15, fol. 944 recto (Lussagnet, p. 193). For a commentary on this passage, see Métraux, *Religions et magies indiennes*, p. 47.

29 The same inversion is seen in certain tales of martyrdom, and in a related epigram by Clément Marot, 'Du lieutenant criminel et de Samblançay' (*Œuvres poétiques*, ed. Y. Giraud, 1973, p. 362). See my *La Cause des Martyrs dans 'Les Tragiques' d'Agrippa d'Aubigné* (Mont-de-Marsan: Editions InterUniversitaires, 1991), pp. 49–50.

30 Thevet, *Cosmographie universelle*, vol. II, book XXI, ch. 15, fol. 944 verso (Lussagnet, p. 194).
31 Ibid. Lussagnet (p. 196, note 1) corrects the rather improbable sequence of events proposed by Thevet. Cf. Métraux, *Religions et magies indiennes*, p. 75.
32 On this seemingly paradoxical rite see Georg Friederici, *Der Tränengruss der Indianer* (Leipzig: Simmel, 1910) and Alfred Métraux, *La Religion des Tupinamba et ses rapports avec celle des autres tribus tupi-guarani* (Paris: E. Leroux, 1928), pp. 180–8.
33 Thevet, *Cosmographie universelle*, vol. II, book XXI, ch. 15, fol. 944 verso (Lussagnet, p. 195). Cf. Métraux, *Religions et magies indiennes*, pp. 52–3.
34 Host, as if from *hostis*, enemy'. José de Acosta, *Historia natural y moral de las Indias*, V, 20. Here, I am drawing on the rather tenuous analysis by Fermín del Pino Díaz, 'Culturas clásicas y americanas en la obra del Padre Acosta', in Francisco de Solano and Fermin del Pino (eds), *América y la España del siglo XVI: homenaje a Gonzalo Fernández de Oviedo* (Madrid: CSIC, Instituto Gonzalo Fernández de Oviedo, 1982), pp. 327–62, esp. pp. 357–8.
35 Joseph-François Lafitau, *Mœurs des Sauvages Ameriquains comparées aux mœurs des premiers temps* (Paris: Saugrain l'aîné et Charles-Etienne Hochereau, 1724), 4 vols, vol. IV, pp. 18–31.
36 Ibid., p. 19. Another remark in the same vein is made during a comparison with the Mexicans (vol. I, p. 165): 'Among the other barbarian Peoples, these kinds of Sacrifices were not so ordinary, nor so marked, unless one sees as a Sacrifice the torment which they inflict on their slaves, or prisoners of war; which I think quite probable.' A little earlier (p. 163), Lafitau had explained what he meant by 'sacrifice': 'Sacrifice is an act of Religion, an Offering made to the Divinity for the same reasons as are included in the obligation of men to worship him as is his due, and especially for reason of gratitude for the good things they receive from him, and which they acknowledge that they owe to him who is their master. It is as ancient as Religion itself, and as widespread as the Nations subject to Religion, since there is not one of them where Sacrifice is not customary, or to whom it is not also a proof of that Religion.'
37 Ibid., vol. IV, p. 25.
38 Ibid., vol. I, ch. IV, 'Of Religion', pp. 152–62: 'Sacred fire in America'. Of particular interest is his remark: 'Fire has always been in some way sacred to all the Nations of America who have the use of it; but the wandering Nations, and most of the sedentary ones, have no perpetual Fire, nor any temple in which to keep it.'
39 Ibid., vol. IV, pp. 22–3.
40 Ibid., p. 28.
41 Ibid., p. 30.
42 See ch. 6 below, and my 'Catholiques et Cannibales. Le thème du cannibalisme dans le discours protestant au temps des guerres de Religion', in J.-C. Margolin and R. Sauzet (eds), *Pratiques et discours alimentaires à la Renaissance* (Paris: Maisonneuve et Larose, 1982), pp. 233–45.
43 This solution has been accepted by some Brazilian anthropologists, such as Eduardo Batalha Viveiros de Castro: *Araweté: os deuses canibais* (Rio de Janeiro: J. Zahar Editor-Anpocs, 1986). See also his study, written with Manuela Carneiro da Cunha: 'Vingança e temporalidade: os Tupinamba', *Journal de la Société des Américanistes* LXXI (1985), pp. 91–298. This theory was partially accepted, but modified, by Isabelle Combès, 'Etre ou ne pas

être. A propose d'*Araweté*. *Os deuses canibais* de Eduardo Viveiros de Castro', *Journal de la Société des Américanistes* LXXII (1986), pp. 211–20; see also her *Tragédie cannibale*, pp. 26, 188 and esp. pp. 197–205.

44 See Pierre François-Xavier de Charlevoix, SJ, *Histoire du Paraguay* (Paris: Didot, Giffart et Nyon, 1756), vol. I, p. 182, on the year 1588. For a commentary on the corresponding passage from Father Antonio Ruiz de Montoya, see Combès, *Tragédie cannibale*, pp. 197–8.

45 André Thevet, *Histoire d'André Thevet Angoumoisin, Cosmographe du Roy, de deux voyages par luy faits aux Indes Australes, et Occidentales, Contenant la façon de vivre des peuples Barbares, et observation des principaux points que doivent tenir en leur route les Pilotes, et mariniers, pour eviter le naufrage, et autres dangers de ce grand Ocean. Avec une response aux libelles d'injures, publiées contre le chevalier de Villegagnon*, c.1587–8 (Paris: BN, MS fr. 15454. Substantial extracts were edited by Suzanne Lussagnet in her *Le Brésil et les Brésiliens*, pp. 237–310. An incomplete and slightly earlier version of the work, under the title *Second voyage d'André Thevet, dans les Terres Australes et Occidentales*, constitutes BN MS fr. 17175.

46 Mathurin Héret handled *Les Singularitez*; François de Belleforest and Philibert Bretin dealt with *Cosmographie universelle*. They fulfilled their thankless (and anonymous) task with varying degrees of zeal. For more about these invariably stormy collaborations, see my *André Thevet, cosmographe des derniers Valois*, chs V, VI and VII.

47 Thevet, *Histoire de deux voyages*, fols 53–4 (Lussagnet, pp. 270–4, esp. p. 273).

48 Ibid., fol. 57 verso (Lussagnet, pp. 277–8).

49 Ibid., fol. 55 verso (Lussagnet, p. 276). 'Nonetheless,' opines Thevet, 'I think that he had no great desire to fall upon her.'

50 Ibid., fol. 56 verso (Lussagnet, p. 279).

51 Ibid., fol. 57 verso (Lussagnet, pp. 279–80). On the significance of these analogous designs, see Combès, *Tragédie cannibale*, p. 252.

52 Ibid., fol. 58 recto (Lussagnet, p. 281).

53 Claude Lévi-Strauss, *Structural Anthropology* (Harmondsworth: Penguin, 1968), p. 217.

54 Thevet, *Cosmographie universelle*, vol. II, fols 913–20 verso; *Histoire de deux voyages*, fols 41–51. See Lévi-Strauss's commentary in *The Story of Lynx*, trans. C. Tihanyi (Chicago: University of Chicago Press, 1995), chs IV and V, pp. 43–4 and 55.

55 It therefore seems dangerous to seek a plausible chronology in this juxtaposition, as Métraux attempts in a celebrated chapter of *La Religion des Tupinamba* (ch. II, pp. 55–66, summarized by Combès in *Tragédie cannibale*, pp. 59–62). We will never know what, in the repetitive structure, derives from the rite itself and what from the narrative dyslexia which infected the first ethnographers of the Tupinamba – the Portuguese Fernão Cardim and the Frenchman André Thevet.

56 Combès adds a 'sixth' act to this cannibal tragedy, though it is not included in the temporal sequence of the sacrificial ritual (*Tragédie cannibale*, pp. 213–55).

Chapter 6: Jean de Léry, or the Cannibal Obsession

1 Léry's only additions to Thevet are a disquisition on the music of the war-dance, and a dialogue 'on the entry or arrival in the land of Brazil'. See Jean de Léry, *Histoire d'un voyage faict en la terre du Brésil* (Geneva: Antoine Chuppin, 1578), ch. XX: 'Colloquy upon the entry or arrival in the land of Brazil among the people of the country called *Tououpinambaoults* and *Toupinenkins* in the savage and in the French languages'. I refer mostly to the 1580 second edition of *Histoire d'un voyage*, reprinted in facsimile with a commentary by J.-C. Morisot (Geneva: Droz, 1975), pp. 306–38. The translations are from Janet Whatley, *History of a Voyage to the Land of Brazil* (Berkeley: University of California Press, 1990); here, pp. 178–95.

2 On the genesis and progressive developments of *Histoire d'un voyage*, see my *Le Huguenot et le Sauvage* (Paris: Aux Amateurs de Livres, 1990), chs II and III, pp. 47–104.

3 Léry, *Histoire d'un voyage*, trans. Whatley, ch. XV, p. 127.

4 Ibid.

5 Ibid., ch. V, p. 29.

6 On this canonical opposition see vol. 1 of Claude Lévi-Strauss's 'Mythologies', in *The Raw and the Cooked* (London: Cape, 1970).

7 On this distinction made by Thevet, which is both onomastic, cultural and geographical, see ch. 4 above, notes 19–21 and corresponding text.

8 Léry, *Histoire d'un voyage*, trans. Whatley, ch. VIII, p. 56.

9 Ibid., p. XV, p. 126. The scene was later illustrated by Thédore de Bry, *Americae tertia pars* (Frankfurt, 1592), p. 179: 'Boucan et Barbarorum culina'. On this narrative and iconographic motif see Bernadette Bucher, *La Sauvage aux seins pendants* (Paris: Hermann, 1977) and my *Le Huguenot et le Sauvage*, p. 53.

10 Léry, *Histoire d'un voyage*, 3rd edn (Geneva: Antoine Chuppin, 1585), ch. XVI, p. 281. In the fourth (1599–1600) and subsequent editions, this chapter is XVII. The passage in question is on p. 317 of the 'fifth' and last edition (Geneva: Jean Vignon, 1611).

11 On this crucial question of the Eucharistic controversy, see Preserved Smith, *A Short History of Christian Theophagy* (Chicago and London: Open Court Publishing, 1922). See also Gary Macy, *The Banquet's Wisdom. A Short History of the Theologies of the Lord's Supper* (New York, 1992). For the connections between this controversy and the colonial venture of France Antarctique, see my 'Tristes Tropistes: du Brésil à la France, une controverse à l'aube des guerres de religion', *Revue de l'Histoire des Religions* CCII-3 (1985), pp. 267–94.

12 Léry, *Histoire d'un voyage*, trans. Whatley, ch. VI, p. 41: 'for when they were shown by other passages that these words and expressions are figures – that is, that Scripture is accustomed to calling the signs of the Sacraments by the names of the things signified ...'

13 Ibid.

14 This is the very argument which Catholic theologians, especially the Jansenists of Port-Royal in the seventeenth century, turned against the Calvinists themselves in the Eucharistic controversy. In *La Logique ou l'art de penser* (I, IV), Antoine Arnauld and Pierre Nicole emphasized that 'one can never conclude with certainty, either from the presence of the sign that the thing signified is present (since there are signs of things that are absent);

nor from the presence of the sign, that the thing signified is absent, since there are signs of things that are present' (addition made in 1683; see the critical edition by P. Clair and F. Girbal, Paris: Vrin, 1981, p. 53; my italics). For a reading of the passages in *La Logique* relating to the Eucharist, see Louis Marin, *Food for Thought,* trans. M. Hjort (Baltimore: Johns Hopkins University Press, 1989), ch. 1 pp. 3–25.

15 Léry, *Histoire d'un voyage,* trans. Whatley, ch. XV, p. 132.

16 Micah 3: 3, as quoted in ibid. On the old anti-Semitic cliché and its use in the Renaissance, see, especially, Anthony Pagden, *The Fall of Natural Man* (Cambridge: Cambridge University Press, 1986), p. 82, citing Norman Cohn, *Europe's Inner Demons* (St Albans, 1976), pp. 1–2. See also Jean-Claude Margolin, 'Liberté de conscience ou intolérance? Réflexions sur quelques "histoires juives" à la Renaissance', in *La Liberté de conscience (XVIe–XVIIe siècles). Actes du Colloque de Mulhouse et Bâle* (Geneva: Droz, 1991), pp. 191–216. As Margolin remarks (p. 209), the legend of Simon of Trent, a Christian youth sacrificed by Jews in a parody of the Crucifixion, became widely known towards the end of the fifteenth century, particularly in the Nuremberg region.

17 Léry, *Histoire d'un voyage,* 3rd edn, ch. XV, p. 232.

18 Ibid., pp. 234–5.

19 Ibid., p. 247.

20 Ibid., pp. 251–6.

21 Ibid., pp. 257–60.

22 Charles de Rochefort, *Histoire naturelle et morale des Iles Antilles* (Rotterdam, 1658), p. 487.

23 Jean de Léry, *Histoire memorable de la ville de Sancerre* (Geneva, 1574); new edition by Géralde Nakam entitled *Au lendemain de la Saint-Barthélemy. Guerre civile et famine* (Paris: Anthropos, 1975), p. 291. The scene is summarized in a less than serious tone by Pierre-Antoine Bernheim and Guy Stavridès in *Cannibales!* (Paris: Plon, 1992); pp. 168–9.

24 Léry, *Histoire memorable,* ed. Nakam, p. 292.

25 Ibid., p. 294.

26 Ibid., p. 295.

27 Léry, 'Sommaire discours de la famine, cherté de vivres, chairs, et autres choses non acoustumées pour la nourriture de l'homme, dont les assiegez de la ville de Sanxerre ont esté affligéz, et en ont usé environ trois mois. Avec une missive escrite à Monseigneur de la Chastre, Gouverneur de Berry, par ung ministre dudit Sanxerre nommé Delery, comme ensuit' (Aix-en-Provence: Bibliothèque Méjanes, MS 445, pp. 333–43.

28 Léry, *Histoire memorable,* ed. Nakam, p. 290.

29 On this ambiguity in the attitude of Léry, who was the principal negotiator on the Protestant side when the terms of surrender for Sancerre were discussed in August 1573, see my *Le Huguenot et le Sauvage,* ch. II, pp. 72–9.

30 On this comparison between the two forms of cannibalism, see ibid., pp. 52–3. For some more general comments on the horror of blood among the Reformers see my *La Cause des martyrs dans 'Les Tragiques' d'Agrippa d'Aubigné* (Mont-de-Marsan: Edition's InterUniversitaires, 1991), esp. pp. 11–17 and 35–7.

31 I quote from the transcription by Bruna Conconi, published as an appendix to her thesis 'Le prove dei testimonie. Scrivere di storia, fare letteratura nella seconda metà del Cinquecento: l'*Histoire memorable* di Jean de Léry'

(University of Milan: Instituto di Lingua e letteratura francese, 1992), fol. 213. On the archetype of the aged Cannibal woman, see Bucher, *La Sauvage aux seins pendants*, and Claude Rawson, ' "Indians" and Irish: Montaigne, Swift and the Cannibal Question', *Modern Language Quarterly* (September 1992), pp. 299–363. See esp. pp. 302–5, which comments in detail on the relevant chapter by Léry and relates it to Montaigne's 'Of Cannibals'.

32 This is noted as early as the *Discours de la famine*, ed. Conconi, fol. 211; cf. Léry *Histoire memorable*, ed. Nakam, p. 291.

33 Regarding the contrast between these two movements, polarized between the two sexes, I agree with the conclusions of Viveiros de Castro, *Araweté* (Rio de Janeiro: J. Zahar Editor-Anpocs, 1986), though Isabelle Combès, *La Tragédie cannibale chez les anciens Tupi-Guarani* (Paris: PUF, 1992), casts some doubt on them.

34 Léry, *Histoire d'un voyage*, trans. Whatley, ch. XVIII, p. 163.

35 Ibid., ch. XXII, p. 213.

36 Léry's word, *Histoire memorable*, ch. X, p. 291. Cf. *Discours de la famine*, ed. Conconi, fol. 211.

37 Léry, *Histoire d'un voyage*, trans. Whatley, ch. XV, p. 132. A marginal note refers to 'the history of our times book 7 pag. 22', meaning Théodore Beza's *Histoire ecclésiastique des Eglises reformées au Royaume de France* (Antwerp: J. Rémy, 1580).

38 On Léry's primitivism, which, like all primitivism, was fundamentally ambiguous, see Christian Marouby, *Utopie et primitivisme: essai sur l'imaginaire anthropologique à l'âge classique* (Paris: Seuil, 1990), pp. 111–12, esp. 126–37. Cf. the concordant remarks by Pagden, *European Encounters*, pp. 42–7.

Chapter 7: The Melancholy Cannibal

1 This chapter takes up a line of thought which I have pursued elsewhere: 'Rage, fureur, folie, cannibales: le Scythe et le Brésilien', in Jean Céard (ed.), *La Folie et le corps* (Paris: Presses de L'Ecole Normale Supérieure, 1985), pp. 49–80.

2 To borrow an expression from the title of Paul Bénichou's *Morales du Grand Siècle* (Paris: Gallimard, 1948).

3 Jean-Pierre Seguin, *L'Information en France avant le périodique* (Geneva: Droz, 1964), nos 40 and 72.

4 See especially the anthology with preface by Claude Gaignebet, *Le Coeur mangé. Récits érotiques et courtois des XIIe et XIIIe siècles*, 'Stock + Plus' collection (Paris: Stock, 1979). For the persistence of cannibalism in the popular French imagination in the nineteenth century, see Alain Corbin, *The Village of Cannibals* (Cambridge: Polity, 1992), pp. 88–101: on 16 August 1870, a 'young nobleman' was killed and roasted in the market-place of the village of Hautefaye in the Dordogne, on the grounds that he was a 'Prussian'.

5 The story was published by N. Dureau of Troyes in 1608. Paris, BN, Rés. G. 2871 (Seguin, no. 40).

6 Ibid., p. 14.

7 Ibid.

8 This description of anthropophagy is by Claude Lévi-Strauss, undoubtedly the leading theorist on incest. On the analogy in numerous societies between

the food taboo and the incest taboo, see his *The Savage Mind* (London, 1966), pp. 97–108.

9 Agrippa d'Aubigné, *Les Tragiques* (1616), I, II. pp. 524–6.

10 Gaignebet, *Le Coeur mangé*, pp. 221–39. One of the cuckolded husbands declares, 'We will make them eat it by cunning, for we could have no better vengeance!' (p. 235).

11 Extracts of this tale are given in ibid., pp. 241–51.

12 In the second of these tales – the story of Nastasio degli Onesti – the heart of the woman whom he cannot have is fed to the dogs: the love-inspired anthropophagy is performed, so to speak, by delegation.

13 Said, with reference to certain myths and folktales, by Jean Pouillon, 'Manières de table, manières de lit, manières de langage', in *Destins du cannibalisme. Nouvelle Revue de Psychanalyse* 6 (Paris: Gallimard, autumn 1972), p. 15.

14 Published by N. Alexandre. Paris: BN, Lk7.1748 (Seguin, no. 72).

15 Ibid., p. 4

16 Ibid., p. 3.

17 Ibid., p. 8.

18 Four oral versions of this famous tale, each with a cannibal element, are reproduced by Yvonne Verdier as an appendix to her article 'Grands-mères, si vouv saviez [Grandmothers, if you only knew!] ... Le Petit Chaperon Rouge dans la tradition orale', *Cahiers de Littérature Orale* 4 (1978), pp. 17–55. The more usual assimilation is between the grandmother and the wolf. On this, see Claude Rawson, ' "Indians" and Irish', *Modern Language Quarterly* (September 1992).

19 On vengeance as a heroic quality and its various avatars in Bandello see Eliott Forsyth, *La Tragédie française de Jodelle à Corneille (1553–1640): le thème de la vengeance* (Paris: Nizet, 1962), pp. 128–30.

20 Montaigne, *Essays*, trans. John Florio (Menston, Yorks: Scholar Press, 1969), p. 50.

21 Jean Bodin, *Methodus ad facilem historiarum cognitionem* (1566), trans. Pierre Mesnard as *La Méthode de l'Histoire* (Paris: Les Belles Lettres, 1941), ch. V, pp. 82–5; Bodin, *Les Six Livres de la République* (Paris, 1576), book V, p. 527, 'Estranges cruautez des peuples de Septentrion' and 528, 'Cruautez terribles des peuples de midy'.

22 Herodotus, *Histories*, book IV, chs 64–80. Cf. Solinus, *Polyhistor*, ch. XXV, 'De Scytharum moribus' (Basle, 1538), fol. 48; Pomponius Mela, *De situ orbis*, book II (Basle, 1538), p. 183.

23 Bodin, *Six Livres*, book V, p. 527. For Léry, see ch. 6 above, note 19 and text.

24 Ibid., p. 528.

25 Ibid., pp. 521ff.

26 Bodin, *Methodus*, trans. Mesnard, p. 86.

27 Ibid. According to Aristotle's *Problemata* (XXX, 1), which Bodin seems to be following in this passage, the destiny of these suicidal heroes, who slay their own offspring or eat their own relations, is explained by an excess of black bile, otherwise defined as the *dyscrasia* of the humours. For this medical explanation, see Jean Starobinski, *Trois Fureurs*, 'Le Chemin' collection (Paris: Gallimard, 1975), ch. 1, 'The sword of Ajax', pp. 64–6. Cf. d'Aubigné, *Les Tragiques*, I, ll. 135–62, in which France, which is tearing itself apart, is compared to a giant 'full of dyscrasia' whose 'bulk degenerates into melancholy'.

28 For instance, the Protestant Innocent Gentillet, in his *Discours d'Estat. Contre Nicolas Machiavel* (1576), describes the extremes to which Italians can be driven by the spirit of vengefulness: 'So that when they can have their enemy at their mercy, to be avenged on him, they beat him in some strange and barbarous way, and as they beat him they remind him of the wrong he has done to them, reproach him and insult him, so as to torment body and soul both together, and sometimes they wash their hands and mouths in his blood, and constrain him to give himself up to the devil, so as to damn his soul while killing his body, if they may.' The author concludes with this prayer: 'May God in His grace guard poor France (which already is stained with other crimes and with the doctrine taught by Machiavelli which is practised by those of his nation) from being fouled and infected with this immortal and irreconcilable vengeance' (part III, p. 311; new edn by C. Edward Rathé, Geneva: Droz, 1968, pp. 325–6). See also Elliott Forsyth, *Tragédie française*, p. 123.

29 Bartolomé de Las Casas, *Brevísima relación de la destrucción de las Indias* (1552) in *Tratados*, vol. II, p. 91: 'this captain was accustomed to take with him as many subject Indians as he could, to make war on the others. And, as he gave no food to the ten or twenty thousand men whom he took with him, he permitted them to eat the Indians whom they captured. There was also in his camp a most solemn butchery of human flesh; children were killed and roasted in his presence.' This scene produced a great sensation, especially after the engraver and printer Théodore de Bry made it into a spectacular illustration (see Las Casas, *Narratio regionum Indicarum per Hispanos quosdam devastatarum verissima* (Frankfurt: Théodore de Bry, 1598), p. 50; reproduced in my *Le Huguenot et le Sauvage* (Paris: Aux Amateurs de Livres, 1990), p. 245.

30 Jacques-Auguste de Thou, *Historia sui temporis* (1576), book II, p. 582A.

31 Pierre de L'Estoile, *Mémoires journaux*, vol. 1, pp. 161–2 (November 1576). This and the previous reference are from Elliott Forsyth, *Tragédie française*, p. 132.

32 Theodore Beza, *Deuxiesme volume de l'histoire ecclesiastique des Eglises reformées au Royaume de France* (Antwerp: J. Rémy, 1580), book VII, p. 454.

33 On this anti-Italianism aroused by the Florentine court of Catherine de' Medici, see J. Mathorez, 'Les Italiens et l'opinion française à la fin du XVIe siècle', *Bulletin du Bibliophile et du Bibliothécaire* (Paris, 1914).

34 Henri Estienne, *De la conformité des merveilles anciennes avec les modernes. Ou traité préparatif à l'Apologie pour Hérodote* (Geneva, 1566), book 1, ch. XIX, pp. 311–12. See Gabriel Maugain, 'L'Italie dans l'*Apologie pour Hérodote* d'Henri Estienne', in *Mélanges Abel Lefranc* (Paris, 1936), pp. 374–92. A few pages further on, in the same chapter, Estienne reports from Matteo Bandello's 'Tragical Histories' the story of a Spanish girl who was clandestinely married and avenged herself by killing the man who had betrayed her. Many details in this topical tale prefigure the adventure of Cécile de Dole as recounted in 1608. The entrapment of the lover by a mechanical bed or chair, the insults done upon his corpse and the public execution of the heroine occur in both versions of the exemplary tale (ibid., p. 313).

35 Thyestes had raped the wife of his brother Atreus. To avenge the outrage, the latter cut the throats of Thyestes' children and served them up to him in a sauce. He did not discover what he had eaten until the meal was over. The sun

then hid its face. On the Thyestes myth and its structural analogy with that of Oedipus, see Alain Moreau, 'A propos d'Œdipe: la liaison entre trois crimes – parricide, inceste et cannibalisme', *Etudes de littérature ancienne* (Paris: Presses de l'Ecole Normale Supérieure, 1979), pp. 97–127.

36 Bodin, *Six Livres*, book V, p. 528. Cf. his *Methodus*, trans. Mesnard, p. 85: 'One should not believe, with Polybius, that excess of cruelty is necessarily the fruit of bad education. Let us rather consider the Americans of the South [i.e. the Brazilians] who plunge their children in the blood of their slain enemies, suck that blood and feed upon the severed limbs of their victims. But the cruelty of the Southerners is very different from that of the Scythians.'

37 Bodin, *Six Livres*, book V, p. 528.

38 Bodin, *Methodus*, trans. Mesnard, p. 86.

39 Lycanthropy was described in antiquity by Galen, Pliny et al. Its symptoms are discussed by, *inter aliis*, André Thevet in his *Cosmographie de Levant* (Lyons: J. de Tournes and G. Gazeau, 1554), ch. VI. Most Renaissance scholars and experts on witchcraft denied that any transformation actually took place, and attributed the effect to a 'prestige', meaning a trick or 'enchantment' of Satan. See, especially, Jean de Nynauld, *De la lycanthropie, transformation et extase des sorciers (1615). Edition critique augmentée d'études sur les lycanthropes et les loups-garous par Nicole Jacques-Chaquin, Jean Céard, Maxime Préaud, Frédéric Max, Michel Meurger, Sophie Houdard et Lise Andries* (Paris: Frénésie Editions, 1990).

40 See ch. 6 above. Cf. Géralde Nakam, *Au lendemain de la Saint-Barthélemy* (Paris: Anthropos, 1975), Preface, pp. 103–4 and text, pp. 291–5.

41 Bodin, *Methodus*, trans. Mesnard, p. 86.

42 Though André Thevet, in *Les Singularitez de la France Antarctique* (Paris: chez les Héritiers de Maurice de la Porte, 1557), laments that the Tupinamba did not earlier encounter the evangelical precepts of gentleness and pardon. But this knowledge of Christianity might be insufficient, 'considering, that the Christian, although [vengeance] is forbidden to him by an express command, cannot refrain from it' (*Les Singularitez*, ch. 4, 'That these Savages are marvellously vindictive', fol. 78).

43 Especially Estienne's *Apologie pour Hérodote* (Geneva, 1566). In his *Serées* (1584–1618), Guillaume Bouchet devotes a good deal of space to Cannibals, as described by Thevet, Léry and Montaigne. See, e.g., the fourteenth 'Serée', 'On persons decapitated, hanged, whipped, banished or with their ears cut off' (book 2 pp. 67ff.).

44 Bodin, *Six Livres*, book V, p. 528.

45 Thevet, *Grand Insulaire et Pilotage*, c.1586–8, vol. 1 (BN, MS fr. 15452), fol. 269: 'Islands of Giants'.

46 Pierre de Dampmartin, *De la connoissance et merveilles du monde et de l'homme* (Paris: Thomas Périer, 1585), book VIII, fol. 112 recto.

47 Ibid., fol. 112 verso.

48 Ibid.

49 Montaigne, *Essais*, II, 11, 'Of cruelty', p. 247: 'Amongst all other vices, there is none I hate more, than cruelty, both by nature and judgement, as the extremest of all vices.'

Chapter 8: The Spitting Cannibal

1 Montaigne, *Essays* trans. John Florio (Menston, Yorks: Scholar Press, 1969), I, 30 [31], p. 101. Cf. Hugo Friedrich, *Montaigne* (Paris: Gallimard, 1968), p. 219. Note that Friedrich, normally one of Montaigne's best commentators, misunderstands the nature of Brazilian cannibalism. They did not 'eat their own dead', as he says (p. 218): they ate their enemies, who were killed at ritual banquets.

2 Alphonse Dupront, 'Espace et Humanisme'; *Bibliothèque d'Humanisme et Renaissance* VIII (1946), pp. 61, 64. Raymond Lebègue, 'Montaigne et le paradoxe des Cannibales', in *Studi di letteratura, storia e filosofia in onore di Bruno Revel* (Florence: Olschki, 1965), pp. 361–2. Joseph R. de Lutri takes this idea of playfulness and gratuitous paradox, which his predecessors at least put in more restrained terms, to absurd lengths. For example, there is no discernible pun in Montaigne's anecdote about the horseman whose 'seat' amazed the Americans, who promptly murdered him: see de Lutri, 'L'humour de la déception dans le chapitre "Des Cannibales" ', *BSAM* 5/14–15 (1975), pp. 105–6. The word 'assiette', used here by Montaigne to mean a seat on a horse, does, of course, also mean 'plate'; but the Cannibals did not use plates, and Montaigne does not say that the unfortunate victim was eaten by his murderers. Similarly, the allusions to hammocks and the 'principal office' of women, which was to 'heat the beverage' of the warriors, do not in the least constitute 'comic asides'. These are cultural characteristics, which had been duly reported, before Montaigne, by Thevet and Léry. What would de Lutri have said if Montaigne had added that this drink might have been fermented using saliva and spit? That was the recipe described by contemporary observers, but Montaigne, seeking to defend and exalt the Cannibals, decided not to mention it. It seems quite clear that such definite comments, far from betraying an omnipresent underlying humour, are intended only to add verisimilitude to the narrative.

3 As felt by Georges Le Gentil, 'La France Equinoxiale (1593–1615)', in *Biblos. Revista da Faculdade de Letras da Universidade de Coimbra* VIII (1932), pp. 555–78. See esp. p. 559: 'Cannibalism itself, however repugnant it might have been, found favour with these anarchistic thinkers'; and p. 575: 'One further step and this spirit of progress, or Utopia, will lead us to total overthrow, to revolution.' Le Gentil agrees here with apologists for the *conquista*, such as Fernández de Oviedo and Cieza de León, that the South American Indians are a 'degenerate race' (p. 578) practising 'crude animism' (p. 558) and exhibiting 'undoubted barbarity' (p. 559). Unfortunately, he is writing well into the twentieth century, when anthropological explanations have gained a right of audience.

4 See Jean Plattard, *Montaigne: 'Des Cannibales'* (Paris: CDU, 1940), p. 38: 'I do not believe that any man was eaten alive during the Wars of Religion', and again, 'it seems improbable that human bodies were roasted piece by piece during the Wars of Religion'. Even a hasty reading of Theodore Beza's *Histoire ecclésiastique* (Antwerp: J. Rémy, 1580), or Agrippa d'Aubigné's *Les Tragiques* would prove the contrary. On this, see Natalie Z. Davis, *Les Cultures du peuple* (Paris: Aubier-Montaigne, 1979), ch. 6, 'Rites of violence'. Cf. my 'Catholiques et Cannibales', in J.-C. Margolin and R. Sauzet (eds), *Pratiques et discours alimentaires à la Renaissance* (Paris: Maisonneuve et Larose, 1982), pp. 233–45.

5 Montaigne, *Essays*, I, 30 [31], p. 107. The idea that this chapter is paradoxical, already suggested by Lebègue in 'Montaigne et la paradoxe' in 1965, was pursued by André Tournon, *Montaigne, la glose et l'essai* (Lyons: Presses Universitaires de Lyon, 1983), pp. 217–21.

6 Ibid., p. 102. Cf. Montaigne, *Essays*, II, 12, p. 304: 'There is neither Corn, nor Wine, no nor any of our beasts seen in that new corner of the World, which our fathers have lately discovered.'

7 Etienne Pasquier, *Les Lettres d'Estienne Pasquier, conseiller et advocat general du Roy en la chambre des comptes de Paris* (Paris: Abel L'Angelier, 1596), book III, fols 62 verso–63 verso. This letter is reproduced in an appendix to my 'La négation des Cannibales: Montaigne et Pasquier', in Marcel Tetel and G. Mallary Masters (eds), *Le Parcours des essais. Montaigne 1588–1988* (Paris: Aux Amateurs de Livres, 1989), pp. 225–37. A more illustrious imitator of this passage from the *Essays*, via Florio's translation, is William Shakespeare, who puts the same approving enumeration into the mouth of Gonzalo in *The Tempest*:

> I'the commonwealth I would by contraries
> Execute all things; for no kind of traffic
> Would I admit; no name of magistrate;
> Letters should not be known; riches, poverty,
> And use of service, none; contract, succession,
> Bourn, bound of land, tilth, vineyard, none;
> No use of metal, corn, or wine, or oil;
> No occupation; all men idle, all;
> And women too, but innocent and pure;
> No sovereignty. (*The Tempest*, II. i. 154ff.)

Spoken by this gaping, doddering old man, the negative formula assumes a distinctly ironic tone: it is scarcely more acceptable than it was in Pasquier. The denizen of the unknown island, the half-Negro Caliban, whose name is an anagram of 'Canibal', soon turns up as a forcible refutation of Gonzalo's senile reverie. For a commentary on this celebrated paraphrase of Montaigne, see Allan H. Gilbert, 'Montaigne and *The Tempest*', *Romantic Review* V (1914), pp. 357–64, and, more recently, Janet Whatley, ' "Sea-Changes": *L'Histoire d'un voyage* de Jean de Léry et *La Tempête* de Shakespeare', in *La France-Amérique. Actes du Colloque de Tours 1992* (Paris: Champion, 1996). More generally, on the 'negative formula' as a favourite and obligatory figure of utopian discourse, see Harry Levin, *The Myth of the Golden Age in the Renaissance* (London: Faber and Faber, 1970), p. 11. Cf. Gérard Defaux, *Marot, Rabelais, Montaigne* (Paris and Geneva: Champion-Slatkine, 1987), p. 172.

8 *La Pazzia* (Venice, 1540; reprinted 1543, 'Stampata in Venegia per Giovanni Andrea Vavassore detto Guadagnino et Florio fratello'). French translation: *Les Louanges de LA FOLIE, Traicté fort plaisant en forme de Paradoxe, traduict d'Italien en François par feu messire Jean du Thier* (Paris: Hertmann Barbé, 1566). This source was identified, with some reservations, by José V. de Piña Martins, 'Modèles portugais et italiens de Montaigne', in *Montaigne et l'Europe. Actes du Colloque International de Bordeaux (1992)* (Mont-de-Marsan: Editions InterUniversitaires, 1992), pp. 139–52. See also his 'Um Livro acerca da Loucoura (*La Pazzia*, 1540), e a sua discutivel originalidade', in *Homenaje a Eugenio Asensio* (Madrid: Editorial Gredos, 1988), pp. 361–78.

9 *Les Louanges de LA FOLIE,* fol. C6 verso.
10 Ibid., fol. C7 recto.
11 Montaigne, *Essays,* I, 30 [31], p. 102.
12 Ibid., p. 104.
13 Lebègue, 'Montaigne et le paradoxe', detects some of the rhetorical slippage in this part of the essay. Tournon, *Montaigne, la glose et l'essai,* concludes his discussion of the chapter: 'The whole remains disquieting, in that logically incompatible ideas are associated instead of contrasted, and added to one another instead of cancelling one another out, just as sophisms sit side by side with solid arguments in *declamatio.*' The internal logic of the purely American part of the chapter 'Des Coches' presents at least a comparable degree of difficulty. In the very first lines, for example, there is an imperceptible slide from the Golden Age to the age of gold, from the naked and innocent peoples encountered by Columbus in the islands to the sophisticated civilization of the Aztecs and Incas, who were acquainted with weaving, architecture and goldsmithing (Montaigne, *Essays,* III, 6, p. 545).
14 Herodotus, *Histories,* book IV, 1–44. On the 'imagined Scythians', see the commentary by François Hartog, *Le Miroir d'Hérodote* (Paris: Gallimard, 1980), part I.
15 d'Aubigné, *Les Tragiques,* I, l. 499: an allusion to the siege of Sancerre in 1573, which ended with a case of cannibalism. See Jean de Léry on the subject in ch. 6 above.
16 That, at least, was the opinion of most Renaissance geographers. For example, André Thevet, in *Les Singularitez de la France Antarctique* (Paris: chez les Héritiers de Maurice de la Porte, 1557), declares that America 'is much bigger than any of the other' parts of the world (ch. 27, fol. 51 recto).
17 This last point has been confirmed by recent historians: when the Europeans arrived, South America was 'a continent devoid of herbivores', though, paradoxically, it contains the most extensive grazing lands in the world. See the very detailed study by Pierre Deffontaines, 'Le rôle du bétail européen dans la conquête de l'Amérique du Sud par les Ibériques', in *Actes du colloque 'La Découverte de l'Amérique' (Tours, 1966)* (Paris: Vrin, 1968), pp. 105–14.
18 Jules Verne, *Les Enfants du Capitaine Grant* (Paris: Hetzel, 1868), part III, ch. VI. See ch. 13 below for an analysis of this colourful passage, which effectively justifies the extermination of the Maoris, the earliest inhabitants of New Zealand.
19 This is the title of a work by Antonello Gerbi, *La Natura delle Indie Nove* (Milan and Naples: Rocciardi, 1975), which traces the prolonged sixteenth-century debate over whether America was specially blessed – or, alternatively, specially accursed – by Divine Providence. The debate was renewed during the Enlightenment after the controversy provoked by Cornelius de Pauw. See ch. 12 below.
20 Montaigne, *Essays,* I, 30 [31], p. 104.
21 Ibid.
22 Ibid., pp. 103–4.
23 Ibid., p. 106. It is necessary to correct note 8, p. 212, of the Villey-Saulnier (Paris: PUF, 1965 and 1978) edition on this point. Montaigne is clearly referring not to 'descriptions', but to actual 'paintings', or, more accurately, woodcuts. For the purposes of comparison, see Thevet, *Les Singularitez,* fol. 76 verso, and *Cosmographie universelle* (1575), vol. II, fol. 945 verso; and Jean de Léry, *Histoire d'un voyage faict en la terre du Bresil,* 2nd edn (Geneva:

Antoine Chuppin, 1580), p. 214. See my new edition of Léry (Montpellier: Max Chaleil, 1992) for a complete iconography of the subject, pp. 150–1.

24 Hans Staden, *Warhaftige Historia und Beschreibung eyner Landtschafft der Wilden, Nacketen, Grimmigen Menschfresser, Leuthen in der Neuenwelt America gelegen* (Marburg: A. Kolbe, 1557), vol. II, p. 29; Théodore de Bry's edition of Hans Staden and Jean de Léry, *Americae tertia pars, provinciae Brasiliae Historiam continens...* (Frankfurt, 1592), p. 125. See Illustration 8.

25 Montaigne, *Essays*, III, 6, 'Of Coaches', p. 546.

26 Ibid., I, 30 [31], p. 106.

27 Etienne de La Boétie, *De la servitude volontaire ou Contr'Un*, critical edition by Malcolm Smith (Geneva: Droz, 1987), p. 35. Cf. Montaigne, *Essays*, I, 30 [31], p. 106. Like 'Of Cannibals', La Boétie's *Contr'Un* follows the rules of declamation, as shown by Jean Lafond, 'Le *Discours de la Servitude volontaire* de La Boétie et la rhétorique de la déclamation', in *Mélanges sur la littérature de la Renaissance à la mémoire de V.-L. Saulnier* (Geneva: Droz, 1984), pp. 735–45.

28 Montaigne, *Essays*, I, 30 [31], p. 106.

29 Ibid., p. 105.

30 Ibid., III, 6, p. 546. On this legal ritual and Montaigne's interpretation of it, see Marcel Bataillon, 'Montaigne et les conquérants de l'or', *Studi Francesi* III/9 (September–December 1959), pp. 353–67.

31 Roger Caillois, preface to Montesquieu's *Œuvres complètes*, Bibliothèque de la Pléiade (Paris: Gallimard, 1947), vol. 1, p. v: 'What I call a sociological revolution is the mental attitude of pretending to be a stranger to the society in which one lives, looking at it from the outside as if one were seeing it for the first time ... It takes a powerful imagination to attempt such a change of outlook, and a good deal of tenacity to persist in it.' For an extended echo of this, see Georges May, 'Sens unique et double sens. Réflexions sur les voyages imaginaires', *Diogène* 152 (October–December 1990), pp. 3–21.

32 Montaigne, *Essays*, III, 6, p. 548.

33 Ibid., I, 30 [31], p. 105. On the 'cannibal economy' which is at work here and which betrays Montaigne's nostalgia for the old aristocratic virtues of gift-giving and heedless extravagance, cf. Philippe Desan's broadly similar approach in *Les Commerces de Montaigne. Le discours économique des 'Essais'* (Paris: Nizet, 1992), ch. VI, pp. 175–98. On interpretations of Tupinamba cannibalism, as described in the sixteenth century both before and after Montaigne, see the classic studies by Alfred Métraux, *Religions et magies indiennes d'Amérique du Sud* (Paris: Gallimard, 1967), ch. II, pp. 45–78, and Florestan Fernandes, 'La guerre et le sacrifice humain chez les Tupinamba', *Journal de la Société des Américanistes* (1952), pp. 139–220, both of which give satisfying answers. However, these interpretations, which were influenced by Marcel Mauss's *Essai sur le don*, have recently been revised by Viveiros de Castro in *Araweté* (Rio de Janeiro: J. Zahar Editor-Anpocs, 1986) and Isabelle Combès in *La Tragédie cannibale chez les anciens Tupi-Guarani* (Paris: PUF, 1992): see ch. 5 above.

34 Montaigne, *Essays*, III, 6, p. 547.

35 Ibid., p. 549.

36 Ibid., p. 548. Rousseau quotes at length from this passage in his 'Dernière Réponse' (Final Answer) to M. Bordes on the refutation of his *Discourse on the Arts and Sciences* (April 1752): see the Pléiade edition of Rousseau (Paris: Gallimard, 1964), vol. III, p. 91.

37 Ibid.
38 Ibid., I, 30 [31], p. 104.
39 Ibid., I, 28, 'Of Friendship'.
40 La Boétie, *Contr'Un*, p. 42.
41 André Thevet, *Les Vrais Pourtraits et vies des hommes illustres* (Paris: Veuve J. Kervert and G. Chauière, 1584), vol. II, book VIII, ch. 149, fols 661–2. On this 'portrait' see my *L'Atelier du cosmographe* (Paris: Albin Michel, 1991), ch. IV, pp. 128–45.
42 As previously noted by Michel de Certeau, *Heterologies: Discourse on the Other* (Minneapolis: University of Minnesota Press, 1985), ch. 5, 'From the body to speech, or cannibalistic utterance', pp. 73–7. For this very reason Montaigne tends to allegorize cannibalism, as is also pointed out by Antoine Compagnon, *Chat en poche. Montaigne et l'allégorie* (Paris: Seuil, 1993), pp. 110–21.

Chapter 9: Cardano, or the Rule of Necessity

1 See the important argument of Elliott Forsyth in *La Tragédie française de Jodelle à Corneille* (Paris: Nizet, 1962), esp. pp. 87–109.
2 For the French adaptation of Cinzio's *Orbecche-Oronte* see *Le Phoenix* by Jan Edouard Du Monin (Paris: Guillaume Bichon, 1585; BN Rés, Ye 1926–7, fols. 73ff.). Orbecche is the name of the heroine; her father has her lover and two sons murdered and brought to her in 'three basins'. She strikes him a mortal blow and hurls a string of epithets at him, as follows:

> Hearken to me, hound, leopard, crocodile, dragon,
> Tartar, cannibal, morphite, lestrigon:
> in your blood my blood pays the debt of mine,
> you are the sepulchre of your nephews and son-in-law.
>   (Act V, fol. 123)

For Favre's tragedy *Les Gordiens et Maximins ou l'Ambition* (1589) see Forsyth, *Tragédie française*, pp. 198–201. *Le Thyeste de Monsieur de Monleon* was published by Pierre Guillemot in Paris, 'at the Palace with the prisoners' gallery' in 1638. To refresh this theme inherited from Seneca, the author does not shrink from effects worthy of the Grand-Guignol: the 'gaping' corpses of the children are brought on stage, and 'the heads, arms and feet' are displayed separately, 'on a table in a flat dish' (p. 100).
3 Forsyth, *Tragédie française*, p. 201.
4 Pierre Mainfray, *Cyrus triomphant, ou la fureur d'Astiages Roy de Mede, tragedie* (Rouen: David du Petit Val, 1618), Act 3 Scene I, p. 27. BN, Yf. 3761–7.
5 Girolamo Cardano, *De rerum varietate libri XVII* (Basle: Heinrich Petri, 1557), book XVII, ch. XCIII, pp. 663–4. This passage is also discussed by Piero Camporesi, *Le Pain sauvage* (Paris: Le Chemin vert, 1981), p. 43.
6 *De rerum*, pp. 663–4: 'quod nos etiam in beluis abhorremus'.
7 The second mention is ibid., book VIII, ch. XL, 'De homine', p. 286: 'Adeo ut cum servabus coeuntes et filios procreantes, illos comedant.' Remarks of this nature may have been suggested to Cardano by the *Mundus Novus* attributed to Vespucci. See ch. 2 above.

8 William C. Sturtevant, 'La tupinambisation des Indiens d'Amérique du Nord', in Giles Thérien (ed.), *Les Figures de l'Indien* (Montreal: Service des Publications de l'Université du Québec à Montréal, 1988), pp. 293–303. See also idem, 'First Visual Images of Native America', in Fredi Chiappelli (ed.), *First Images of America. The Impact of the New World on the Old* (Berkeley, Los Angeles and London: University of California Press, 1976), pp. 417–54.

9 In the arrangement of the *Essays* this 'prolongation' or codicil immediately precedes 'Des Cannibales' (I, 30 [31]), although the former was written eight years before the latter. Hence the jolting contrast now felt between the two chapters: from the violence of the Aztecs (end of I, 29 [30]) we pass directly to the Eden of the free Cannibals (I, 30 [31]).

10 *Essays*, I, 29 [30], p. 99. On the role of this codicil, added in 1588, see especially the article by Juan Duran Luzio, 'Las Casas y Montaigne: escritura y lectura del Nuevo Mundo', *Montaigne Studies. An Interdisciplinary Forum*, First Issue (Hestia Press, 1989), pp. 88–106, esp. pp. 93–5. This study is resumed and extended in idem, *Bartolomé de Las Casas ante la Conquista de América. Las voces del historiador* (Heredia, Costa Rica: Euna, 1992), ch. IV, pp. 233–85. Cf. Géralde Nakam, *Les Essais, miroir et procès de leur temps* (Paris: Nizet, 1984), p. 344.

11 The volcano image is borrowed from Tzvetan Todorov, *The Conquest of America* (New York: Harper and Row, 1984), pp. 143–4.

12 This ceremony was described many times by the Spanish historians of the conquest of Mexico, notably by Fray Toribio Motolinea, *Historia de los Indios de la Nueva España (1, 6)* and D. Duran, *Historia de las Indias de Nueva España e Islas de la Tierra Firma* (III, 23). Duran emphasizes the symbolic importance of the sacrificial east–west journey, which culminates in the murder at the zenith, on the top of the Aztec pyramid. Cf. Bernardino de Sahagún, *Historia general de las cosas de Nueva España* (III, 2). All these references are in Todorov, *Conquest of America*, pp. 229–31.

13 These diverse elements are from Christian Duverger, *La Fleur Létale. Economie du sacrifice aztèque* (Paris: Editions du Seuil, 1979), pp. 123ff.

14 *Essays*, I, 29 [30], p. 100.

15 Jean de Léry, *Histoire d'un voyage faict en la terre du Brésil* (1580), trans. Janet Whatley (Berkeley: University of California Press, 1990), ch. XV, p. 128. The reader's attention is drawn to this detail by the marginal note 'Horrible and incomparable cruelty'. Cf. André Thevet, *Cosmographie universelle* (1575), vol. II, book XXI, ch. XV, fol. 944 verso; in Suzanne Lussagnet, *Les Français en Amérique* (Paris: PUF, 1953), p. 194.

16 On this see Lussagnet, *Les Français en Amérique*, p. 195, note 1.

17 Thevet, *Cosmographie universelle*, vol. II, book XXI, ch. X, fol. 934 recto (Lussagnet, p. 139): 'In consideration of which, and being firmly persuaded, that the son is the Image of the father, and that he receives the same humours and apprehensions, they kill all the males, that they take from their enemies, however small and of tender years'. For his part, the Protestant captain Bruneau, gentleman of Rivedoux, remarks in his *Histoire veritable de certain voiages perilleux et hasardeux sur la mer, auxquels reluit la justice de Dieu sur les uns et la misericorde sur les autres* (Niort, 1599; Paris, BN, Rés. G. 2889, p. 204) that to the native mind it was not 'alimentary incest' for a woman to eat the offspring of her union with the enemy prisoner: 'What is very strange about this is that during the life and marriage of the prisoner if the women has

children, when the captor so wishes he will eat them with his neighbours, and the mother shows no reluctance to eat them, telling those among the French who chided her for it, that the children were not hers, that they belonged only to her husband, who was not of her nation, but an enemy of her nation.' Gabriel Soares de Souza, *Noticia do Brasil*, II, 279, even alleges that the mother must be the first to eat her child's flesh – a detail that is not found in the French accounts except for one late piece of writing by Thevet. This kind of assertion, who must derive partly from the fantasies of the observer, is of course unverifiable. On this see again Lussagnet, *Les Français en Amérique*, p. 195, note 1.

18 André Thevet, *Les Singularitez de la France Antarctique* (Paris: chez les Héritiers de Maurice de la Porte, 1557), ch. 40, fol. 76 verso: 'As for the women and girls who are taken in war, they remain prisoners for a time, like the men, and are treated the same, save that they are given no husband.'

19 François de Belleforest, *Histoire universelle du Monde* (Paris: Gervais Mallot, 1570), book IV, fols 315 verso–316 recto.

20 This approach lies open to Montaigne's brand of irony: 'They leave things, and run to causes. O conceited discoursers!' (*Essays* III, 11, p. 612). [Translator's note: the original includes an untranslatable triple pun between *chose* 'thing', *cause* 'cause' and *causer* 'to chatter'.] Cardano pronounces the following learned and contrary principle: 'Ergo desinet admirari qui causas norit. Tantum potest causarum cognitio, etiam in incredibilibus' ('Therefore he who knows the causes will cease to be surprised, because such is the power of a knowledge of causes, even in unbelievable things'): *De rerum varietate*, p. 664.

21 *Essays*, 1, 30 [31], p. 106.

22 Cardano, *De rerum varietate*, p. 664. Another very similar argument appears in the contemporary writings of Julius Caesar Scaliger, *Exotericae Exercitationes* (Paris: Vascosan, 1557), 261st *exercitatio*, fol. 335 recto: 'Quae de Anthropophagia. Canibales. Tentiritae. Corsi.' It is impossible to be sure which of them influenced the other, or whether both Cardano and Scaliger were inspired by another, unknown text predating 1557. I owe this valuable piece of information to a book review by Michel Magnien, in *Bulletin du bibliophile* 2 (1995), pp. 372–6.

23 Thevet, *Les Singularitez*, ch. 41, fol. 78 recto. Quoted above in ch. 7, note 42.

24 Cardano, *De rerum varietate*: 'nam ibi nullum quadrupes erat animal, cujus caro suavis esset gustui, non sues, boves, pecudes, caprae, cervi, equi asinive. Ob inopiam igitur hanc eo progressi sunt.'

25 See Pierre Deffontaines, 'Le rôle du bétail européen', in *Actes du colloque 'la Découverte de l'Amérique' (Tours, 1966)* (Paris: Vrin, 1968), pp. 105–14, and the remarks by Thomas Robert Malthus in *An Essay on the Principle of Population* (5th edn, 1817; London: Dent, 1958), book I, ch. IV, 'On the obstacles to population among the indigenous nations of America'. On Malthus see further below, ch. 11.

Chapter 10: Brébeuf and Robinson: The Missionary and the Colonist

1 Claude d'Abbeville, *Histoire de la mission des Peres Capucins en l'Isle de Maragnan et terres circonvoysines* (Paris: de l'imprimerie de François Huby, 1614), ch. XLIX, fol. 294 verso. Cf. Jean de Léry, *Histoire d'un voyage faict*

en la terre du Brésil (2nd edn, 1580), ch. XV, p. 220 (see my edition, Montpellier: Max Chaleil, 1992, pp. 146–7). On d'Abbeville's extensive debts to Léry, see the article by Elena Semeria, 'Jean de Léry e Claude d'Abbeville: parentele e dipendenze', *Studi Francesi* XXX/1 (January–April 1986), pp. 65–71.

2 Ibid. (continues the passage quoted above).

3 Ibid., fol. 295 verso.

4 Ibid., fol. 296 verso, marginal note.

5 Yves d'Evreux, *Suite de l'Histoire des choses plus memorables advenues en Maragnan es annees 1613 et 1614* (Paris: François Huby, 1615), fol. 75 verso; new edition by Ferdinand Denis (Leipzig and Paris: A Franck, 1864), p. 72.

6 Ibid., fol. 67 recto (Denis, p. 63).

7 D'Abbeville, *Histoire de la mission des Peres Capucins*, ch. XLIX, fol. 287 verso.

8 Abbé G.-Th. Raynal, *Histoire des deux Indes* (1770 Amsterdam edn), vol. III, p. 336. See also ch. 11 below.

9 For a fairly comprehensive treatment of the subject, see Pierre-Antoine Bernheim and Guy Stavridès, *Cannibales!* (Paris: Plon, 1992), pp. 106–9, 'De la physiologie du goût'.

10 Urbain Chauveton (translating and annotating Girolamo Benzoni), *Histoire nouvelle du Nouveau Monde* (Geneva, 1579), pp. 258–9, 'discourse of the translator' on book I, ch. 23, note 2.

11 Raymond Breton, *Relation de l'Isle de la Guadeloupe* (Basse-Terre: Société d'Histoire de la Guadeloupe, 1978), vol. 1, part 2: *Relation de l'Isle de Guadeloupe*, ch. XI, p. 77.

12 Jean-Baptiste du Tertre, *Histoire des Isles de S. Christophe, de la Guadeloupe, de la Martinique, et autres dans l'Amérique* (Paris: Jacques Langlois, 1654), part V, ch. X, p. 451.

13 Ibid., p. 452.

14 Ibid., p. 451. Cf. ch. 6 above, notes 9 and 31 and text.

15 Ibid., p. 452.

16 Ibid., p. 450. Du Tertre also emphasizes that the Caribs take their desire for vengeance to such lengths 'that they kill and eat the male children which they have from these [captive] women, and they even eat the male children who are born of the daughters of these slave women'. This information should be treated with caution.

17 Charles de Rochefort, *Histoire naturelle et morale des Iles Antilles de l'Amerique, enrichie de plusieurs belles figures des raretez les plus considerables qui y sont décrites. Avec un vocabulaire caraibe* (Rotterdam, 1658), book II, ch. 11, p. 403. The reference is to Léry, 'Chap. 13'. Cf. Léry, *Histoire d'un voyage* (1580), ch. XIII, pp. 176–7 (1992 edn, pp. 126–7). *Les Voyages fameux du sieur Vincent le Blanc Marsellois*, from the library of Peiresc, compiled by Pierre Bergeron and subsequently by Louis Coulon, SJ, had appeared in 1648 (Paris: Gervais Clousier). Their authenticity is more than doubtful: see G. Chinard, *L'Amérique et le rêve exotique* (Paris, 1934), p. 79, and J.-P. Duviols, *Voyageurs français en Amérique* (Paris: Bordas, 1978), pp. 92–4. On Rochefort, see Philip P. Boucher, *Cannibal Encounters* (Baltimore and London: Johns Hopkins University Press, 1992), pp. 57–8.

18 Rochefort, *Histoire naturelle et morale*, continuing passage cited above. Cf. *Essays*, III, 6, p. 547: 'Lo here an example of the stammering of this infancy.'

19 Rochefort, *Histoire naturelle et morale*, book II, ch. XXI, p. 480: 'A thing which even the Pagans, in their thick darkness, found so full of execration, that they feigned that the Sun had set so as not to shine upon such repasts'. Cf. p. 483: 'I admit that the Sun would be right to abandon those Barbarians, rather than attending upon such detestable solemnities.'

20 Ibid., p. 480.

21 Ibid., p. 487: 'But too much of this. Let us draw a veil over these horrors.' Cf. Agrippa d'Aubigné, *Les Tragiques*, I, ll. 561–2: 'The sun cannot look on the other smoking table: / Over this let us draw the veil of Timanthus.'

22 Ibid., p. 482.

23 Ibid., pp. 480–1.

24 On the concept of martyrdom during the Reformation, see my *La Cause des martyrs dans 'Les Tragiques' d'Agrippa d'Aubigné* (Mont-de-Marzan: Editions InterUniversitaires, 1991), and Denis Crouzet, *Les Guerriers de Dieu* (Paris: Champ Vallon, 1990).

25 Pierre François-Xavier de Charlevoix, SJ, *Histoire et description générale de la Nouvelle France* (Paris: chez Nyon fils, 1744), vol. 1, book VI, p. 294.

26 Ibid., continuing previous quotation. On ritual anthropophagy among the Iroquois, and the refined cruelty which it involved, see Urszula Chodowiec, 'La hantise et la pratique. Le cannibalisme iroquois', *Nouvelle Revue de Psychanalyse* 6 (Autumn 1972), 'Destins du cannibalisme', pp. 55–69.

27 Charlevoix, *Histoire et description générale*, p. 276. The event took place in 1646. A very similar anecdote was reported by Charlevoix in his *Histoire du Paraguay* (Paris: Didot, Giffart et Nyon, 1756), vol. I, book VIII, pp. 423–4. In 1635 the Jesuit Mendoza, missionary in the Capé, was tortured and murdered by the natives: 'Finally they threw him in a stream and went to feast upon the corpses of two young Indians who served the holy Man at the Altar, and who had been killed at his side the day before.'

28 Charlevoix, *Histoire et description générale*, pp. 258–9. Bressani's death is dated to the year 1644.

29 Isaac Jogues, who had suffered the same misadventure during his first mission to New France, got permission from the Pope to celebrate the divine mysteries with his mutilated hands. It would not have been fair to 'refuse a Martyr of Jesus Christ the right to drink the blood of Jesus Christ, *Indignum esset Christi Martyrum Christ non bibere Sanguinem*'. Quoted in Charlevoix, *Histoire et description*, vol. I, vook VI, p. 250.

30 Claude Lévi-Strauss, *Tristes Tropiques* (Harmondsworth: Penguin, 1976), p. 508.

31 Charlevoix, *Histoire et description*, vol. 1, p. 294. On the imitation of Christ in Canadian martyrology, see Pierre Berthiaume, *L'Aventure américaine au XVIIIe siècle* (Ottawa: Les Presses de l'Université d'Ottawa, 1990), ch. 4, pp. 261–5; cf. Guy Laflèche, *Les Saints Martyrs canadiens* (Montréal: Ed. Singulier, 1988–9), 2 vols published to date.

32 Charlevoix, *Histoire et description* p. 309, years 1650–1: 'No longer did the most fearful wildernesses and the most impenetrable Cantons of the North offer any refuge against the fury of those Barbarians [the Iroquois] and against the hydropic thirst they had for human blood.'

33 Abbé Antoine-François Prévost, *Le Philosophe Anglois, ou Histoire de Monsieur Cleveland, fils naturel de Cromwell, écrite par lui-meme, et traduite de l'Anglois. Nouvelle Edition* (Utrecht: Etienne Neaulme, 1736–9; new edition by Jean Sgard, Grenoble, 1978). On the design of *Cleveland*, see especially J. Sgard, *Prévost romancier* (Paris: Corti, 1989), pp. 119–26.

34 Prévost, *Cleveland*, vol. IV, book V, p. 7.
35 Ibid., vol. III, book IV, p. 216.
36 Ibid., vol. IV, book V, p. 48.
37 Ibid., vol. VI, book X, p. 359.
38 Ibid., vol. IV, book V, pp. 46–7.
39 Ibid., p. 41.
40 Ibid., p. 71.
41 Ibid., vol. V, book VI, p. 14.
42 On this, see the fine analysis by Jean-Michel Racault, *L'Utopie narrative en France et en Angleterre 1675–1761*, Studies on Voltaire 280 (Oxford: The Voltaire Foundation, 1991), pp. 601–59, esp. pp. 622–33.
43 On this obsession, see Neil Heims, 'Robinson Crusoe and the Fear of Being Eaten', *Colby Library Quarterly* 19/4 (December 1983), pp. 190–3. For the possible origins of this terror in Defoe's personal life and its connection with his journalistic activities and various sojourns in prison, cf. Maximilian E. Novak, 'Imaginary Islands and Real Beasts: The Imaginative Genesis of *Robinson Crusoe*', *Tennessee Studies in Literature* 19 (1974), pp. 57–8.
44 Daniel Defoe, *Robinson Crusoe* (Harmondsworth: Penguin, 1994), p. 152.
45 Ibid., p. 163.
46 See above, ch. 1, note 12 and text.
47 Defoe, *Robinson Crusoe*, p. 190: 'the excellent advice of my father, the opposition to which was, as I may call it, my *original sin*'.
48 Ibid., p. 212.
49 Ibid., p. 228.
50 Ibid., p. 181.
51 Ibid., pp. 178–9.
52 Ibid., p. 180.
53 Ibid., p. 204.
54 Ibid., p. 219.
55 Ibid., p. 207.
56 For all the above remarks see the excellent analysis by Boucher in *Cannibal Encounters*, pp. 125–7.
57 Daniel Defoe, *Serious Reflections of Robinson Crusoe*, in Defoe, *Romances and Narratives*, ed. George Aitken (New York: AMS Press, 1974), vol. 3, pp. 115–16. Cited by Boucher, *Cannibal Encounters*, p. 127.
58 Here I am summarizing Boucher's conclusions, ibid., pp. 127–9.
59 Rochefort, *Histoire naturelle et morale*, book II, ch. 20, p. 476.
60 On this question, which we glanced at earlier when dealing with Léry (ch. 6), see my 'Catholiques et Cannibales', in J.-C. Margolin and R. Sauzet (eds), *Pratiques et discours alimentaires à la Renaissance* (Paris: Maisonneuve et Larose, 1982).
61 See, e.g. E. Pearlman, 'Robinson and the Cannibals', *Mosaic* 10 (Winnipeg, 1976), pp. 39–55.
62 On the political economy of Robinson's island, see Racault, *Utopie narrative*, pp. 239–42.

Chapter 11: The Enlightenment Cannibal: From Bougainville to Voltaire

1 Denis Diderot, *Supplément au voyage de Bougainville* (*c.*1771–80), in Jean de Varloot and Nivole Evrard (eds), *Le Neveu de Rameau et autres dialogues*

philosophiques. Folio series (Paris: Gallimard). I shall refer to this easily accessible edition rather than to the standard edition edited by Herbert Dieckmann (Geneva: Droz, 1955). Also worth consulting is the edition by Gilbert Chinard, *Supplément au voyage de Bougainville, publié d'après le manuscrit de Leningrad* (Paris: Droz and Baltimore: Johns Hopkins University Press, 1935), with its very useful and comprehensive introduction. For *Histoire philosophique et politique des établissements et du commerce des Européens dans les deux Indes,* by Abbé G.-Th. Raynal, of which a good ten editions were published between 1770 and 1786, I have compared two versions of the text: that of 1770, mainly written by Raynal with only limited contributions from Diderot, and that of 1780, which was copiously 'interglossed' and substantially rewritten by Diderot (Geneva: chez Jean-Léonard Pellet, 4 quarto vols). The passage in question, relating to cannibalism in early Britain and reproduced almost word for word in the *Supplément,* is in vol. I, book III, ch. 1 of the 1780 edition; it is not in earlier versions.

2 Denis Diderot, 'Supplement to Bougainville's "Voyage"' in *Rameau's Nephew and Other Works,* trans. Jacques Barzun and Ralph H. Bowen (New York: Bobbs-Merrill Co., Inc., 1964), p. 182.

3 Louis-Antoine de Bougainville, *Voyage autour du monde par la frégate du Roi 'La Boudeuse' et la flûte 'L'Etoile' en 1766, 1767, 1768, 1769,* p. 180. Cited in Chinard's edition of the *Supplément,* p. 107, note 1.

4 Report in Denis Diderot, *Œuvres complètes,* ed. R. Lewinter, vol. IX (Paris: Le Club français du Livre, 1971), pp. 965–73. Quotation on p. 968.

5 On the island as a framework for classification and study, see my 'Insulaires', in *Cartes et figures de la terre* (Paris: Centre Georges-Pompidou, 1980), pp. 470–5. Cf. 'L'Insulaire des Lumières. Esquisse introductive', in J.-M. Racault and J.-C. Carpanin Marimoutou (eds), *L'Insularité. Actes du Colloque de Saint-Denis de la Réunion (1992)* (Saint-Denis: Université de la Réunion, 1994).

6 Denis Diderot, *Lettre apologétique de l'abbé Raynal.* I have slightly altered the expression quoted by Michèle Duchet in her *Diderot et l'Histoire des deux Indes, ou l'Ecriture fragmentaire* (Paris: Nizet, 1978), p. 157.

7 Raynal (Diderot), *Histoire des deux Indes* (Geneva, 1780), vol. I, book III, ch. I, 'Idea of the ancient commerce of the English', p. 262. Duchet, *Diderot et l'Histoire,* p. 68, note 5, also notes this 'striking resemblance' to the text of the *Supplément.* This passage was not added to the original text of the *Histoire* until 1780, but thereafter constituted the bulk of the chapter.

8 Raynal, *Histoire des deux Indes* (Amsterdam, 1770), vol. III, p. 336. This ch. V of book IX, on the 'Portuguese settlement in Brazil', was completely rewritten in editions from 1774 onwards (Duchet, *Diderot et l'Histoire,* p. 80). It appears in vol. II of the 1780 Geneva edition, pp. 371–2. The text goes on to give an interesting piece of information which appears in 1770 (vol. III, book IX, ch. VII, pp. 541–2) and subsequent editions. Raynal, as compiler, was the indirect heir of a continuous line of texts going back to the sixteenth century, as evidenced by the oblique reference to Léry in a passage concerning the 'Irruption of the French into Brazil': 'The only valuable monument of their fruitless endeavours is a dialogue which shows the natural good sense of the savages all the better in that it is written in the naive style which characterized the French language of two centuries ago, in which we still find graces which are sadly lacking today.' This dialogue, the 'Colloquy of the author and a savage, showing that they are not such blockheads as they were thought to be' (Jean de Léry, *Histoire d'un voyage faict en la terre du*

Brésil, ch. XIII), quite closely prefigures the 'Farewell of the old man' to Bougainville in the second part of Diderot's *Supplément*. On this link, see the paper by Gianluigi Goggi, 'Quelques remarques sur la collaboration de Diderot à la première édition de l'*Histoire des deux Indes*', in Hans-Jürgen Lüsebrink and Manfred Tietz (eds), *Lectures de Raynal. L'"Histoire des deux Indes' en Europe et en Amérique au XVIIIe siècle* (Oxford: The Voltaire Foundation, 1991), pp. 17–52, esp. pp. 41–8.

9 Raynal (Diderot), *Histoire des deux Indes* (1780), vol. I, book III, ch. I, p. 262. This comment does not appear in the earlier editions.

10 Thomas Robert Malthus, *An Essay on the Principle of Population*, 2 vols (London: Dent, 1958), vol. I, book I, ch. V, 'Of the checks to population in the islands of the South Sea', p. 44.

11 Ibid.

12 Ibid., vol. I, book II, ch. I: Norway; ch. II: Sweden; ch. III: Russia, etc.

13 Ibid., vol. II, book IV, ch. XIV, 'Of our rational expectations respecting the future improvement of society', p. 257. This is the concluding chapter of Malthus's *Essay*.

14 Diderot, who bequeathed a copy of the *Essays* to Sophie Volland, was an enthusiastic reader of Montaigne. Some passages in the *Supplément* bear an undeniable resemblance to parts of 'Des Cannibales' and 'Des Coches'. *B*'s reflection that 'The Tahitian is close to the origin of the world, while the European is close to its old age' (trans. Barzun and Bowen, p. 186) is strangely reminiscent of a sentence in Montaigne's *Essays*, trans. John Florio (Menston, Yorks: Scholar Press, 1969): 'If we conclude aright of our end, and the aforesaid Poet of the infancy of his age, this late-world shall but come to light, when ours shall fall into darkness', III, 6, p. 545. Another maxim from *B* (again!), that 'there is less harm to be suffered in being mad among madmen than in being sane all by oneself' (Barzun and Bowen, p. 227) has an unmistakeably Montaignian ring.

15 Voltaire, *Philosophical Dictionary*, vol. 1, trans. Peter Gay (New York: Basic Books, 1962), pp. 86–8. For the article referred to above, see under the French heading 'Anthropophages'. That Voltaire interviewed an 'ash-coloured woman' who was a native of the Mississippi region is confirmed in chapter 146 of his *Essai sur les mœurs*, vol. 2 (Paris: Bordas, Classiques Garnier, 1990), ed. René Pomeau, p. 344.

16 Voltaire, *Philosophical Dictionary*, trans. Gay, p. 24. In his annotated edition of Voltaire's *Candide* (Paris: Magnard, 1987), Jean Goldzink observes that the transition from one oral activity to the other features both in the story and in the *Dictionary*.

17 Here I echo an observation by the psychoanalyst André Green in 'Le cannibalisme: réalité ou fantasme agi?', *Nouvelle Revue de Psychanalyse* 6 (Autumn 1972), p. 51: 'There is more than one way of loving a person to the point of becoming one with him. One of them is anthropophagy.'

18 Montaigne, *Essays*, I, 30 [31], p. 104.

19 Voltaire, *Candide* (London: Oxford University Press, 1966), ch. XVI, p. 155. This passage is discussed by Antonello Gerbi in *La disputa del Nuovo Mondo. Storia di una polemica: 1750–1900* (Milan and Naples: Riccardo Ricciardi, 1983), p. 66.

20 Voltaire, *Candide*, ch. XVII: 'When they came to the frontier of the Oreillons, Cacambo said to Candide: "You can see that the new world is no better than the old" ' (p. 161).

21 Voltaire, *Histoire de Jenni* (1775), ch. VII: 'What happened in America'. Birton cruelly adds a little later that 'For a long time I had been very displeased with that horrible woman, Clife-Hart: I care no more about her than if someone had put a fat hen on the spit.' Mr Freind [sic], the deist, eventually succeeds in restoring this militant atheist to a more humane way of thinking.

22 Voltaire, *Philosophical Dictionary*, trans. Gay, p. 87.

23 Ibid. To Voltaire's cannibal writings we must also add the section of *Essai sur les mœurs* devoted to the anthropophagi of America (1761 edn, vol. IV, pp. 103–5). It was written in 1758, which makes it contemporary with *Candide*.

24 The expression is Diderot's in his summary of the *Voyage autour du monde* in *Œuvres complètes*, vol. IX, p. 967: the Jesuits of Paraguay, who had just been expelled, are described as 'those cruel black-robed Spartans'. Voltaire would have been proud to have invented the description.

Chapter 12: Cruel Nature: De Pauw and Sade

1 Voltaire, *Candide* (London: Oxford University Press, 1966), ch. XVII, p. 163.

2 Cornelius de Pauw, *Recherches philosophiques sur les Américains* (2nd edn; Berlin: 1771), vol. I, p. xiii.

3 Montaigne, *Essays*, III, 6, p. 547.

4 On this line of reasoning see Antonello Gerbi, *La Disputa del Nuovo Mondo* (Milan and Naples: Riccardo Ricciardi, 1983), p. 79.

5 *De l'Amérique et des Américains, ou Observations curieuses du philosophe La Douceur qui a parcouru cet Hémisphère pendant la dernier guerre, en faisant le noble métier de tuer des hommes sans les manger* (Berlin: S. Pitra, 1771), title of ch. 1. This short (80-page) anonymous work, which defends the opinion of Dom Pernety against 'Mr. de P**', has been attributed to Zacharie de Pazzi de Bonneville. Gerbi, *Disputa del Nuovo Mondo*, p. 148, makes some prudent observations against this assumption.

6 De Pauw, *Recherches*, vol. I, p. 221.

7 Ibid., 'Discours préliminaire', p. ix.

8 Buffon, *Additions à l'Histoire de l'homme* (1777), 'Des Américains'. On this volte-face by Buffon, see Gerbi, *Disputa del Nuovo Mondo*, pp. 218–21. Cf. Michèle Duchet, *Anthropologie et histoire au siècle des Lumières* (Paris: François Maspéro, 1971), p. 214.

9 Gerbi, *Disputa del Nuovo Mondo*, p. 81.

10 De Pauw, *Recherches*, vol. I, 'Discours préliminaire', p. v.

11 Ibid.

12 Ibid., pp. v–vi.

13 Ibid., p. vi.

14 Ibid., p. iv.

15 Duchet, *Anthropologie et histoire*, pp. 203, 205, 410. Cf. Gerbi, *Disputa del Nuovo Mondo*, p. 81.

16 De Pauw, *Recherches*, vol. II, part V, title of section I, p. 153. For the Hermaphrodites of Florida see vol. II, part IV, section III, pp. 83ff. Cf. vol. II, part IV, section IV: 'On circumcision and infibulation'; part V, section III: 'On the use of poisoned arrows'.

17 Ibid., vol. I, part II, section III, 'On anthropophagi', p. 221.

18 Ibid., pp. 208–9.

19 Ibid., pp. 214–5.

20 Ibid., p. 216. Cf. ch. 3 above, note 14 and text.
21 Ibid., p. 217.
22 Ibid., p. 218.
23 Ibid., p. 225.
24 Ibid., pp. 222–3.
25 Ibid., pp. 232–3.
26 Ibid., p. 233.
27 Ibid.: 'Although the Authors of the *Universal History* claim that the Jagas practised all these abominations, and had made it a law never to live save on human flesh, one can boldly say that it is not true or even likely. *Non cadit in quemquam tantum nefas.*' The article 'JAGAS, GIAGAS OR GIAGUES' in the *Encyclopédie*, which repeats the legend without casting the slightest doubt upon it, notes as a source *The modern part of an universal history*, vol. XVI – i.e. the work that de Pauw calls the *Histoire universelle*.
28 Ibid., p. 222: 'one cannot believe what is reported by certain Portuguese concerning the States of the Grand-Macoco, whom they depict as a powerful and magnificent Monarch who serves human flesh at his table and those of his Courtesans. It seems almost impossible that a People civilized enough to have elected a Sovereign, built Cities and cultivated the Arts should still feed upon such disgusting foods.' For Sade's narrative use of Grand-Macoco (alias Grand-Macoro, whom he rechristens by the – as he sees it – more exotic name Ben Mácoro), see below, notes 40ff. and text.
29 Ibid., p. 223.
30 Francis Bacon, *Sylva sylvarum: or, A naturall historie. In ten centuries. Written by the Right Honourable Francis Io. Verulam viscount St. Alban. Published after the authors death, by William Rawley doctor of divinitie, late his Lordships chaplaine* (London: 'Printed by J. H. for William Lee at the Turks Head in Fleet-street', 1626), Century I, 26: 'Experiment Solitary touching the Venemous Quality of Mans Flesh', p. 7. On the scientific tradition of *Sylva sylvarum* and its subsequent history, see Ann Blair, 'Humanist Methods in Natural Philosophy: the Commonplace Book', *Journal of the History of Ideas* (1992), pp. 541–51.
31 De Pauw, *Recherches*, vol. I, pp. 228–38.
32 Ibid., p. 226.
33 See above, ch. 10.
34 De Pauw, *Recherches*, vol. I, p. 226.
36 Ibid., pp. 220–1.
36 Ibid., p. 220.
37 Ibid., p. 208.
38 See Beatrice C. Fink, 'Sade and Cannibalism', *L'Esprit Créateur* 15/4 (Winter 1975), pp. 403–12. The author argues that cannibalism is the 'central metonymy' of Sade's work. Cf. Jean Biou, 'Lumières et anthropophagie', *Revue des Sciences Humaines* 37 (1972), pp. 223–33. He looks only at de Pauw and his opponent, Dom Pernety, skating over Sade, who gives little support to the author's Marxist line of argument.
39 Sade, *Aline et Valcour*, in Michel Delon (ed.), *Œuvres*, vol. I (Paris: Gallimard, 1990), letter XXXV, 'Déterville to Valcour', p. 592.
40 Ibid., p. 563, note *. Besides this essential source, Sade also draws ethnographical information on cannibalism from accounts by voyagers, historians and compilers, including Cook, Forster, and, in particular, Jean-Nicolas Démeunier, *L'Esprit des usages et coutumes des differens peuples ou*

Observations tirées des Voyageurs et des Historiens (London: Pissot, 1776), vol. I. For the 'Sadean copy', see Michel Delon in *Littérature* 69 (1988) and his learned annotations to *Aline et Valcour*, esp. pp. 1259–65.

41 Sade, *La Nouvelle Justine*, in *Œuvres complètes* (Paris: Cercle du livre précieux, 1963), vol. VII, pp. 127–218. For a reading of this episode, see Fink, 'Sade and Cannibalism', pp. 407–9.

42 Sade, *Juliette* (London: Arrow Books, 1968), pp. 579–99.

43 Sade, *Aline et Valcour*, letter XXXV.

44 For this relatively precise geography, see Christopher L. Miller, *Blank Darkness. Africanist Discourse in French* (Chicago: University of Chicago Press, 1985), ch. 5, pp. 184–200, esp. pp. 197–9.

45 For this antithetical binary archipelago, which is *de rigueur* in imaginary voyages from Rabelais to Swift, see Yves Giraud, 'La ville du bout du monde (Sade, *Aline et Valcour*)', *Studi di letteratura francese* XI (1985), pp. 85–100.

46 Sade, *Aline et Valcour*, p. 559.

47 Ibid., p. 565.

48 In fact this applies mostly to the libertines that the 'story-tellers' introduce into their daily narratives. See Sade, *The Hundred and Twenty Days of Sodom* (New York: Grove Press, 1987), part III, story 143; part IV, stories 89, 106, 111, 144, pp. 621, 647, 652, 653, 664. The stories also include numerous other cases of cannibalism associated with torture.

49 Sade, *Aline et Valcour*, p. 582.

50 Ibid.

51 Ibid., p. 597.

52 Ibid., p. 562.

53 Ibid., p. 597.

54 Ibid., p. 566.

55 Ibid., p. 577. Here I am drawing on Michel Delon's note to the same passage.

56 Ibid., p. 592.

57 Ibid., p. 591.

58 Ibid.

59 Sade, *The Hundred and Twenty Days*, p. 672.

60 Sade, *Juliette*, p. 578. For explicit references to Hell and Charon's boat, thought to be accessible from near Cumae and Baiae in Campania, cf. pp. 953–4.

61 See above, ch. 3, note 20 and text.

62 Sade, *Juliette*, p. 581.

63 Ibid., p. 1017.

64 Sade, *Aline et Valcour*, letter XXXV, p. 552.

65 Sade, *Juliette*, part III, p. 580.

66 Annie Le Brun, *Soudain un bloc d'abîme. Sade. Introduction aux œuvres complètes* (Paris: Jean-Jacques Pauvert, 1986).

Chapter 13: Cannibalism and Colonialism: Jules Verne

1 As shown by the passage from Chateaubriand in Appendix II.

2 Jules Verne, *Les Enfants du Capitaine Grant* (Paris: Hetzel, 1868), part III, ch. VI.

3 Ibid., p. 478.

4 Ibid., ch. XII, 'The funeral of a Maori chief', p. 535. Even the deliberate

omissions ('In less time than a fluent pen could write it...'), imitate the 'energetic' stylistics of the classical epic.

5 Ibid.

6 Verne, *Five Weeks in a Balloon* (London: New English Library, 1974), ch. XII, p. 76. Before Verne saddled them with this bogus etymology, the Nyam-Nyams or Niam-Niams already had a substantial history. In 1851 Francis de Castelnau published his *Renseignements sur l'Afrique centrale et sur une nation de Niam-Niam ou 'hommes à queue' qui s'y trouverait, d'après les nègres de Soudan* ('Information concerning central Africa and a nation of Niam-Niams 'or "men with tails" who are to be found there according to the negroes of the Sudan') (Paris: P. Bertrand). The book caused quite a stir in the learned circles of its time. On this, see Christopher L. Miller, *Blank Darkness* (Chicago: University of Chicago Press, 1985), pp. 3–4.

7 Verne, *Five Weeks in a Balloon*, ch. XIII, p. 84.

8 Ibid. Verne continues: ' "No, no," cried the Doctor quickly. "Why should we mix ourselves up in this quarrel? How do you know who is right and who is wrong, that you should play the part of Providence? Let us fly from this repulsive exhibition.'

9 In fact, Malthus was obliged to defend his own view against Robertson's: see *An Essay on the Principle of Population* (London: Dent, 1958), vol. I, book I, ch. IV, p. 34.

10 All these details are from the highly prejudiced narrative of two survivors: Jean-Baptiste Henri Savigny and Alexandre Corréard, *Relation du naufrage de la frégate 'La Méduse', faisant partie de l'expédition du Sénégal en 1816* (Paris, 1817). A 'Fourth Edition', revised and enlarged, was published by Corréard in 1821 (reissued Paris: Jean de Bonnot, 1968). The work was translated into English under the title *Narrative of a Voyage to Senegal in 1816: undertaken by order of the French government, comprising an account of the shipwreck of the Medusa, the sufferings of the crew ... Illustrated with the notes of M. Bredif* (London: H. Colburn, 1818). The story was later dramatized by William Thomas Moncrieff: *Shipwreck of the Medusa: or, the Fatal Raft. A drama in three acts* (London: J. Cumberland, c.1830). According to the author, the play was 'founded on facts, contained in a French narrative... "Naufrage de la frégate la Meduse ... par J. B. Savigny et Alexandre Corréard" '. Their narrative is neatly summarized by Julian Barnes in *A History of the World in 10½ Chapters* (Cambridge University Press, 1995), pp. 117–27.

11 *Géricault. Catalogue de l'exposition du Grand Palais* (Paris: Réunion des Musées Nationaux, 1991), no. 234, p. 147 (from a private collection). See the comments by Régis Michel, p. 136.

12 Verne's novel was published in 1875, showing that the memory of the *Medusa* was still vivid nearly sixty years after the event.

13 Verne, *Le Pays des fourrures* (Paris: J. Hetzel, 1873).

14 Verne, *Le Jangada* (Paris: J. Hetzel, 1881).

15 Arthur Rimbaud, *Le Bateau ivre*, I. 11.

16 Verne *Le Chancellor* (Paris: J. Hetzel, 1875; Lausanne, Editions Rencontre), ch. XLVI, p. 196: 'As for Robert Kurtis, I cannot tell ... I dared not ask him.'

17 Ibid., ch. XLI, p. 169.

18 Here I agree with Claude Rawson, who has shown (' "Indians" and Irish', *Modern Language Quarterly* (September 1992), pp. 306–7) that Montaigne's use of language in 'Of Cannibals' modulates imperceptibly from the literal to the figurative.

19 Verne, *Le Chancellor*, ch. LIII, p. 211.
20 Ibid., p. 213.
21 These facts are reported quite frankly by Savigny and Corréard. Cf. Julian Barnes's ironical explanation of why Géricault decided not to include the mutiny scene which appears in some of the sketches: 'On the raft, it was not virtue that triumphed, but strength; and there was little mercy to be had. The subtext of this version would say that God was on the side of the officer class. Perhaps he used to be in those days. Was Noah officer class?' (*A History of the World in 10½ Chapters*, p. 132).
22 Verne, *Le Chancellor*, ch. LV, pp. 219–20.
23 Clément Marot, *L'Adolescence clémentine*, refrain of Ballade XIII, 'De la Passion de Notre Seigneur Jésus-Christ', in 'Poésie' edition (Paris: Gallimard, 1987), pp. 166–7.
24 Verne, *Le Chancellor*, ch. LVII, p. 223.
25 Ibid., p. 219.
26 On this, see the article by Roger Dadoun, commenting on evidence given by Anatoly Marshenko: 'Du cannibalisme comme stade suprême du stalinisme', *Nouvelle Revue de Psychanalyse* 6 (Autumn 1972), 'Destins du cannibalisme', pp. 269–72.
27 Verne, *Le Chancellor*, ch. XLVII, p. 196: 'To see men becoming wild animals ... How dreadful!'

Epilogue: The Return of the Cannibal

1 Gustave Flaubert, in Jean Bruneau (ed.), *Correspondance* (Paris: Gallimard 'Pléiade', 1980), vol. III, p. 186.
2 Ibid., 2 January 1862, p. 195.
3 Ibid., to Louis Bouilhet, 1 October 1860, p. 116.
4 Ibid., to Madame Jules Sandeau, 30 September (1 October) 1859, p. 42.
5 Ibid., to Jules Duplan, Wednesday, 25 September 1861: 'I'm just finishing the siege of Carthage, and I'm coming to the grilled kiddies.' To Ernest Feydeau, Monday, 7 October 1861: 'The day after tomorrow I shall start the last movement of my penultimate chapter: the grilled kiddies' (pp. 176, 178). Cf. letter to Feydeau, 17 August 1861 (p. 170): 'My colours are turning rather dark. We are starting to walk in blood and guts and burn the little kiddies. Baudelaire will like this!'
6 Ibid., to Edmond and Jules de Goncourt, 30 April/May 1861, p. 152.
7 Ibid., to Ernest Feydeau, Saturday, 17 August 1861, p. 170.
8 On Flaubert's sadism and how it is transcended in his literary work, see Claude Rawson, 'Cannibalism and Fiction: Reflections on Narrative Form and "Extreme" Situations', *Genre* 10/4 (Winter 1977), pp. 667–711, esp. pp. 691–9. To the abundant evidence gleaned by Rawson from the *Correspondance* we may add the reference to *Par les champs et par les grèves. Touraine et Bretagne* (1847), in René Dumesnil (ed.), *Voyages* (Paris: Les Belles Lettres, 1948), vol. I, pp. 289–90.
9 *Observations sur les effets de la faim et de la soif éprouvés après la naufrage de la frégate du roi 'La Méduse' en 1816* (Paris: Eynmery, 1818), 56pp. This ex-naval surgeon was the same Savigny who co-wrote the *Relation du naufrage de la frégate 'La Médus'* with Alexandre Corréard. In the latter book, which was both an apology and an accusation, the authors exaggerated their own

importance by putting all the blame on Chaumareys and Lieutenant d'Anglas de Praviel. Praviel was goaded into making a rejoinder (1818).

10 Jonathan Swift, *A Modest Proposal for Preventing the Children of Poor People in Ireland, from being a Burden to their Parents or Country; and for making them Beneficial to the Publick* (Dublin, 1729). In Herbert Davis et al. (eds), *Prose Works* (Oxford: Blackwell, 1955), vol. XII, pp. 109–18. This text was selected by André Breton to open his 'Anthology of Black Humour'. On Breton's admiration for Swift, whom he sees as the 'real initiator' of black humour, see Claude Rawson, *Gulliver and the Gentle Reader. Studies in Swift and our Time* (London and Boston: Routledge and Kegan Paul, 1973), pp. 34–5.

11 Claude Rawson, ' "Indians" and Irish', *Modern Language Quarterly* (September 1992), pp. 344–54.

12 Swift, *Modest Proposal*, p. 116.

13 For the ambiguity of Swift's humour see Claude Rawson, *Order from Confusion Sprung* (New Jersey and London: Humanities Press, 1992), pp. 79–80.

14 Gustave Flaubert, *Salammbô* (1862), ed. E. Maynial (Paris: Garnier, 1961), ch. XIV.

15 Jules Verne, *Les Enfants du Captaine Grant* (Paris: Hetzel, 1868), part III, ch. XII, p. 535.

16 Flaubert, *Salammbô*, p. 319.

17 Quoted by Maynial in his edition of the novel, p. xi.

18 Montaigne, *Essays*, trans. John Florio (Menston, Yorks: Scholar Press, 1969), I, 30 [31], p. 104.

19 André Thevet, *Les Singularitez de la France Antarctique* (Paris: chez les Héritiers de Maurice de la Porte, 1557), ch. 38, fol. 71; Jean de Léry, *History of a Voyage to the Land of Brazil* (1580) trans. Janet Whatley (Berkeley: University of California Press, 1990), ch. XIV, p. 120. Léry continues: 'I will say this about it, however: although I have often seen men of arms over here, both on foot and on horseback, nevertheless I have never taken so much pleasure in seeing the infantry, with their gilded helmets and shining arms, as I delighted then in seeing those savages do battle. There was not only the entertainment of seeing them leap, whistle, and wield their swords so dexterously in circles and passades; it was also a marvel to see so many arrows fly in the air and sparkle in the sunbeams.'

20 Jacques Derrida, *Of Grammatology*, trans. G. Spivak (Baltimore: Johns Hopkins University Press, 1976), part II/1, 'The Violence of the Letter: From Lévi-Strauss to Rousseau', p. 115.

21 Claude Lévi-Strauss, *Tristes Tropiques* (Harmondsworth: Penguin, 1976), p. 508.

22 Montaigne, *Essays*, I, 30 [31] pp. 105–6.

23 Here, I am drawing, not quite uncritically, on the stimulating and rewarding study by David Quint, 'A Reconsideration of Montaigne's Des Cannibales', *Modern Language Quarterly* 51/4 (December 1990), pp. 459–89.

24 Montaigne, *Essays*, II, 32, pp. 415–16.

25 Ibid., II, 2, p. 202.

26 Ibid.

27 Agrippa d'Aubigné, *Les Tragiques*, I, l. 1189. On martyrdom as seen by this great Protestant poet, see my *La Cause des Martyrs dans 'Les Tragiques' d'Agrippa d'Aubigné* (Mont-de-Marzan: Editions InterUniversitaires, 1991).

28 Montaigne, *Essays*, I, 30 [31], p. 105.

29 Flaubert, *Salammbô*, ch. XIV, p. 308.

30 Ibid., p. 312.
31 Joseph Conrad, *The Nigger of the 'Narcissus'* (Harmondworth: Penguin, 1988), cited by Maynial (ed.), *Salammbô*, p. 432, note 917. Also cf. Verne, *Le Chancellor*, ch. LI, p. 105. Flaypol, one of the sailors, laughs, sings and waves his hand at an imaginary coast: 'Thus he talks to absent friends. He takes them to a Cardiff tavern, the George and the Dragon. He offers them gin, whisky, water – especially water, intoxicating water! . . . He looks as if he is dead drunk.'

Appendix I: The Cannibal Speaks

1 Montaigne, *Essays*, trans. John Florio (Menston, Yorks: Scholar Press, 1969), I, 30 [31], p. 106.
2 Jean-Jacques Rousseau, *Discours sur l'origine et les fondements de l'inégalité parmi les hommes*, in *Œuvres complètes*, Pléiade edn (Paris: Gallimard, 1964), p. 132: 'Let us therefore begin by setting aside all the facts, because they do not affect the question. Researches which may be undertaken on this Subject must not be taken for historical truths, but only for hypothetical and conditional suggestions.'
3 In his commentary in the Pléiade edition, Jean Starobinski suggests the comparison with Montaigne and, among other more distant literary sources, with Etienne de La Boétie's *De la Servitude volontaire ou Contr'Un*, ed. Malcolm Smith (Geneva: Droz, 1987).
4 Rousseau, *Discours*, p. 194. I am grateful to Dominic Thomas, a graduate student at Yale, for suggesting that Rousseau is in some way making up for Montaigne's lapse of memory.
5 On this see James Supple, *Arms versus Letters: the Military and Literary Ideals in the 'Essays' of Montaigne* (Oxford: Clarendon Press, 1984).
6 Jean-Jacques Rousseau, *Emile*, book II, in *Œuvres complètes*, vol. IV (Paris, 1969), p. 414: 'O unnatural murderer, if you persist in saying that Nature made you to devour your fellow creatures, creatures of flesh and blood, who live and feel as you do, stifle the horror which she inspires in you for such repasts; kill the animals yourself, I say with your own hands, without weapons, without knives; tear them apart with your nails like Lions and bears . . .' This passage is a paraphrase of Plutarch's *Moralia*: 'If it be permissible to eat flesh.'

Appendix II: The Cannibal in Canada

1 See Victor Bouillier, 'Montaigne et Goethe', *Revue de littérature comparée* 5 (1925), pp. 572–93, esp. pp. 575–8.
2 Chateaubriand, *Mémoires d'outre-tombe*, ed. Maurice Levaillant and Georgers Moulinier, Pléiade edn, vol. I (Paris: Gallimard, 1964), book VII, ch. 9, pp. 247–8: 'In Rouen the author of the *Essays* saw certain Iroquois who, he says, were very sensible persons: "But what of that," he adds, "they wear no kind of breeches or hosen!"' Before Chateaubriand, Rousseau, in a note on the *Premier Discours*, part I, had alluded with some admiration to the 'simple and natural polity' of the Cannibals and borrowed Montaigne's final shaft: ' "But what of that!" he said, "they wear no breeches." ' (*Œuvres complètes*, vol. III, p. 11).

Bibliography

This bibliography is restricted to works of reference. For other works the reader is referred to the notes.

Arens, William, *The Man-Eating Myth: Anthropology and Anthropophagy*. New York: Oxford University Press, 1979.

Arveiller, Raymond, *Contribution à l'étude des termes de voyage en français (1505–1722)*. Paris: Editions D'Artrey, 1963.

Atkinson, Geoffroy, *Les Nouveaux Horizons de la Renaissance française*. Paris: Droz, 1935.

Balmas, Enea, *Il buon selvaggio nella cultura francese del settecento*. Fasano di Puglia: Schena, 1984.

——(ed.) *La scoperta dell'America e le lettere francesi*. Milan: Cisalpino-Istituto Editoriale Universitario, 1992.

Bataille, Georges, *La Part maudite*. Paris: Editions de Minuit and Editions du Seuil, 'Points', 1967.

Bedini, Silvio A. (ed.), *The Christopher Columbus Encyclopaedia*. New York and London: Simon and Schuster, 1991.

Benzi Grupioni, Luis Donisete (ed.), *Indios no Brasil*. São Paulo: Secretaria Municipal de Cultura, 1992.

Bernand, Carmen and Gruzinski, Serge, *Histoire du Nouveau Monde*, vol. I: *De la découverte à la conquête, une expérience européene 1492–1550*. Paris: Fayard, 1991.

Bernheim, Pierre-Antoine and Stavridès, Guy, *Cannibales!* Paris: Plon, 1992.

Berthiaume, Pierre, *L'Aventure américaine au XVIIIe siècle. Du voyage à l'écriture*. Ottawa: Les Presses de l'Université d'Ottawa, 1990.

Blanchard, Marc E., *Trois Portraits de Montaigne: essai sur la représentation à la Renaissance*. Paris: Nizet, 1990. ch. II: 'Cannibale', pp. 107–202.

Blanckaert, Claude (ed.), *Naissance de l'ethnologie? Anthropologie et missions en Amérique XVIe–XVIIe siècle*. Paris: Editions du Cerf, 1985.

Boucher, Philip P., *Cannibal Encounters. Europeans and Island Caribs, 1492–1763*. Baltimore and London: Johns Hopkins University Press, 1992.

Bucher, Bernadette, *La Sauvage aux seins pendants*. Paris: Hermann, 1977. English translation, *Icon and Conquest: A Structural Analysis of the Illustrations of De Bry's Great Voyages*, trans. B. M. Gulati. Chicago: University of Chicago Press, 1981.

Céard, Jean (ed.), *La Folie et le corps*. Paris: Presses de l'Ecole Normale Supérieure, 1985.

Certeau, Michel de, *Heterologies: Discourse on the Other*, trans. B. Massumi. Minneapolis: University of Minnesota Press, 1985.

——*The Writing of History*, trans. T. Conley. New York: Columbia University Press, 1988.

Chaunu, Pierre, *L'Amérique et les Amériques*. Paris: Armand Colin, 1964.
——*Conquête et exploitation des nouveaux mondes (XVIe siècle)*. Paris: PUF, 'Nouvelle Clio', 1969.
Chavagnac, Béatrice de and Andrade, Oswald de, *Premier Volume de la Grande Encyclopédie 'Miam-Miam' qui traite, pour cette fois, du Cannibalisme*. Paris: A l'Imprimerie Quotidienne/Le Couteau dans la plaie, 1979.
Chiappelli, Fredi (ed.), *First Images of America. The Impact of the New World on the Old*. Berkeley, Los Angeles and London: University of California Press, 1976.
Chinard, Gilbert, *L'Exotisme américain dans la littérature française au XVIe siècle*. Paris: Hachette, 1911 (reprint Geneva: Slatkine, 1978).
——*L'Amérique et le rêve exotique dans la littérature française au XVIe siècle*. Paris: Hachette, 1913 and 1934.
Clendinnen, Inga, *Aztecs: An Interpretation*. Cambridge: Cambridge University Press, 1991 and 1993.
Combès, Isabelle, *La Tragédie cannibale chez les anciens Tupi-Guarani*. Paris: PUF, 1992.
Corbin, Alain, *Le Village des Cannibales*. Paris: Aubier, 1990. English translation, *The Village of Cannibals: Rage and Murder in France, 1870*, trans. A. Goldhammer. Cambridge: Polity Press, 1992.
Defaux, Gérard, *Marot, Rabelais, Montaigne: l'écriture comme présence*. Paris and Geneva: Champion-Slatkine, 1987.
Derrida, Jacques, *Of Grammatology*, trans. G. Spivak. Baltimore: Johns Hopkins University Press, 1976.
Desan, Philippe, *Les Commerces de Montaigne. Le discours économique des 'Essais'*. Paris: Nizet, 1992.
Droixhe, D. and Gossiaux, Pol.-P. (ed.), *L'Homme des Lumières et la découverte de l'autre*. Brussels: Editions de l'Université de Bruxelles, 1985.
Duchet, Michèle, *Anthropologie et histoire au siècle des Lumières*. Paris: François Maspéro, 1971.
——*Diderot et l'Histoire des deux Indes, ou l'Ecriture fragmentaire*. Paris: Nizet, 1978.
——(ed.), *L'Amérique de Théodore de Bry*, Paris: Editions du CNRS, 1987.
Duverger, Christian, *La Fleur Létale. Economie du sacrifice aztèque*. Paris: Editions du Seuil, 1979.
Eitner, Lorenz, *Géricault, his Life and Work*. London: Orbis Books, 1983.
Forsyth, Donald W., 'The Beginnings of Brazilian Anthropology. Jesuits and Tupinamba Cannibalism', *Journal of Anthropological Research* 39/2 (Summer 1983), pp. 147–78.
Gerbi, Antonello, *La disputa del Nuovo Mondo. Storia di una polemica: 1750–1900*. Final edition. Milan and Naples: Riccardo Ricciardi, 1983.
Gewecke, Frauke, *Wie die neue Welt in die alte kam*. Stuttgart: Klett-Cotta, 1986.
Girard, René, *Violence and the Sacred*, trans. P. Gregory. Baltimore: Johns Hopkins University Press, 1977.
Gliozzi, Giuliano, *Adamo e il nuovo mondo. La nascita dell'antropologia come ideologia coloniale dalle genealogie bibliche alle teorie razziali (1500–1700)*. Florence: La Nuova Italia, 1977.
Greenblatt, Stephen, *Marvelous Possessions. The Wonder of the New World*. Oxford: Clarendon Press, 1991.
——(ed.) *New World Encounters*. Berkeley and Los Angeles: University of California Press, 1992.

Harris, Marvin, *Cannibals and Kings: The Origins of Cultures.* New York: Random House, 1977.

Hulme, Peter, *Colonial Encounters: Europe and the Native Caribbean 1492–1797.* London: Methuen, 1986.

Hulme, Peter and Whitehead, Neil L. (eds), *Wild Majesty. Encounters with Caribs from Columbus to the Present Day. An Anthology.* Oxford: Clarendon Press, 1992.

Kohl, Karl-Heinz (ed.), *Mythen der Neuen Welt. Zur Entdeckungsgeschichte Lateinamerikas.* Berlin: Frölich and Kaufmann, 1982.

Lestringant, Frank, 'Le cannibalisme des "Cannibales"', *Bulletin de la Société des Amis de Montaigne,* series 6, 9–10 (January–June 1982), pp. 27–40, and 11–12 (July–December 1982), pp. 19–38.

——'Le Cannibale et ses paradoxes. Images du cannibalisme au temps des guerres de Religion', *Mentalités/Mentalities* 1/2. Hamilton, New Zealand: Outrigger Publishers, 1983, pp. 4–19.

——'Le Nom des "Cannibales", de Christophe Colomb à Michel de Montaigne', *Bulletin de la Société des Amis de Montaigne,* series 6, 17–18 (January–June 1984), pp. 51–74.

——*Le Huguenot et le Sauvage. L'Amérique et la controverse coloniale, en France, au temps des guerres de Religion.* Paris: Aux Amateurs de Livres (Klincksieck), 1990.

——*Mapping the Renaissance World,* trans. D. Fausett. Cambridge: Polity Press and Berkeley: University of California Press, 1994.

——*André Thevet, cosmographe des derniers Valois.* Geneva: Droz, 1991.

——*Ecrire le monde à la Renaissance. Quinze études sur Rabelais, Postel, Bodin et la littérature géographique.* Caen: Editions Paradigme, 1993.

Lévi-Strauss, Claude, *Tristes Tropiques.* Harmondsworth: Penguin, 1976.

——*The Savage Mind.* London, 1966.

——*The Story of Lynx,* trans. C. Tihanyi. Chicago: University of Chicago Press, 1995.

Macy, Gary. *The Theologies of the Eucharist in the Early Scholastic Period. A Study of the Salvific Function of the Sacrament According to the Theologians c.1080–1220.* Oxford, 1984.

——*The Banquet's Wisdom. A Short History of the Theologies of the Lord's Supper.* New York, 1992.

Margolin, Jean-Claude and Sauzet, Robert (eds), *Pratiques et discours alimentaires à la Renaissance.* Paris: G.-P. Maisonneuve et Larose, 1982.

Marin, Louis, *Food for Thought,* trans. M. Hjort. Baltimore: Johns Hopkins University Press, 1989.

Marouby, Christian, *Utopie et primitivisme: essai sur l'imaginaire anthropologique à l'âge classique.* Paris: Seuil, 1990.

Mello Franco, Afonso Arinos de, *O Indio brasileiro e a Revolução francesa.* Rio de Janeiro: José Olimpio, 1937.

Métraux, Alfred, *La Religion des Tupinamba et ses rapports avec celle des autres tribus tupi-guarani.* Paris: E. Leroux, 1928.

——*Religions et magies indiennes d'Amérique du Sud.* Paris: Gallimard, 1967.

Miller, Christopher, *Blank Darkness. Africanist Discourse in French.* Chicago and London: University of Chicago Press, 1985.

'Montaigne et le Nouveau Monde'. Actes du Colloque de Paris 18–20 mai 1992. *Bulletin de la Société des Amis de Montaigne,* series 7, 29–32 (July–December 1992 and January–June 1993).

Mouralis, Bernard, *Montaigne et le mythe du bon sauvage, de l'Antiquité à Rousseau.* Paris: Editions Pierre Bordas, 1989.

Nouvelle Revue de Psychanalyse 6 (Autumn 1972): 'Destins du cannibalisme'.

Pagden, Anthony, 'Cannibalismo e contagio: sull'importanza dell'antropofagia nell'Europa preindustriale', *Quaderni storici* 50 (1982), pp. 535–50.

——*The Fall of Natural Man: The American Indian and the Origins of Comparative Ethnology.* Cambridge: Cambridge University Press, 1982 and 1986.

——*European Encounters with the New World. From Renaissance to Romanticism.* New Haven and London: Yale University Press, 1993.

Pot, Olivier, *L'Inquiétante Etrangeté. Montaigne: la pierre, le cannibale, la mélancolie.* Paris: Champion, 1993.

Racault, Jean-Michel, *L'Utopie narrative en France et en Angleterre 1675–1761.* Oxford: The Voltaire Foundation, 1991.

Rawson, Claude J., *Gulliver and the Gentle Reader, Studies in Swift and our Time.* London and Boston: Routledge and Kegan Paul, 1973. Ch. V, 'Catalogues, Corpses and Cannibals. Swift and Mailer, with Reflections on Whitman, Conrad and Others', pp. 100–52.

——'Cannibalism and Fiction: Reflections on Narrative Form and "Extreme" Situations', *Genre* 10/4 (Winter 1977), pp. 667–711.

——'Narrative and Proscribed Act: Homer, Euripides and the Literature of Cannibalism', in *Literary Theory and Criticism: Festschrift in Honor of René Wellek* (2nd edn), Bern: Peter Lang, 1986, vol. II, pp. 1159–97.

——*Order from Confusion Sprung. Studies in Eighteenth-Century Literature from Swift to Cowper.* New Jersey and London: Humanities Press, 1992 (1st edn 1985).

——' "Indians" and Irish: Montaigne, Swift, and the Cannibal Question', *Modern Language Quarterly* (September 1992), pp. 299–363.

Smith, Preserved, *A Short History of Christian Theophagy.* Chicago and London: Open Court Publishing, 1922.

Tannahill, Reay, *Flesh and Blood: A History of the Cannibal Complex.* London and New York: Stein and Day, 1975.

——*The World, the Flesh and the Devil.* New York: Crown Publishers, 1987.

Todorov, Tzvetan, *The Conquest of America. The Question of the Other.* New York: Harper and Row, 1984.

——*On Human Diversity,* trans. C. Porter. Cambridge, MA: Harvard University Press, 1993.

——*The Morals of History,* trans. A. Haters. Minneapolis: University of Minnesota Press, 1995.

Viveiros de Castro, Eduardo Batalha, *Araweté: os deuses canibais.* Rio de Janeiro: Jorge Zahar Editor-Anpocs, 1986.

Whatley, Janet, 'Food and the Limits of Civility: the Testimony of Jean de Léry', *The Sixteenth Century Journal* 15/4 (Winter 1984), pp. 387–400.

White, David Gordon, *Myths of the Dog-Man.* Chicago and London: University of Chicago Press, 1991.

Index

Page numbers in italics indicate illustrations

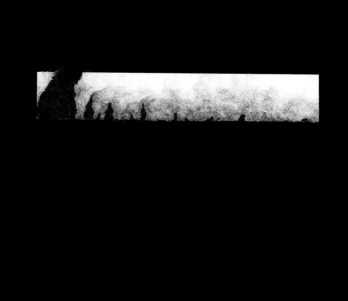